CAMBRIDGE GREEK AND LATIN CLASSICS

GENERAL EDITORS

E. J. KENNEY

Emeritus Kennedy Professor of Latin, University of Cambridge

AND

P. E. EASTERLING

Regius Professor of Greek, University of Cambridge

VIRGIL

GEORGICS

VOLUME 2: BOOKS III–IV

EDITED BY

RICHARD F. THOMAS

Professor of Greek and Latin,
Harvard University

 CAMBRIDGE
UNIVERSITY PRESS

PUBLISHED BY THE PRESS SYNDICATE OF THE UNIVERSITY OF CAMBRIDGE
The Pitt Building, Trumpington Street, Cambridge, United Kingdom

CAMBRIDGE UNIVERSITY PRESS
The Edinburgh Building, Cambridge CB2 2RU, UK
40 West 20th Street, New York, NY 10011–4211, USA
10 Stamford Road, Oakleigh, VIC 3166, Australia
Ruiz de Alarcón 13, 28014 Madrid, Spain
Dock House, The Waterfront, Cape Town 8001, South Africa

http://www.cambridge.org

© Cambridge University Press 1988

First published 1988
Reprinted 1990, 1994, 1997, 2001

British Library Cataloguing in Publication data
Virgil
Georgics. –
(Cambridge Greek and Latin classics).
Vol. 2: Books 3–4
I. Title   II. Thomas, Richard F.   III. Series
871'.01   PA6804

Library of Congress Cataloguing in Publication data
Virgil.
Georgics. Vol. 2: Books 3–4
(Cambridge Greek and Latin classics)
Text in Latin; commentary in English.
I. Thomas, Richard F.   II. Title.   III. Series
PA6804.A6   1988 873'.01   87-23834

ISBN 0 521 34653 3 hardback
ISBN 0 521 34678 9 paperback

Transferred to digital printing 2003

AO

CONTENTS

THE GEORGICS
BOOKS III–IV

GEORGICON III

Te quoque, magna Pales, et te memorande canemus
pastor ab Amphryso, uos, siluae amnesque Lycaei.
cetera, quae uacuas tenuissent carmine mentes,
omnia iam uulgata: quis aut Eurysthea durum
aut inlaudati nescit Busiridis aras?   5
cui non dictus Hylas puer et Latonia Delos
Hippodameque umeroque Pelops insignis eburno,
acer equis? temptanda uia est, qua me quoque possim
tollere humo uictorque uirum uolitare per ora.
primus ego in patriam mecum, modo uita supersit,   10
Aonio rediens deducam uertice Musas;
primus Idumaeas referam tibi, Mantua, palmas,
et uiridi in campo templum de marmore ponam
propter aquam, tardis ingens ubi flexibus errat
Mincius et tenera praetexit harundine ripas.   15
in medio mihi Caesar erit templumque tenebit:
illi uictor ego et Tyrio conspectus in ostro
centum quadriiugos agitabo ad flumina currus.
cuncta mihi Alpheum linquens lucosque Molorchi
cursibus et crudo decernet Graecia caestu.   20
ipse caput tonsae foliis ornatus oliuae
dona feram. iam nunc sollemnis ducere pompas
ad delubra iuuat caesosque uidere iuuencos,
uel scaena ut uersis discedat frontibus utque
purpurea intexti tollant aulaea Britanni.   25
in foribus pugnam ex auro solidoque elephanto
Gangaridum faciam uictorisque arma Quirini,
atque hic undantem bello magnumque fluentem
Nilum ac nauali surgentis aere columnas.
addam urbes Asiae domitas pulsumque Niphaten   30

3

fidentemque fuga Parthum uersisque sagittis,
et duo rapta manu diuerso ex hoste tropaea
bisque triumphatas utroque ab litore gentes.
stabunt et Parii lapides, spirantia signa,
Assaraci proles demissaeque ab Ioue gentis   35
nomina, Trosque parens et Troiae Cynthius auctor.
Inuidia infelix Furias amnemque seuerum
Cocyti metuet tortosque Ixionis anguis
immanemque rotam et non exsuperabile saxum.
interea Dryadum siluas saltusque sequamur   40
intactos, tua, Maecenas, haud mollia iussa:
te sine nil altum mens incohat. en age segnis
rumpe moras; uocat ingenti clamore Cithaeron
Taygetique canes domitrixque Epidaurus equorum,
et uox adsensu nemorum ingeminata remugit.   45
mox tamen ardentis accingar dicere pugnas
Caesaris et nomen fama tot ferre per annos,
Tithoni prima quot abest ab origine Caesar.
    Seu quis Olympiacae miratus praemia palmae
pascit equos, seu quis fortis ad aratra iuuencos,   50
corpora praecipue matrum legat. optima toruae
forma bouis cui turpe caput, cui plurima ceruix,
et crurum tenus a mento palearia pendent;
tum longo nullus lateri modus: omnia magna,
pes etiam, et camuris hirtae sub cornibus aures.   55
nec mihi displiceat maculis insignis et albo,
aut iuga detrectans interdumque aspera cornu
et faciem tauro propior, quaeque ardua tota
et gradiens ima uerrit uestigia cauda.
aetas Lucinam iustosque pati hymenaeos   60
desinit ante decem, post quattuor incipit annos;
cetera nec feturae habilis nec fortis aratris.
interea, superat gregibus dum laeta iuuentas,
solue mares; mitte in Venerem pecuaria primus,
atque aliam ex alia generando suffice prolem.   65

optima quaeque dies miseris mortalibus aeui
prima fugit; subeunt morbi tristisque senectus
et labor, et durae rapit inclementia mortis.
semper erunt quarum mutari corpora malis:
semper enim refice ac, ne post amissa requiras,   70
ante veni et subolem armento sortire quotannis.
    Nec non et pecori est idem dilectus equino:
tu modo, quos in spem statues summittere gentis,
praecipuum iam inde a teneris impende laborem.
continuo pecoris generosi pullus in aruis   75
altius ingreditur et mollia crura reponit;
primus et ire uiam et fluuios temptare minacis
audet et ignoto sese committere ponti,
nec uanos horret strepitus. illi ardua ceruix
argutumque caput, breuis aluus obesaque terga,   80
luxuriatque toris animosum pectus. honesti
spadices glaucique, color deterrimus albis
et giluo. tum, si qua sonum procul arma dedere,
stare loco nescit, micat auribus et tremit artus,
collectumque premens uoluit sub naribus ignem.   85
densa iuba, et dextro iactata recumbit in armo;
at duplex agitur per lumbos spina, cauatque
tellurem et solido grauiter sonat ungula cornu.
talis Amyclaei domitus Pollucis habenis
Cyllarus et, quorum Grai meminere poetae,   90
Martis equi biiuges et magni currus Achilli.
talis et ipse iubam ceruice effundit equina
coniugis aduentu pernix Saturnus, et altum
Pelion hinnitu fugiens impleuit acuto.
    Hunc quoque, ubi aut morbo grauis aut iam segnior
                                                  annis   95
deficit, abde domo, nec turpi ignosce senectae.
frigidus in Venerem senior, frustraque laborem
ingratum trahit, et, si quando ad proelia uentum est,
ut quondam in stipulis magnus sine uiribus ignis,

incassum furit. ergo animos aeuumque notabis   100
praecipue: hinc alias artis prolemque parentum
et quis cuique dolor uicto, quae gloria palmae.
nonne uides, cum praecipiti certamine campum
corripuere, ruuntque effusi carcere currus,
cum spes arrectae iuuenum, exsultantiaque haurit   105
corda pauor pulsans? illi instant uerbere torto
et proni dant lora, uolat ui feruidus axis;
iamque humiles iamque elati sublime uidentur
aëra per uacuum ferri atque adsurgere in auras.
nec mora nec requies; at fuluae nimbus harenae   110
tollitur, umescunt spumis flatuque sequentum:
tantus amor laudum, tantae est uictoria curae.
primus Ericthonius currus et quattuor ausus
iungere equos rapidusque rotis insistere uictor.
frena Pelethronii Lapithae gyrosque dedere   115
impositi dorso, atque equitem docuere sub armis
insultare solo et gressus glomerare superbos.
aequus uterque labor, aeque iuuenemque magistri
exquirunt calidumque animis et cursibus acrem,
quamuis saepe fuga uersos ille egerit hostis   120
et patriam Epirum referat fortisque Mycenas,
Neptunique ipsa deducat origine gentem.
   His animaduersis instant sub tempus et omnis
impendunt curas denso distendere pingui,
quem legere ducem et pecori dixere maritum,   125
florentisque secant herbas fluuiosque ministrant
farraque, ne blando nequeat superesse labori
inualidique patrum referant ieiunia nati.
ipsa autem macie tenuant armenta uolentes,
atque, ubi concubitus primos iam nota uoluptas   130
sollicitat, frondesque negant et fontibus arcent.
saepe etiam cursu quatiunt et sole fatigant,
cum grauiter tunsis gemit area frugibus, et cum
surgentem ad Zephyrum paleae iactantur inanes.

hoc faciunt, nimio ne luxu obtunsior usus   135
sit genitali aruo et sulcos oblimet inertis,
sed rapiat sitiens Venerem interiusque recondat.
    Rursus cura patrum cadere et succedere matrum
incipit. exactis grauidae cum mensibus errant,
non illas grauibus quisquam iuga ducere plaustris,   140
non saltu superare uiam sit passus et acri
carpere prata fuga fluuiosque innare rapacis.
saltibus in uacuis pascunt et plena secundum
flumina, muscus ubi et uiridissima gramine ripa,
speluncaeque tegant et saxea procubet umbra.   145
est lucos Silari circa ilicibusque uirentem
plurimus Alburnum uolitans, cui nomen asilo
Romanum est, oestrum Grai uertere uocantes,
asper, acerba sonans, quo tota exterrita siluis
diffugiunt armenta; furit mugitibus aether   150
concussus siluaeque et sicci ripa Tanagri.
hoc quondam monstro horribilis exercuit iras
Inachiae Iuno pestem meditata iuuencae;
hunc quoque (nam mediis feruoribus acrior instat)
arcebis grauido pecori, armentaque pasces   155
sole recens orto aut noctem ducentibus astris.
    Post partum cura in uitulos traducitur omnis;
continuoque notas et nomina gentis inurunt,
et quos aut pecori malint summittere habendo
aut aris seruare sacros aut scindere terram   160
et campum horrentem fractis inuertere glaebis.
cetera pascuntur uiridis armenta per herbas:
tu quos ad studium atque usum formabis agrestem
iam uitulos hortare uiamque insiste domandi,
dum faciles animi iuuenum, dum mobilis aetas.   165
ac primum laxos tenui de uimine circlos
ceruici subnecte; dehinc, ubi libera colla
seruitio adsuerint, ipsis e torquibus aptos
iunge pares, et coge gradum conferre iuuencos;

atque illis iam saepe rotae ducantur inanes   170
per terram, et summo uestigia puluere signent;
post ualido nitens sub pondere faginus axis
instrepat, et iunctos temo trahat aereus orbis.
interea pubi indomitae non gramina tantum
nec uescas salicum frondes uluamque palustrem,   175
sed frumenta manu carpes sata; nec tibi fetae
more patrum niuea implebunt mulctraria uaccae,
sed tota in dulcis consument ubera natos.
    Sin ad bella magis studium turmasque ferocis,
aut Alphea rotis praelabi flumina Pisae   180
et Iouis in luco currus agitare uolantis,
primus equi labor est animos atque arma uidere
bellantum lituosque pati, tractuque gementem
ferre rotam et stabulo frenos audire sonantis,
tum magis atque magis blandis gaudere magistri   185
laudibus et plausae sonitum ceruicis amare.
atque haec iam primo depulsus ab ubere matris
audeat, inque uicem det mollibus ora capistris
inualidus etiamque tremens, etiam inscius aeui.
at tribus exactis ubi quarta accesserit aestas,   190
carpere mox gyrum incipiat gradibusque sonare
compositis, sinuetque alterna uolumina crurum,
sitque laboranti similis; tum cursibus auras
tum uocet, ac per aperta uolans ceu liber habenis
aequora uix summa uestigia ponat harena,   195
qualis Hyperboreis Aquilo cum densus ab oris
incubuit, Scythiaeque hiemes atque arida differt
nubila: tum segetes altae campique natantes
lenibus horrescunt flabris, summaeque sonorem
dant siluae, longique urgent ad litora fluctus;   200
ille uolat simul arua fuga simul aequora uerrens.
hic uel ad Elei metas et maxima campi
sudabit spatia et spumas aget ore cruentas,
Belgica uel molli melius feret esseda collo.

tum demum crassa magnum farragine corpus   205
crescere iam domitis sinito; namque ante domandum
ingentis tollent animos, prensique negabunt
uerbera lenta pati et duris parere lupatis.
    Sed non ulla magis uiris industria firmat
quam Venerem et caeci stimulos auertere amoris,   210
siue boum siue est cui gratior usus equorum.
atque ideo tauros procul atque in sola relegant
pascua post montem oppositum et trans flumina lata,
aut intus clausos satura ad praesepia seruant.
carpit enim uiris paulatim uritque uidendo   215
femina, nec nemorum patitur meminisse nec herbae
dulcibus illa quidem inlecebris, et saepe superbos
cornibus inter se subigit decernere amantis.
pascitur in magna Sila formosa iuuenca:
illi alternantes multa ui proelia miscent   220
uulneribus crebris; lauit ater corpora sanguis,
uersaque in obnixos urgentur cornua uasto
cum gemitu; reboant siluaeque et longus Olympus.
nec mos bellantis una stabulare, sed alter
uictus abit longeque ignotis exsulat oris,   225
multa gemens ignominiam plagasque superbi
uictoris, tum quos amisit inultus amores,
et stabula aspectans regnis excessit auitis.
ergo omni cura uiris exercet et inter
dura iacet pernox instrato saxa cubili   230
frondibus hirsutis et carice pastus acuta,
et temptat sese atque irasci in cornua discit
arboris obnixus trunco, uentosque lacessit
ictibus, et sparsa ad pugnam proludit harena.
post, ubi collectum robur uiresque refectae,   235
signa mouet praecepsque oblitum fertur in hostem,
fluctus uti medio coepit cum albescere ponto,
longius ex altoque sinum trahit, utque uolutus
ad terras immane sonat per saxa neque ipso

monte minor procumbit, at ima exaestuat unda   240
uerticibus nigramque alte subiectat harenam.
    Omne adeo genus in terris hominumque ferarumque
et genus aequoreum, pecudes pictaeque uolucres,
in furias ignemque ruunt: amor omnibus idem.
tempore non alio catulorum oblita leaena   245
saeuior errauit campis, nec funera uulgo
tam multa informes ursi stragemque dedere
per siluas; tum saeuus aper, tum pessima tigris;
heu, male tum Libyae solis erratur in agris.
nonne uides ut tota tremor pertemptet equorum   250
corpora, si tantum notas odor attulit auras?
ac neque eos iam frena uirum neque uerbera saeua,
non scopuli rupesque cauae atque obiecta retardant
flumina correptosque unda torquentia montis.
ipse ruit dentesque Sabellicus exacuit sus   255
et pede prosubigit terram, fricat arbore costas
atque hinc atque illinc umeros ad uulnera durat.
quid iuuenis, magnum cui uersat in ossibus ignem
durus amor? nempe abruptis turbata procellis
nocte natat caeca serus freta, quem super ingens   260
porta tonat caeli, et scopulis inlisa reclamant
aequora; nec miseri possunt reuocare parentes,
nec moritura super crudeli funere uirgo.
quid lynces Bacchi uariae et genus acre luporum
atque canum? quid quae imbelles dant proelia ceruei?   265
scilicet ante omnis furor est insignis equarum,
et mentem Venus ipsa dedit, quo tempore Glauci
Potniades malis membra absumpsere quadrigae.
illas ducit amor trans Gargara transque sonantem
Ascanium; superant montis et flumina tranant.   270
continuoque auidis ubi subdita flamma medullis
(uere magis, quia uere calor redit ossibus), illae
ore omnes uersae in Zephyrum stant rupibus altis,
exceptantque leuis auras, et saepe sine ullis

coniugiis uento grauidae (mirabile dictu)   275
saxa per et scopulos et depressas conuallis
diffugiunt, non, Eure, tuos neque solis ad ortus,
in Borean Caurumque aut unde nigerrimus Auster
nascitur et pluuio contristat frigore caelum.
hic demum, hippomanes uero quod nomine dicunt   280
pastores, lentum destillat ab inguine uirus,
hippomanes, quod saepe malae legere nouercae
miscueruntque herbas et non innoxia uerba.
   Sed fugit interea, fugit inreparabile tempus,
singula dum capti circumuectamur amore.   285
hoc satis armentis; superat pars altera curae,
lanigeros agitare greges hirtasque capellas;
hic labor, hinc laudem fortes sperate coloni.
nec sum animi dubius uerbis ea uincere magnum
quam sit et angustis hunc addere rebus honorem;   290
sed me Parnasi deserta per ardua dulcis
raptat amor; iuuat ire iugis, qua nulla priorum
Castaliam molli deuertitur orbita cliuo.
nunc, ueneranda Pales, magno nunc ore sonandum.
   Incipiens stabulis edico in mollibus herbam   295
carpere ouis, dum mox frondosa reducitur aestas,
et multa duram stipula filicumque maniplis
sternere subter humum, glacies ne frigida laedat
molle pecus scabiemque ferat turpisque podagras.
post hinc digressus iubeo frondentia capris   300
arbuta sufficere et fluuios praebere recentis,
et stabula a uentis hiberno opponere soli
ad medium conuersa diem, cum frigidus olim
iam cadit extremoque inrorat Aquarius anno.
hae quoque non cura nobis leuiore tuendae,   305
nec minor usus erit, quamuis Milesia magno
uellera mutentur Tyrios incocta rubores.
densior hinc suboles, hinc largi copia lactis;
quam magis exhausto spumauerit ubere mulctra,

laeta magis pressis manabunt flumina mammis.   310
nec minus interea barbas incanaque menta
Cinyphii tondent hirci saetasque comantis
usum in castrorum et miseris uelamina nautis.
pascuntur uero siluas et summa Lycaei,
horrentisque rubos et amantis ardua dumos,   315
atque ipsae memores redeunt in tecta suosque
ducunt et grauido superant uix ubere limen.
ergo omni studio glaciem uentosque niualis,
quo minor est illis curae mortalis egestas,
auertes, uictumque feres et uirgea laetus   320
pabula, nec tota claudes faenilia bruma.
    At uero Zephyris cum laeta uocantibus aestas
in saltus utrumque gregem atque in pascua mittet,
Luciferi primo cum sidere frigida rura
carpamus, dum mane nouum, dum gramina canent,   325
et ros in tenera pecori gratissimus herba.
inde, ubi quarta sitim caeli collegerit hora
et cantu querulae rumpent arbusta cicadae,
ad puteos aut alta greges ad stagna iubebo
currentem ilignis potare canalibus undam;   330
aestibus at mediis umbrosam exquirere uallem,
sicubi magna Iouis antiquo robore quercus
ingentis tendat ramos, aut sicubi nigrum
ilicibus crebris sacra nemus accubet umbra;
tum tenuis dare rursus aquas et pascere rursus 335
solis ad occasum, cum frigidus aëra Vesper
temperat, et saltus reficit iam roscida luna,
litoraque alcyonen resonant, acalanthida dumi.
    Quid tibi pastores Libyae, quid pascua uersu
prosequar et raris habitata mapalia tectis?   340
saepe diem noctemque et totum ex ordine mensem
pascitur itque pecus longa in deserta sine ullis
hospitiis: tantum campi iacet. omnia secum
armentarius Afer agit, tectumque laremque

armaque Amyclaeumque canem Cressamque pharetram;   345
non secus ac patriis acer Romanus in armis
iniusto sub fasce uiam cum carpit, et hosti
ante exspectatum positis stat in agmine castris.
    At non qua Scythiae gentes Maeotiaque unda,
turbidus et torquens flauentis Hister harenas,   350
quaque redit medium Rhodope porrecta sub axem.
illic clausa tenent stabulis armenta, neque ullae
aut herbae campo apparent aut arbore frondes;
sed iacet aggeribus niueis informis et alto
terra gelu late septemque adsurgit in ulnas.   355
semper hiems, semper spirantes frigora Cauri;
tum Sol pallentis haud umquam discutit umbras,
nec cum inuectus equis altum petit aethera, nec cum
praecipitem Oceani rubro lauit aequore currum.
concrescunt subitae currenti in flumine crustae,   360
undaque iam tergo ferratos sustinet orbis,
puppibus illa prius, patulis nunc hospita plaustris,
aeraque dissiliunt uulgo, uestesque rigescunt
indutae, caeduntque securibus umida uina,
et totae solidam in glaciem uertere lacunae,   365
stiriaque impexis induruit horrida barbis.
interea toto non setius aëre ningit:
intereunt pecudes, stant circumfusa pruinis
corpora magna boum, confertoque agmine cerui
torpent mole noua et summis uix cornibus exstant.   370
hos non immissis canibus, non cassibus ullis
puniceaeue agitant pauidos formidine pennae,
sed frustra oppositum trudentis pectore montem
comminus obtruncant ferro grauiterque rudentis
caedunt et magno laeti clamore reportant.   375
ipsi in defossis specubus secura sub alta
otia agunt terra, congestaque robora totasque
aduoluere focis ulmos ignique dedere.
hic noctem ludo ducunt, et pocula laeti

fermento atque acidis imitantur uitea sorbis.   380
talis Hyperboreo Septem subiecta trioni
gens effrena uirum Riphaeo tunditur Euro
et pecudum fuluis uelatur corpora saetis.
  Si tibi lanitium curae, primum aspera silua,
lappaeque tribolique, absint; fuge pabula laeta;   385
continuoque greges uillis lege mollibus albos.
illum autem, quamuis aries sit candidus ipse,
nigra subest udo tantum cui lingua palato,
reice, ne maculis infuscet uellera pullis
nascentum, plenoque alium circumspice campo.   390
munere sic niueo lanae, si credere dignum est,
Pan deus Arcadiae captam te, Luna, fefellit
in nemora alta uocans; nec tu aspernata uocantem.
  At cui lactis amor, cytisum lotosque frequentis
ipse manu salsasque ferat praesepibus herbas: 395
hinc et amant fluuios magis, et magis ubera tendunt
et salis occultum referunt in lacte saporem.
multi etiam excretos prohibent a matribus haedos,
primaque ferratis praefigunt ora capistris.
quod surgente die mulsere horisque diurnis,   400
nocte premunt; quod iam tenebris et sole cadente,
sub lucem: exportant calathis (adit oppida pastor),
aut parco sale contingunt hiemique reponunt.
  Nec tibi cura canum fuerit postrema, sed una
uelocis Spartae catulos acremque Molossum   405
pasce sero pingui. numquam custodibus illis
nocturnum stabulis furem incursusque luporum
aut impacatos a tergo horrebis Hiberos.
saepe etiam cursu timidos agitabis onagros,
et canibus leporem, canibus uenabere dammas;   410
saepe uolutabris pulsos siluestribus apros
latratu turbabis agens, montisque per altos
ingentem clamore premes ad retia ceruum.
  Disce et odoratam stabulis accendere cedrum

galbaneoque agitare grauis nidore chelydros.   415
saepe sub immotis praesepibus aut mala tactu
uipera delituit caelumque exterrita fugit,
aut tecto adsuetus coluber succedere et umbrae
(pestis acerba boum) pecorique aspergere uirus
fouit humum. cape saxa manu, cape robora, pastor,   420
tollentemque minas et sibila colla tumentem
deice! iamque fuga timidum caput abdidit alte,
cum medii nexus extremaeque agmina caudae
soluuntur, tardosque trahit sinus ultimus orbis.
est etiam ille malus Calabris in saltibus anguis   425
squamea conuoluens sublato pectore terga
atque notis longam maculosus grandibus aluum,
qui, dum amnes ulli rumpuntur fontibus et dum
uere madent udo terrae ac pluuialibus Austris,
stagna colit ripisque habitans hic piscibus atram   430
improbus ingluuiem ranisque loquacibus explet;
postquam exusta palus terraeque ardore dehiscunt,
exsilit in siccum, et flammantia lumina torquens
saeuit agris asperque siti atque exterritus aestu.
ne mihi tum mollis sub diuo carpere somnos   435
neu dorso nemoris libeat iacuisse per herbas,
cum positis nouus exuuiis nitidusque iuuenta
uoluitur, aut catulos tectis aut oua relinquens,
arduus ad solem et linguis micat ore trisulcis.
    Morborum quoque te causas et signa docebo.   440
turpis ouis temptat scabies, ubi frigidus imber
altius ad uiuum persedit et horrida cano
bruma gelu, uel cum tonsis inlotus adhaesit
sudor, et hirsuti secuerunt corpora uepres.
dulcibus idcirco fluuiis pecus omne magistri   445
perfundunt, udisque aries in gurgite uillis
mersatur, missusque secundo defluit amni,
aut tonsum tristi contingunt corpus amurca,
et spumas miscent argenti uiuaque sulpura

Idaeasque pices et pinguis unguine ceras   450
scillamque elleborosque grauis nigrumque bitumen.
non tamen ulla magis praesens fortuna laborum est
quam si quis ferro potuit rescindere summum
ulceris os: alitur uitium uiuitque tegendo,
dum medicas adhibere manus ad uulnera pastor   455
abnegat et meliora deos sedet omina poscens.
quin etiam, ima dolor balantum lapsus ad ossa
cum furit atque artus depascitur arida febris,
profuit incensos aestus auertere et inter
ima ferire pedis salientem sanguine uenam,   460
Bisaltae quo more solent acerque Gelonus,
cum fugit in Rhodopen atque in deserta Getarum,
et lac concretum cum sanguine potat equino.
quam procul aut molli succedere saepius umbrae
uideris aut summas carpentem ignauius herbas   465
extremamque sequi, aut medio procumbere campo
pascentem et serae solam decedere nocti,
continuo culpam ferro compesce, priusquam
dira per incautum serpant contagia vulgus.
non tam creber agens hiemem ruit aequore turbo   470
quam multae pecudum pestes. nec singula morbi
corpora corripiunt, sed tota aestiua repente,
spemque gregemque simul cunctamque ab origine gentem.
tum sciat, aërias Alpis et Norica si quis
castella in tumulis et Iapydis arua Timaui   475
nunc quoque post tanto uideat, desertaque regna
pastorum et longe saltus lateque uacantis.
    Hic quondam morbo caeli miseranda coorta est
tempestas totoque autumni incanduit aestu
et genus omne neci pecudum dedit, omne ferarum,   480
corrupitque lacus, infecit pabula tabo.
nec uia mortis erat simplex, sed ubi ignea uenis
omnibus acta sitis miseros adduxerat artus,
rursus abundabat fluidus liquor omniaque in se

ossa minutatim morbo conlapsa trahebat.   485
saepe in honore deum medio stans hostia ad aram,
lanea dum niuea circumdatur infula uitta,
inter cunctantis cecidit moribunda ministros;
aut si quam ferro mactauerat ante sacerdos,
inde neque impositis ardent altaria fibris,   490
nec responsa potest consultus reddere uates,
ac uix suppositi tinguntur sanguine cultri
summaque ieiuna sanie infuscatur harena.
hinc laetis uituli uulgo moriuntur in herbis
et dulcis animas plena ad praesepia reddunt,   495
hinc canibus blandis rabies uenit, et quatit aegros
tussis anhela sues ac faucibus angit obesis.
labitur infelix studiorum atque immemor herbae
uictor equus fontisque auertitur et pede terram
crebra ferit; demissae aures, incertus ibidem   500
sudor et ille quidem morituris frigidus; aret
pellis et ad tactum tractanti dura resistit.
haec ante exitium primis dant signa diebus;
sin in processu coepit crudescere morbus,
tum uero ardentes oculi atque attractus ab alto   505
spiritus, interdum gemitu grauis, imaque longo
ilia singultu tendunt, it naribus ater
sanguis, et obsessas fauces premit aspera lingua.
profuit inserto latices infundere cornu
Lenaeos; ea uisa salus morientibus una.   510
mox erat hoc ipsum exitio, furiisque refecti
ardebant, ipsique suos iam morte sub aegra
(di meliora piis, erroremque hostibus illum!)
discissos nudis laniabant dentibus artus.
ecce autem duro fumans sub uomere taurus   515
concidit, et mixtum spumis uomit ore cruorem
extremosque ciet gemitus. it tristis arator
maerentem abiungens fraterna morte iuuencum,
atque opere in medio defixa reliquit aratra.

non umbrae altorum nemorum, non mollia possunt   520
prata mouere animum, non qui per saxa uolutus
purior electro campum petit amnis; at ima
soluuntur latera, atque oculos stupor urget inertis
ad terramque fluit deuexo pondere ceruix.
quid labor aut benefacta iuuant? quid uomere terras   525
inuertisse grauis? atqui non Massica Bacchi
munera, non illis epulae nocuere repostae:
frondibus et uictu pascuntur simplicis herbae,
pocula sunt fontes liquidi atque exercita cursu
flumina, nec somnos abrumpit cura salubris.   530
tempore non alio dicunt regionibus illis
quaesitas ad sacra boues Iunonis et uris
imparibus ductos alta ad donaria currus.
ergo aegre rastris terram rimantur, et ipsis
unguibus infodiunt fruges, montisque per altos   535
contenta ceruice trahunt stridentia plaustra.
non lupus insidias explorat ouilia circum
nec gregibus nocturnus obambulat: acrior illum
cura domat; timidi dammae ceruique fugaces
nunc interque canes et circum tecta uagantur.   540
iam maris immensi prolem et genus omne natantum
litore in extremo ceu naufraga corpora fluctus
proluit; insolitae fugiunt in flumina phocae.
interit et curuis frustra defensa latebris
uipera et attoniti squamis astantibus hydri.   545
ipsis est aër auibus non aequus, et illae
praecipites alta uitam sub nube relinquunt.
praeterea iam nec mutari pabula refert,
quaesitaeque nocent artes; cessere magistri,
Phillyrides Chiron Amythaoniusque Melampus.   550
saeuit et in lucem Stygiis emissa tenebris
pallida Tisiphone Morbos agit ante Metumque,
inque dies auidum surgens caput altius effert.
balatu pecorum et crebris mugitibus amnes

arentesque sonant ripae collesque supini.   555
iamque cateruatim dat stragem atque aggerat ipsis
in stabulis turpi dilapsa cadauera tabo,
donec humo tegere ac foueis abscondere discunt.
nam neque erat coriis usus, nec uiscera quisquam
aut undis abolere potest aut uincere flamma;   560
ne tondere quidem morbo inluuieque peresa
uellera nec telas possunt attingere putris;
uerum etiam inuisos si quis temptarat amictus,
ardentes papulae atque immundus olentia sudor
membra sequebatur, nec longo deinde moranti   565
tempore contactos artus sacer ignis edebat.

GEORGICON IV

Protinus aërii mellis caelestia dona
exsequar: hanc etiam, Maecenas, aspice partem.
admiranda tibi leuium spectacula rerum
magnanimosque duces totiusque ordine gentis
mores et studia et populos et proelia dicam.   5
in tenui labor; at tenuis non gloria, si quem
numina laeua sinunt auditque uocatus Apollo.
    Principio sedes apibus statioque petenda,
quo neque sit uentis aditus (nam pabula uenti
ferre domum prohibent) neque oues haedique petulci   10
floribus insultent, aut errans bucula campo
decutiat rorem et surgentis atterat herbas.
absint et picti squalentia terga lacerti
pinguibus a stabulis meropesque aliaeque uolucres
et manibus Procne pectus signata cruentis;   15
omnia nam late uastant ipsasque uolantis
ore ferunt dulcem nidis immitibus escam.
at liquidi fontes et stagna uirentia musco
adsint et tenuis fugiens per gramina riuus,
palmaque uestibulum aut ingens oleaster inumbret,   20

ut, cum prima noui ducent examina reges
uere suo ludetque fauis emissa iuuentus,
uicina inuitet decedere ripa calori
obuiaque hospitiis teneat frondentibus arbos.
in medium, seu stabit iners seu profluet umor,   25
transuersas salices et grandia conice saxa,
pontibus ut crebris possint consistere et alas
pandere ad aestiuum solem, si forte morantis
sparserit aut praeceps Neptuno immerserit Eurus.
haec circum casiae uirides et olentia late   30
serpylla et grauiter spirantis copia thymbrae
floreat, inriguumque bibant uiolaria fontem.
ipsa autem, seu corticibus tibi suta cauatis
seu lento fuerint aluaria uimine texta,
angustos habeant aditus; nam frigore mella   35
cogit hiems, eademque calor liquefacta remittit.
utraque uis apibus pariter metuenda; neque illae
nequiquam in tectis certatim tenuia cera
spiramenta linunt, fucoque et floribus oras
explent, collectumque haec ipsa ad munera gluten   40
et uisco et Phrygiae seruant pice lentius Idae.
saepe etiam effossis, si uera est fama, latebris
sub terra fouere larem, penitusque repertae
pumicibusque cauis exesaeque arboris antro.
tu tamen et leui rimosa cubilia limo   45
ungue fouens circum, et raras superinice frondes.
neu propius tectis taxum sine, neue rubentis
ure foco cancros, altae neu crede paludi,
aut ubi odor caeni grauis aut ubi concaua pulsu
saxa sonant uocisque offensa resultat imago.   50
    Quod superest, ubi pulsam hiemem sol aureus egit
sub terras caelumque aestiua luce reclusit,
illae continuo saltus siluasque peragrant
purpureosque metunt flores et flumina libant
summa leues. hinc nescio qua dulcedine laetae   55

progeniem nidosque fouent, hinc arte recentis
excudunt ceras et mella tenacia fingunt.
hinc ubi iam emissum caueis ad sidera caeli
nare per aestatem liquidam suspexeris agmen
obscuramque trahi uento mirabere nubem,   60
contemplator: aquas dulcis et frondea semper
tecta petunt. huc tu iussos asperge sapores,
trita melisphylla et cerinthae ignobile gramen,
tinnitusque cie et Matris quate cymbala circum:
ipsae consident medicatis sedibus, ipsae   65
intima more suo sese in cunabula condent.
    Sin autem ad pugnam exierint – nam saepe duobus
regibus incessit magno discordia motu,
continuoque animos uulgi et trepidantia bello
corda licet longe praesciscere; namque morantis   70
Martius ille aeris rauci canor increpat, et uox
auditur fractos sonitus imitata tubarum.
tum trepidae inter se coeunt pennisque coruscant
spiculaque exacuunt rostris aptantque lacertos
et circa regem atque ipsa ad praetoria densae   75
miscentur magnisque uocant clamoribus hostem.
ergo ubi uer nactae sudum camposque patentis,
erumpunt portis, concurritur, aethere in alto
fit sonitus, magnum mixtae glomerantur in orbem
praecipitesque cadunt; non densior aëre grando,   80
nec de concussa tantum pluit ilice glandis.
ipsi per medias acies insignibus alis
ingentis animos angusto in pectore uersant,
usque adeo obnixi non cedere dum grauis aut hos
aut hos uersa fuga uictor dare terga subegit.   85
hi motus animorum atque haec certamina tanta
pulueris exigui iactu compressa quiescent.
    Verum ubi ductores acie reuocaueris ambo,
deterior qui uisus, eum, ne prodigus obsit,
dede neci; melior uacua sine regnet in aula.   90

alter erit maculis auro squalentibus ardens –
nam duo sunt genera: hic melior insignis et ore
et rutilis clarus squamis; ille horridus alter
desidia latamque trahens inglorius aluum.
ut binae regum facies, ita corpora plebis: 95
namque aliae turpes horrent, ceu puluere ab alto
cum uenit et sicco terram spuit ore uiator
aridus; elucent aliae et fulgore coruscant
ardentes auro et paribus lita corpora guttis.
haec potior suboles, hinc caeli tempore certo   100
dulcia mella premes, nec tantum dulcia quantum
et liquida et durum Bacchi domitura saporem.
　　At cum incerta uolant caeloque examina ludunt
contemnuntque fauos et frigida tecta relinquunt,
instabilis animos ludo prohibebis inani.   105
nec magnus prohibere labor: tu regibus alas
eripe; non illis quisquam cunctantibus altum
ire iter aut castris audebit uellere signa.
inuitent croceis halantes floribus horti
et custos furum atque auium cum falce saligna   110
Hellespontiaci seruet tutela Priapi.
ipse thymum pinosque ferens de montibus altis
tecta serat late circum, cui talia curae;
ipse labore manum duro terat, ipse feracis
figat humo plantas et amicos inriget imbris.   115
　　Atque equidem, extremo ni iam sub fine laborum
uela traham et terris festinem aduertere proram,
forsitan et pinguis hortos quae cura colendi
ornaret canerem biferique rosaria Paesti,
quoque modo potis gauderent intiba riuis   120
et uirides apio ripae, tortusque per herbam
cresceret in uentrem cucumis; nec sera comantem
narcissum aut flexi tacuissem uimen acanthi
pallentisque hederas et amantis litora myrtos.
namque sub Oebaliae memini me turribus arcis,   125

qua niger umectat flauentia culta Galaesus,
Corycium uidisse senem, cui pauca relicti
iugera ruris erant, nec fertilis illa iuuencis
nec pecori opportuna seges nec commoda Baccho.
hic rarum tamen in dumis olus albaque circum   130
lilia uerbenasque premens uescumque papauer
regum aequabat opes animis, seraque reuertens
nocte domum dapibus mensas onerabat inemptis.
primus uere rosam atque autumno carpere poma,
et cum tristis hiems etiamnum frigore saxa   135
rumperet et glacie cursus frenaret aquarum,
ille comam mollis iam tondebat hyacinthi
aestatem increpitans seram Zephyrosque morantis.
ergo apibus fetis idem atque examine multo
primus abundare et spumantia cogere pressis   140
mella fauis; illi tiliae atque uberrima pinus,
quotque in flore nouo pomis se fertilis arbos
induerat, totidem autumno matura tenebat.
ille etiam seras in uersum distulit ulmos
eduramque pirum et spinos iam pruna ferentis   145
iamque ministrantem platanum potantibus umbras.
uerum haec ipse equidem spatiis exclusus iniquis
praetereo atque aliis post me memoranda relinquo.
   Nunc age, naturas apibus quas Iuppiter ipse
addidit expediam, pro qua mercede canoros   150
Curetum sonitus crepitantiaque aera secutae
Dictaeo caeli regem pauere sub antro.
solae communis natos, consortia tecta
urbis habent magnisque agitant sub legibus aeuum,
et patriam solae et certos nouere penatis;   155
uenturaeque hiemis memores aestate laborem
experiuntur et in medium quaesita reponunt.
namque aliae uictu inuigilant et foedere pacto
exercentur agris; pars intra saepta domorum
narcissi lacrimam et lentum de cortice gluten   160

prima fauis ponunt fundamina, deinde tenacis
suspendunt ceras; aliae spem gentis adultos
educunt fetus; aliae purissima mella
stipant et liquido distendunt nectare cellas;
sunt quibus ad portas cecidit custodia sorti,   165
inque uicem speculantur aquas et nubila caeli,
aut onera accipiunt uenientum, aut agmine facto
ignauum fucos pecus a praesepibus arcent:
feruet opus, redolentque thymo fraglantia mella.
ac ueluti lentis Cyclopes fulmina massis   170
cum properant, alii taurinis follibus auras
accipiunt redduntque, alii stridentia tingunt
aera lacu; gemit impositis incudibus Aetna;
illi inter sese magna ui bracchia tollunt
in numerum, uersantque tenaci forcipe ferrum: 175
non aliter, si parua licet componere magnis,
Cecropias innatus apes amor urget habendi
munere quamque suo. grandaeuis oppida curae,
et munire fauos et daedala fingere tecta.
at fessae multa referunt se nocte minores,   180
crura thymo plenae; pascuntur et arbuta passim
et glaucas salices casiamque crocumque rubentem
et pinguem tiliam et ferrugineos hyacinthos.
omnibus una quies operum, labor omnibus unus:
mane ruunt portis, nusquam mora; rursus easdem   185
Vesper ubi e pastu tandem decedere campis
admonuit, tum tecta petunt, tum corpora curant;
fit sonitus, mussantque oras et limina circum.
post, ubi iam thalamis se composuere, siletur
in noctem, fessosque sopor suus occupat artus.   190
nec uero a stabulis pluuia impendente recedunt
longius, aut credunt caelo aduentantibus Euris,
sed circum tutae sub moenibus urbis aquantur
excursusque breuis temptant, et saepe lapillos,
ut cumbae instabiles fluctu iactante saburram,   195
tollunt, his sese per inania nubila librant.

Illum adeo placuisse apibus mirabere morem,
quod neque concubitu indulgent, nec corpora segnes
in Venerem soluunt aut fetus nixibus edunt;
uerum ipsae e foliis natos, e suauibus herbis   200
ore legunt, ipsae regem paruosque Quirites
sufficiunt, aulasque et cerea regna refingunt.
saepe etiam duris errando in cotibus alas
attriuere, ultroque animam sub fasce dedere:
tantus amor florum et generandi gloria mellis.   205
ergo ipsas quamuis angusti terminus aeui
excipiat (neque enim plus septima ducitur aestas),
at genus immortale manet, multosque per annos
stat fortuna domus, et aui numerantur auorum.
　　Praeterea regem non sic Aegyptus et ingens   210
Lydia nec populi Parthorum aut Medus Hydaspes
obseruant. rege incolumi mens omnibus una est;
amisso rupere fidem, constructaque mella
diripuere ipsae et cratis soluere fauorum.
ille operum custos, illum admirantur et omnes   215
circumstant fremitu denso stipantque frequentes,
et saepe attollunt umeris et corpora bello
obiectant pulchramque petunt per uulnera mortem.
　　His quidam signis atque haec exempla secuti
esse apibus partem diuinae mentis et haustus   220
aetherios dixere; deum namque ire per omnis
terrasque tractusque maris caelumque profundum;
hinc pecudes, armenta, uiros, genus omne ferarum,
quemque sibi tenuis nascentem arcessere uitas:
scilicet huc reddi deinde ac resoluta referri   225
omnia, nec morti esse locum, sed uiua uolare
sideris in numerum atque alto succedere caelo.
　　Si quando sedem angustam seruataque mella
thesauris relines, prius haustu sparsus aquarum
ora foue, fumosque manu praetende sequacis.   230
bis grauidos cogunt fetus, duo tempora messis:
Taygete simul os terris ostendit honestum

Pleas et Oceani spretos pede reppulit amnis,
aut eadem sidus fugiens ubi Piscis aquosi
tristior hibernas caelo descendit in undas.   235
illis ira modum supra est, laesaeque uenenum
morsibus inspirant, et spicula caeca relinquunt
adfixae uenis, animasque in uulnere ponunt.
sin duram metues hiemem parcesque futuro
contususosque animos et res miserabere fractas,   240
at suffire thymo cerasque recidere inanis
quis dubitet? nam saepe fauos ignotus adedit
stelio et lucifugis congesta cubilia blattis
immunisque sedens aliena ad pabula fucus;
aut asper crabro imparibus se immiscuit armis,   245
aut dirum tiniae genus, aut inuisa Mineruae
laxos in foribus suspendit aranea cassis.
quo magis exhaustae fuerint, hoc acrius omnes
incumbent generis lapsi sarcire ruinas
complebuntque foros et floribus horrea texent.   250
    Si uero, quoniam casus apibus quoque nostros
uita tulit, tristi languebunt corpora morbo –
quod iam non dubiis poteris cognoscere signis:
continuo est aegris alius color; horrida uultum
deformat macies; tum corpora luce carentum   255
exportant tectis et tristia funera ducunt;
aut illae pedibus conexae ad limina pendent
aut intus clausis cunctantur in aedibus omnes
ignauaeque fame et contracto frigore pigrae.
tum sonus auditur grauior, tractimque susurrant,   260
frigidus ut quondam siluis immurmurat Auster,
ut mare sollicitum stridit refluentibus undis,
aestuat ut clausis rapidus fornacibus ignis.
hic iam galbaneos suadebo incendere odores
mellaque harundineis inferre canalibus, ultro   265
hortantem et fessas ad pabula nota uocantem.
proderit et tunsum gallae admiscere saporem

arentisque rosas, aut igni pinguia multo
defruta uel psithia passos de uite racemos,
Cecropiumque thymum et graue olentia centaurea.   270
est etiam flos in pratis, cui nomen amello
fecere agricolae, facilis quaerentibus herba;
namque uno ingentem tollit de caespite siluam
aureus ipse, sed in foliis, quae plurima circum
funduntur, uiolae sublucet purpura nigrae;   275
saepe deum nexis ornatae torquibus arae;
asper in ore sapor; tonsis in uallibus illum
pastores et curua legunt prope flumina Mellae.
huius odorato radices incoque Baccho
pabulaque in foribus plenis appone canistris.   280
    Sed si quem proles subito defecerit omnis
nec genus unde nouae stirpis reuocetur habebit,
tempus et Arcadii memoranda inuenta magistri
pandere, quoque modo caesis iam saepe iuuencis
insincerus apes tulerit cruor. altius omnem   285
expediam prima repetens ab origine famam.
nam qua Pellaei gens fortunata Canopi
accolit effuso stagnantem flumine Nilum
et circum pictis uehitur sua rura phaselis,
quaque pharetratae uicinia Persidis urget,   290
et diuersa ruens septem discurrit in ora   292
usque coloratis amnis deuexus ab Indis,   293
et uiridem Aegyptum nigra fecundat harena,   291
omnis in hac certam regio iacit arte salutem.
exiguus primum atque ipsos contractus in usus   295
eligitur locus; hunc angustique imbrice tecti
parietibusque premunt artis, et quattuor addunt
quattuor a uentis obliqua luce fenestras.
tum uitulus bima curuans iam cornua fronte
quaeritur; huic geminae nares et spiritus oris   300
multa reluctanti obstruitur, plagisque perempto
tunsa per integram soluuntur uiscera pellem.

sic positum in clauso linquunt et ramea costis
subiciunt fragmenta, thymum casiasque recentis.
hoc geritur Zephyris primum impellentibus undas,   305
ante nouis rubeant quam prata coloribus, ante
garrula quam tignis nidum suspendat hirundo.
interea teneris tepefactus in ossibus umor
aestuat, et uisenda modis animalia miris,
trunca pedum primo, mox et stridentia pennis,   310
miscentur, tenuemque magis magis aëra carpunt,
donec ut aestiuis effusus nubibus imber
erupere, aut ut neruo pulsante sagittae,
prima leues ineunt si quando proelia Parthi.
      Quis deus hanc, Musae, quis nobis extudit artem?   315
unde noua ingressus hominum experientia cepit?
pastor Aristaeus fugiens Peneia Tempe,
amissis, ut fama, apibus morboque fameque,
tristis ad extremi sacrum caput astitit amnis
multa querens, atque hac adfatus uoce parentem: 320
'mater, Cyrene mater, quae gurgitis huius
ima tenes, quid me praeclara stirpe deorum
(si modo, quem perhibes, pater est Thymbraeus Apollo)
inuisum fatis genuisti? aut quo tibi nostri
pulsus amor? quid me caelum sperare iubebas?   325
en etiam hunc ipsum uitae mortalis honorem,
quem mihi uix frugum et pecudum custodia sollers
omnia temptanti extuderat, te matre relinquo.
quin age et ipsa manu felicis erue siluas,
fer stabulis inimicum ignem atque interfice messis,   330
ure sata et ualidam in uitis molire bipennem,
tanta meae si te ceperunt taedia laudis.'
      At mater sonitum thalamo sub fluminis alti
sensit. eam circum Milesia uellera Nymphae
carpebant hyali saturo fucata colore,   335
Drymoque Xanthoque Ligeaque Phyllodoceque,
caesariem effusae nitidam per candida colla,

[Nisaee Spioque Thaliaque Cymodoceque]
Cydippe et flaua Lycorias, altera uirgo,
altera tum primos Lucinae experta labores,   340
Clioque et Beroe soror, Oceanitides ambae,
ambae auro, pictis incinctae pellibus ambae,
atque Ephyre atque Opis et Asia Deiopea
et tandem positis uelox Arethusa sagittis.
inter quas curam Clymene narrabat inanem   345
Volcani Martisque dolos et dulcia furta,
aque Chao densos diuum numerabat amores.
carmine quo captae dum fusis mollia pensa
deuoluunt, iterum maternas impulit auris
luctus Aristaei, uitreisque sedilibus omnes   350
obstipuere; sed ante alias Arethusa sorores
prospiciens summa flauum caput extulit unda,
et procul: 'o gemitu non frustra exterrita tanto,
Cyrene soror, ipse tibi, tua maxima cura,
tristis Aristaeus Penei genitoris ad undam   355
stat lacrimans, et te crudelem nomine dicit.'
huic percussa noua mentem formidine mater
'duc, age, duc ad nos; fas illi limina diuum
tangere' ait. simul alta iubet discedere late
flumina, qua iuuenis gressus inferret. at illum   360
curuata in montis faciem circumstetit unda
accepitque sinu uasto misitque sub amnem.
iamque domum mirans genetricis et umida regna
speluncisque lacus clausos lucosque sonantis
ibat, et ingenti motu stupefactus aquarum   365
omnia sub magna labentia flumina terra
spectabat diuersa locis, Phasimque Lycumque,
et caput unde altus primum se erumpit Enipeus,
unde pater Tiberinus et unde Aniena fluenta
saxosusque sonans Hypanis Mysusque Caicus   370
et gemina auratus taurino cornua uultu
Eridanus, quo non alius per pinguia culta

in mare purpureum uiolentior effluit amnis.
postquam est in thalami pendentia pumice tecta
peruentum et nati fletus cognouit inanis   375
Cyrene, manibus liquidos dant ordine fontis
germanae, tonsisque ferunt mantelia uillis;
pars epulis onerant mensas et plena reponunt
pocula, Panchaeis adolescunt ignibus arae.
et mater 'cape Maeonii carchesia Bacchi: 380
Oceano libemus' ait. simul ipsa precatur
Oceanumque patrem rerum Nymphasque sorores,
centum quae siluas, centum quae flumina seruant.
ter liquido ardentem perfundit nectare Vestam,
ter flamma ad summum tecti subiecta reluxit.   385
omine quo firmans animum sic incipit ipsa:
   'Est in Carpathio Neptuni gurgite uates
caeruleus Proteus, magnum qui piscibus aequor
et iuncto bipedum curru metitur equorum.
hic nunc Emathiae portus patriamque reuisit   390
Pallenen; hunc et Nymphae ueneramur et ipse
grandaeuus Nereus: nouit namque omnia uates,
quae sint, quae fuerint, quae mox uentura trahantur;
quippe ita Neptuno uisum est, immania cuius
armenta et turpis pascit sub gurgite phocas.   395
hic tibi, nate, prius uinclis capiendus, ut omnem
expediat morbi causam euentusque secundet.
nam sine ui non ulla dabit praecepta, neque illum
orando flectes; uim duram et uincula capto
tende; doli circum haec demum frangentur inanes.   400
ipsa ego te, medios cum sol accenderit aestus,
cum sitiunt herbae et pecori iam gratior umbra est,
in secreta senis ducam, quo fessus ab undis
se recipit, facile ut somno adgrediare iacentem.
uerum ubi correptum manibus uinclisque tenebis,   405
tum uariae eludent species atque ora ferarum.
fiet enim subito sus horridus atraque tigris

squamosusque draco et fulua ceruice leaena,
aut acrem flammae sonitum dabit atque ita uinclis
excidet, aut in aquas tenuis dilapsus abibit.   410
sed quanto ille magis formas se uertet in omnis,
tam tu, nate, magis contende tenacia uincla,
donec talis erit mutato corpore qualem
uideris incepto tegeret cum lumina somno.'
    Haec ait et liquidum ambrosiae defundit odorem,   415
quo totum nati corpus perduxit; at illi
dulcis compositis spirauit crinibus aura
atque habilis membris uenit uigor. est specus ingens
exesi latere in montis, quo plurima uento
cogitur inque sinus scindit sese unda reductos,   420
deprensis olim statio tutissima nautis;
intus se uasti Proteus tegit obice saxi.
his iuuenem latebris auersum a lumine Nympha
conlocat; ipsa procul nebulis obscura resistit.
iam rapidus torrens sitientis Sirius Indos   425
ardebat caelo et medium sol igneus orbem
hauserat, arebant herbae et caua flumina siccis
faucibus ad limum radii tepefacta coquebant,
cum Proteus consueta petens e fluctibus antra
ibat; eum uasti circum gens umida ponti   430
exsultans rorem late dispergit amarum.
sternunt se somno diuersae in litore phocae;
ipse, uelut stabuli custos in montibus olim,
Vesper ubi e pastu uitulos ad tecta reducit
auditisque lupos acuunt balatibus agni,   435
consedit scopulo medius, numerumque recenset.
cuius Aristaeo quoniam est oblata facultas,
uix defessa senem passus componere membra
cum clamore ruit magno, manicisque iacentem
occupat. ille suae contra non immemor artis   440
omnia transformat sese in miracula rerum,
ignemque horribilemque feram fluuiumque liquentem.

uerum ubi nulla fugam reperit fallacia, uictus
in sese redit atque hominis tandem ore locutus
'nam quis te, iuuenum confidentissime, nostras   445
iussit adire domos? quidue hinc petis?' inquit. at ille:
'scis, Proteu, scis ipse, neque est te fallere quicquam:
sed tu desine uelle. deum praecepta secuti
uenimus hinc lassis quaesitum oracula rebus.'
tantum effatus. ad haec uates ui denique multa   450
ardentis oculos intorsit lumine glauco,
et grauiter frendens sic fatis ora resoluit:
    'Non te nullius exercent numinis irae;
magna luis commissa: tibi has miserabilis Orpheus
haudquaquam ob meritum poenas, ni fata resistant,   455
suscitat, et rapta grauiter pro coniuge saeuit.
illa quidem, dum te fugeret per flumina praeceps,
immanem ante pedes hydrum moritura puella
seruantem ripas alta non uidit in herba.
at chorus aequalis Dryadum clamore supremos   460
impleuit montis; flerunt Rhodopeiae arces
altaque Pangaea et Rhesi Mauortia tellus
atque Getae atque Hebrus et Actias Orithyia.
ipse caua solans aegrum testudine amorem
te, dulcis coniunx, te solo in litore secum,   465
te ueniente die, te decedente canebat.
Taenarias etiam fauces, alta ostia Ditis,
et caligantem nigra formidine lucum
ingressus, Manisque adiit regemque tremendum
nesciaque humanis precibus mansuescere corda.   470
at cantu commotae Erebi de sedibus imis
umbrae ibant tenues simulacraque luce carentum,
quam multa in foliis auium se milia condunt,
Vesper ubi aut hibernus agit de montibus imber,
matres atque uiri defunctaque corpora uita   475
magnanimum heroum, pueri innuptaeque puellae,
impositique rogis iuuenes ante ora parentum,

quos circum limus niger et deformis harundo
Cocyti tardaque palus inamabilis unda
alligat et nouies Styx interfusa coercet.   480
quin ipsae stupuere domus atque intima Leti
Tartara caeruleosque implexae crinibus anguis
Eumenides, tenuitque inhians tria Cerberus ora,
atque Ixionii uento rota constitit orbis.
iamque pedem referens casus euaserat omnis,   485
redditaque Eurydice superas ueniebat ad auras
pone sequens (namque hanc dederat Proserpina legem),
cum subita incautum dementia cepit amantem,
ignoscenda quidem, scirent si ignoscere Manes:
restitit, Eurydicenque suam iam luce sub ipsa   490
immemor heu! uictusque animi respexit. ibi omnis
effusus labor atque immitis rupta tyranni
foedera, terque fragor stagnis auditus Auernis.
illa 'quis et me' inquit 'miseram et te perdidit, Orpheu,
quis tantus furor? en iterum crudelia retro   495
fata uocant, conditque natantia lumina somnus.
iamque uale: feror ingenti circumdata nocte
inualidasque tibi tendens, heu non tua, palmas.'
dixit et ex oculis subito, ceu fumus in auras
commixtus tenuis, fugit diuersa, neque illum   500
prensantem nequiquam umbras et multa uolentem
dicere praeterea uidit; nec portitor Orci
amplius obiectam passus transire paludem.
quid faceret? quo se rapta bis coniuge ferret?
quo fletu Manis, qua numina uoce moueret?   505
illa quidem Stygia nabat iam frigida cumba.
septem illum totos perhibent ex ordine mensis
rupe sub aëria deserti ad Strymonis undam
flesse sibi, et gelidis haec euoluisse sub astris
mulcentem tigris et agentem carmine quercus: 510
qualis populea maerens philomela sub umbra
amissos queritur fetus, quos durus arator

obseruans nido implumis detraxit; at illa
flet noctem, ramoque sedens miserabile carmen
integrat, et maestis late loca questibus implet.   515
nulla Venus, non ulli animum flexere hymenaei:
solus Hyperboreas glacies Tanaimque niualem
aruaque Riphaeis numquam uiduata pruinis
lustrabat, raptam Eurydicen atque inrita Ditis
dona querens. spretae Ciconum quo munere matres   520
inter sacra deum nocturnique orgia Bacchi
discerptum latos iuuenem sparsere per agros.
tum quoque marmorea caput a ceruice reuulsum
gurgite cum medio portans Oeagrius Hebrus
uolueret, Eurydicen uox ipsa et frigida lingua,   525
a miseram Eurydicen! anima fugiente uocabat:
Eurydicen toto referebant flumine ripae.'
   Haec Proteus, et se iactu dedit aequor in altum,
quaque dedit, spumantem undam sub uertice torsit.
at non Cyrene; namque ultro adfata timentem: 530
'nate, licet tristis animo deponere curas.
haec omnis morbi causa, hinc miserabile Nymphae,
cum quibus illa choros lucis agitabat in altis,
exitium misere apibus. tu munera supplex
tende petens pacem, et facilis uenerare Napaeas;   535
namque dabunt ueniam uotis, irasque remittent.
sed modus orandi qui sit prius ordine dicam:
quattuor eximios praestanti corpore tauros,
qui tibi nunc uiridis depascunt summa Lycaei,
delige, et intacta totidem ceruice iuuencas.   540
quattuor his aras alta ad delubra dearum
constitue, et sacrum iugulis demitte cruorem,
corporaque ipsa boum frondoso desere luco.
post, ubi nona suos Aurora ostenderit ortus,
inferias Orphei Lethaea papauera mittes   545
et nigram mactabis ouem, lucumque reuises;
placatam Eurydicen uitula uenerabere caesa.'

haud mora, continuo matris praecepta facessit:
ad delubra uenit, monstratas excitat aras,
quattuor eximios praestanti corpore tauros   550
ducit et intacta totidem ceruice iuuencas.
post, ubi nona suos Aurora induxerat ortus,
inferias Orphei mittit, lucumque reuisit.
hic uero subitum ac dictu mirabile monstrum
aspiciunt, liquefacta boum per uiscera toto   555
stridere apes utero et ruptis efferuere costis,
immensasque trahi nubes, iamque arbore summa
confluere et lentis uuam demittere ramis.
    Haec super aruorum cultu pecorumque canebam
et super arboribus, Caesar dum magnus ad altum   560
fulminat Euphraten bello uictorque uolentis
per populos dat iura uiamque adfectat Olympo.
illo Vergilium me tempore dulcis alebat
Parthenope studiis florentem ignobilis oti,
carmina qui lusi pastorum audaxque iuuenta,   565
Tityre, te patulae cecini sub tegmine fagi.

COMMENTARY

Georgics 3

1–48   Proem

V.'s most extensive, and most complex, programmatic statement comes in the centre of the poem. After two lines invoking the deities appropriate to the book, he proceeds to reject various themes which have now become commonplace (3–8; *omnia iam uulgata*, 4). They are in essence Alexandrian and neoteric (3–8n.). He substitutes for them a metaphorical construct, a temple, to be built on the banks of his native Mincius, with Octavian occupying the centre, and with Rome's conquests represented in the form of statuary (13–36). V. himself will establish the temple, will be a victor along with Octavian, and will award the prizes at the contests that accompany the foundation. This will result in the banishment of *Inuidia* (37–9). The proposed project is delayed, as V. turns back to the business at hand, the completion of the *Georgics* (40–5; *interea*, 40); he will soon return to it (46–8; *mox*, 46).

The temple clearly represents an epic, and though the details of the description are contemporary and political (22–33, 46–8; *pugnas/Caesaris*), the lines look to the *Aeneid*, where the implicit presence of Augustus is constant; and V. could hardly be expected to provide a plot summary of a poem whose details must still have been shadowy in his own mind. The proem contains references to the eastern consolidation after Actium and the triple triumph of 29 B.C. (30, 32–33nn.), and may well be the last part of the poem composed (also 26, 29nn.). The view that the temple represents the *Georgics* will not stand (see Wilkinson (1969) 323–4); and see 11n.

It is tempting to look at the lines as a *recusatio* (Wimmel (1960) 177–87), and to see the reference to a future epic as a traditional Callimachean feature (like the *recusatio* of *E.* 6 or Prop. 2.1), and if the *Aeneid* did not exist, that is how they would doubtless be read. But given the date of the proem, and the fact that reference to Callimachus in these lines constitutes precisely a *rejection* of the letter of Callimacheanism (3–8, 19–20nn.), such a view cannot be tolerated; indeed the proem is if anything an 'anti-*recusatio*', capturing, as no other passage of V. does, the moment at which the inevitability of the *Aeneid* must have come to him. It is nevertheless replete with Callimachean (not just Pindaric) reference, as can be appreciated since the publication in 1975 of Callimachus' *Victoria Berenices* (cf. *SH* frr. 254–69), an epinician situated at the same relative point of the *Aetia* – the beginning of the third book (7–8, 13, 19–20, 37–9nn.); on the programme of the *Georgics*, see Thomas (1983b), (1985), Introduction, pp. 1–3.

1–2   As at the beginning of 2 (but not 1 or 4), the appropriate deities are invoked, there Bacchus, here Pales, Apollo and indirectly Pan (2.1–8n.).

Te quoque ... canemus: cf. 2.2 *nunc te ... canam. quoque* connects the two halves of the *Aeneid* in precisely the same way (7.1 *tu quoque ...*).

Pales: the deity (normally female) of flocks and herds; at *E.* 5.35 too she is with Apollo, as the two desert the countryside after the death of Daphnis. V. invokes her again in the second proem of the book (284–94), and in a way which superficially recalls this line: 294 *ueneranda Pales, magno ...*

pastor ab Amphryso: i.e. Apollo Nomius. The manner of reference is Alexandrian, the actual reference to Callimachus. *pastor* is a gloss on the Greek Νόμιος (as Servius saw: ἀπὸ τῆς νομῆς, *id est a pascuis*), and the identification with Apollo depends on a knowledge that the River Amphrysus is in Thessaly, where the god served Admetus as a shepherd. Indeed the river, which is not mentioned before the Alexandrians, figures in this connection only at Callim. *H.* 2.47–9, which V. is clearly adapting and which specifies Apollo: Φοῖβον καὶ Νόμιον κικλήσκομεν ἐξέτι κείνου, | ἐξότ' ἐπ' ᾿Αμφρυσσῶι ζευγίτιδας ἔτρεφεν ἵππους | ἠιθέου ὑπ' ἔρωτι κεκαυμένος ᾿Αδμήτοιο, 'we call him Phoebus and Nomius ever since that time when by Amphryssus he tended the yoke-mares, fired by love for the young Admetus'. V.'s *ab Amphryso* is in the same position as Callimachus' ἐπ' ᾿Αμφρυσσῶι. For the Alexandrian affiliations of this manner of reference, see 1.14–15n.; also Thomas (1983b) 93.

siluae amnesque Lycaei: an oblique invocation of Pan; cf. 1.16; also *E.* 10.15 *saxa Lycaei*.

3–8   The rejected themes are generally Alexandrian, some specifically Callimachean; see 5, 6, 7–8nn. V. heralds a departure from the chief authors and influences that have inspired his career to date – his grounds however, are partly Callimachean (4n.; Introduction, pp. 1–3).

3 quae ... mentes 'which might have charmed idle fancies with song'; *tenuissent* is potential, sc. 'had they not already been treated'. With *uacuas* V. makes a second point; not only are the 'old' Alexandrian themes hackneyed, they are, unlike the new Virgilian themes, trivial.

uacuas ... mentes: cf. 2.285 *animum ... inanem* (but see n.).

4 omnia iam uulgata: the grounds for rejection are Callimachus' own; cf. *Epigr.* 27.4 σιχχαίνω πάντα τὰ δημόσια, 'I hate everything common' – translated by Horace, also at the beginning of a third book: *odi profanum uulgus et arceo, Odes* 3.1.1; the Virgilian novelty is that it is *Callimachean* themes that have become commonplace.

Eurysthĕă: Greek acc. sing., like *Typhoea*, 1.279; *Orphea*, *E.* 6.30, where, however, it is read as *-ēā* through synizesis.

5 inlaudati ... Busiridis: 'unpraised' (litotes for 'accursed') because this Egyptian king was in the habit of sacrificing strangers (hence *aras*), for which Hercules killed him. Euripides wrote a satyr-play on the man, but V. is surely thinking of the treatment, all but lost, at the end of Callim. *Aet.* 2 (fr. 44 Pf.) – as, doubtless, was Ovid (*A.A.* 1.647-50).

6 cui non dictus Hylas puer: *cui* is dative of agent ('by whom', not 'to whom'). Hylas, a good-looking youth taken along by Hercules on the expedition of the Argonauts, and lost to some nymphs in Mysia, is a figure of Alexandrian and neoteric poetry, which exploited the traditionally conflicting themes of heroism and pederastic love. His story occupies the end of Ap. Rhod. *Arg.* 1 (1207-1357) and Theocritus 13 is an epyllion on the theme. Callimachus probably treated the subject (Thomas (1983b) 94), Varro of Atax will not have omitted him from his version of the *Argonautica*, and there are good grounds for suggesting that Cornelius Gallus also dealt with the theme (Ross (1975) 80-1). V. himself refers not just to the myth but clearly to its place in literature at *E.* 6.43-4. Given such a tradition, the question is an implicit rejection of the themes and genres (but not the manner; see 11 n.) of Alexandrian and neoteric poetry (3-8n.).

Latonia Delos: looks to Callim. *H.* 4, on Leto's wanderings and the eventual birth of Apollo on the island.

7-8 Hippodameque ... equis: Pelops won the hand of Hippodamia by his treacherous defeat of her father, Oenomaus, in a chariot race. With *umeroque ... insignis eburno* V. refers to the myth that Pelops' father Tantalus served him up as a meal to the gods who, when they realized, reassembled him, replacing a shoulder (eaten by Ceres or

Thetis, or lost in the dismembering) with ivory. The wording looks directly to Pindar, *Ol.* 1: cf. 27 ἐλέφαντι φαίδιμον ὦμον κεκαδμένον, 'equipped with a shoulder gleaming with ivory'. But V.'s reference constitutes not so much a rejection of Pindaric poetry (with which he had never been involved), as a transition to the theme of epinician at 17–22 (hence *acer equis*). Besides, 'Pindaric' and 'epinician' are not interchangeable terms, the latter being the context of the beginning of *Aetia* 3, the primary model at this point (1–48, 19–20nn.). In fact Callimachus was influenced by *Olympian* 1 (Pfeiffer, *Index Rerum Notabilium* s.v. 'Pind.'), and reference to Pindar may be only apparent (Thomas (1983b) 94–5). The matter of the shoulder, involving the possibility of cannibalism by the gods, was one which must have appealed to Callimachus, since even in Pindar it is the subject of debate (ζήτημα). The chariot race between Pelops and Oenomaus also figured as a subject on the cloak of Jason (Ap. Rhod. *Arg.* 1.752–8), a sure indication that it interested the Alexandrians.

8 uia: also perhaps indebted to Callimachus, who refers to 'untrodden paths' (κελεύθους | ἀτρίπτους, *Aet.* 1, fr. 1.27–8); cf. 292–3n. and Prop. 3.1.17–18 *opus hoc de monte Sororum | detulit intacta pagina nostra uia* (also 3.1.14); on which see 10–15, 17–22nn. That V.'s path is to be 'untrodden' is clear from 10–15 (see n.).

me: the first of a number of emphatic intrusions by V. (not here as didactic narrator, for which see 1.45n., but in a new, programmatic aspect); cf. 10 *primus ego ... mecum*, 16 *mihi*, 17 *ego*, 19 *mihi*, 21 *ipse*.

9 uictorque uirum uolitare per ora: *uictor* begins the epinician language to be developed at 17–22 (and see 17n.). As at *A.* 12.235 *uiuusque per ora feretur*, a reference to metaphorical flight on the lips of men, developed from Enn. *Epigr.* 18 V. *uolito uiuus per ora uirum*. Some (most recently Putnam (1979) 166) see the image as that of a bird 'flying before the faces of men' (which fits the literal sense of *tollere humo*, but not the restraint of V.). Ennius and V. are both adapting the common Greek phrase διὰ στόματος εἶναι, 'to be on the lips of' (Theocr. 12.21 and Gow ad loc.). Cf. 4.226 *uiua uolare*.

10–15 Cf. 292–3 (and n.). The claim for primacy (*primus ... primus ...*) is traditional in Augustan poetry, or became so, and the details recur as poets claim to accommodate a *Greek* genre to an *Italian* setting (10–11, 15–19; see too 12n.): Prop. 3.1.3–4 *primus ego ingredior puro de fonte sacerdos | Itala per Graios orgia ferre choros* (without doubt in imitation

and emulation of the present passage; see 17-22, 37-9nn.); Hor. *Odes*
3.30.10-14 *dicar ... | princeps Aeolium carmen ad Italos | deduxisse modos*;
Epist. 1.19.23-4 *Parios ego primus iambos | ostendi Latio*. V. may have in
mind Lucr. 1.921-30, though there the adjectives *primus* or *princeps*
(which become a trademark of such claims) and the opposition between
Greece and Italy are missing (19-20n). Lucretius did, however, make
the same claim of Ennius, and that is doubtless the nearest source of V.'s
figure: *Ennius ut noster cecinit, qui primus amoeno | detulit ex Helicone perenni
fronde coronam | per gentis Italas hominum quae clara clueret*, 1.117-19 (11n.).

10   modo uita supersit: suggesting a future project, not completion of the present task (1-48n.).

11 An important, polemical line. Lucretius had said (1.118) of
Ennius *detulit ex Helicone perenni fronde coronam*, which has led some to
explain *primus* at 10 as *primus Mantuanorum* ('*non Romanorum, quod superbum
esset*', Wagner). But poetic *superbia* is acceptable in Roman poetry
(37-9n.), and V.'s claim is for a larger primacy. *Aonio ... uertice* is not
simply a variant for *Helicone*; the adjective is first attested in Callimachus
(fr. 572 Pf.; *H.* 4.75), and seems to have occurred in the *Somnium* (*Aet.* 1,
fr. 2a, 30 Addend. 11 Pf.), Callimachus' programmatic account of his
initiation into the tradition of Hesiodic poetry on Mt Helicon. The
association with Hesiod has led some to see the temple at 16-36 as a
reference to the *Georgics*, but V. is claiming to bring to Italy the Hesiodic
Muses as transformed by Callimachus (see 2.176n. for the same association of *Ascraeum ... carmen*), and his choice of the verb *deduco* specifies
this as a *stylistic*, not a generic, affiliation; *deduco* means not only 'to lead
down (from the mountain)', but, unavoidably in this context, 'to compose in attenuated, Callimachean style' – only the themes of
Callimachus are to be rejected. When Ovid began his epic with the
words *ad mea perpetuum deducite tempora carmen* (*M.* 1.4), the verb had the
same secondary sense: 'compose a continuous song [the despised ἄεισμα
διηνεκές of Callim. *Aet.* 1, fr. 1.3] in a Callimachean mode'. For V. it
here has another appropriate force, that of leading back in triumph; cf.
Hor. *Odes* 1.37.31-2 *priuata deduci superbo | non humilis mulier triumpho*.

12   Idumaeas: at 11 the Hesiodic–Callimachean Muses are to be
adapted to the Virgilian Italy (*patriam*); and at 19-20 Greece, leaving
the Alpheus, and the exclusively Callimachean 'groves of Molorchus'
(see n.), is to compete in the Virgilian temple by the Mincius. Here the
'palms of Idumaea' are to come to the Virgilian Mantua. The place, in

Palestine, appears in Strabo and Josephus, and in Latin here for the first time. The adjective contrasts *palmas* and *Mantua*, as *Aonio* and *Alpheum* ... *lucosque Molorchi* are pointedly contrasted with *patriam* and *Mincius*. That is to say, the adjective appeared before Strabo, doubtless in a writer from Alexandria, from which Idumaea is distant some 300 miles, and given *Aonio* and *Molorchi*, Callimachus is the likely candidate. The alternative is to find V. guilty of complete ineptitude at one of the most important points in his corpus. As with *deducam* (11n.), so with *palmas*, literary and triumphal imagery are both present.

13   templum de marmore ponam 'I shall set up a temple of marble'; cf. *A.* 4.457 *fuit* ... *de marmore templum* (with the same pendant prepositional phrase); also *E.* 7.31-2 *leui de marmore tota* | ... *stabis*.

The metaphor of a temple standing for a work of art has been thought to be Pindaric: 'raising golden pillars to support the fair-walled porch of our house, we shall build, as it were, a wondrous hall', *Ol.* 6.1-3. This may be the ultimate impulse, though V.'s image is sustained throughout, while Pindar's is brief and is softened with the words ὡς ὅτε ('as it were'); but the image may have been developed at some length by Callimachus: *Aet.* inc. lib., fr. 118 Pf., though severely lacunose, seems to describe two temples, one well-finished, the other not, in terms elsewhere used to describe care, or lack of it, in the writing of poetry (Thomas (1983b) 97-9). See 16n.

14   propter aquam: cf. *E.* 8.87 *propter aquae riuum.*

14-15   ubi ... ripas: this tributary of the Po, which flows from L. Benacus through V.'s native Mantua, was dear to his heart: 2.199 *herboso flumine*; *E.* 1.51 *flumina nota*; and *E.* 7.12-13, which is reshaped here, *hic uiridis tenera praetexit harundine ripas* | *Mincius.*

Cf. Horace on the setting of his own fame: *dicar, qua uiolens obstrepit Aufidus* | *et qua pauper aquae Daunus agrestium* | *regnauit populorum ...*, *Odes* 3.30.10-12 - with an element of mock-elevation.

16   A statue of Octavian will be the centrepiece of the temple. On this as a feature of ecphrasis see Thomas (1983a). Octavian occupies the centre and the end (4.560-2) of the poem, just as Berenice held the centre (*SH* frr. 254-69) and end (fr. 110 Pf.) of the *Aetia* (see too 1.32-5n.).

mihi 'I will have Caesar in the middle ...', a strongly felt dative of interest; Page's 'to oblige me', 'at my behest' ignores the architect's role.

16-17   mihi ... erit ... | illi ... ego: the chiastic syntax underscores the close relationship between poet and ruler.

17–22 The imagery combines elements of epinician and triumph, as V. imagines the games he will set up to celebrate the foundation of his temple – games which will supplant those at Olympia and Nemea; see 19–20n. on the influence of Callimachean epinician here.

Propertius 3.1, a poem whose first word is *Callimachi*, and which emulates V.'s proem (8–9, 10–15nn.), uses the same imagery, though it is more exclusively triumphal (18n.).

17   illi 'in his honour'.

uictor: cf. 9 *uictorque* (where it refers to the success of the poetry; cf. 289 *uincere*). V. acts as triumphal victor and president of the games.

Tyrio conspectus in ostre: cf. *A.* 8.588 (of Pallas) *pictis conspectus in armis*, the only other use of *conspectus* in V.

For *Tyrio . . . ostro*, cf. 2.506–7n.

18 'I shall drive [i.e. cause to be driven] a hundred four-horse chariots beside the stream'; the hyperbole suits the grandeur of the occasion. Cf. 180–1 (of the Olympian games).

quadriiugos: cf. 113–14 *currus et quattuor . . . | iungere equos*.

agitabo: cf. 287n.

19–20 All Greece will desert Olympia and Nemea and compete in V.'s Italian games on the banks of his native Mincius. The import of the statement is literary, and goes to the heart of the sense of achievement that Augustan poetry was coming to feel. As Horace in the programmatic *Odes* 3.4 does not need to be transported to Helicon, but can find his initiation in the towns of southern Italy, and be received and transported into the Sabine hills by those Italic muses, the Camenae, so V., having brought the Hesiodic–Callimachean muses back to Italy (11 and n.), will, when his future poem is completed, hold celebratory games which will surpass the traditional games of Greece. The specific triumph is conveyed by the words *lucosque Molorchi*, an apparent periphrasis for Nemea. In fact it is a reference to the opening of the third book of Callimachus' *Aetia* (*SH* frr. 254–69), the epinician to Berenice (her relationship to Callimachus parallels that between Octavian and V.) whose inner panel is the epyllion on the impoverished Molorchus, who entertained Heracles before he killed the Nemean lion and established the games. The name Molorchus appears first in Callimachus, second here. In the same third book of the *Aetia* Callimachus seems to have treated Heracles' founding of the games at Olympia (frr. 76–77a, and Dieg. 1, fr. 77 Pf.); if so *Alpheum* also has a specific reference. V.'s own foundation of his Italian games is to eclipse the Callimachean foundations of *Aetia* 3, just as his poetry will eclipse that of Callimachus (1–48, 3–8nn.; Introduction, pp. 1–3).

For a periphrasis similar to *lucosque Molorchi*, cf. 181 *Iouis in luco* (Olympia).

Graecia caestu: a pointed juxtaposition; Greece will compete in *Roman* events (see n. above). The *caestus* is an exclusively Roman glove, weighted with lead or steel and often spiked; the Greeks, on the other hand, merely bound their hands with thongs as a protection.

21–2   ipse . . . feram: for V.'s depiction of himself cf. that of Aeneas at *A.* 5.774 (where he likewise presides over the games) *ipse caput tonsae foliis euinctus oliuae*; also *A.* 6.808–9.

tonsae 'trimmed'; cf. *A.* 5.556 *tonsa coma pressa corona*.

22–5   Sacrifice and theatrical performance will be included in the festivities.

22–3   iam nunc . . . iuuat: with the excited urgency of *iam nunc* and the change to the present tense, the games are no longer in the future, as V. actually sees himself participating in them. Page well notes the identical feature, with a very similar effect, at Hor. *Odes* 2.1.17–20 *iam nunc minaci murmure cornuum | perstringis auris, iam litui strepunt, | iam fulgor armorum fugaces | terret equos equitumque uultus*. Similar is *Odes* 2.20.9–10 *iam iam residunt cruribus asperae | pelles*, where, again, a future prediction (*non . . . obibo*) becomes a present reality in the poet's imagination.

23–5   The construction with *uidere* changes from direct object (*caesosque . . . iuuencos*) to indirect question (*ut . . . discedat . . . utque | . . . tollant*).

24   uel scaena ut uersis discedat frontibus 'or to see how the scene retreats when the sets have been rotated'; the reference seems to be to the *scaena uersilis*, wherein the whole stage was turned around to display a different scene. Conington and Page, following Servius, see the reference to two actions, reflecting two types of stage, the *scaena ductilis*, with which the back-drop was removed, revealing a new central scene (*scaena ut . . . discedat*), and the *scaena uersilis*, sets on both sides shaped like prisms, which were rotated at the same time, their scenes complementing that of the back-drop: 'or to see how the backdrop is removed, and [at the same time] the side-sets are rotated'. Though it may have present aspect, *uersis* perhaps supports the first interpretation, but it is hard to know.

24-5   utque ... Britanni: the raising of the curtain signalled the end of the play (blocking the stage from the sight of the audience); the Britons, woven on to the curtain, seem to 'lift it up'. Ovid developed the image brilliantly, using the appearance of a gradually rising curtain to exemplify the gradual growth of the warriors from the dragon's teeth sown by Cadmus (*M*. 3.111–14). The Britons serve as an example of the extent of Rome's power; cf. *E*. 1.66 *et penitus toto diuisos orbe Britannos*. Line 25 is a golden one (1.117n.).

26-36   V. describes the engraved doors and statuary of his temple in the style of an ecphrasis; see 26, 34nn.

26   in foribus: the phrase otherwise occurs at the beginning of the line only at *A*. 6.20, at the opening of the ecphrasis on the doors of the temple of Apollo at Cumae (34n.). In both cases V. perhaps alludes to the temple of Apollo on the Palatine (cf. 36n.), whose doors were illustrated (see Prop. 2.31.12–16). If so, since the temple was dedicated in 28, the date of composition of the present passage will have been late (1–48n.).

ex auro solidoque elephanto: i.e. chryselephantine; cf. *A*. 3.464 *dona dehinc auro grauia ac secto elephanto*.

27   Gangaridum: for *Gangaridarum*; the epithet, representing Greek Γαγγαρίδαι (not extant), occurs here first, next in silver Latin. It is intended as a general reference to easterners.

Quirini: provides with *Gangaridum* a contrasting frame for the line. The title, strictly a reference to the deified Romulus, suggests Octavian, the new founder of Rome who had considered adopting the first founder's name (Suet. *Aug*. 7). It also has a more general reference to the people of Rome.

28   undantem bello 'billowing with war'; a powerful image. Cf., in a transferred sense, 2.437 (and n.) *undantem buxo*.

magnumque fluentem: the adverbial use of *magnus* with *fluens* (cf. Hor. *Sat*. 1.7.28 *multoque fluenti*) comes from the Greek μέγας/πολὺς ῥέω ('to be in full stream'), often metaphorical for excess, as here. Cf. Herod. 2.25, on the flood-waters of the Nile, ῥέουσι μεγάλοι, 'they flow full'; also Callim. *H*. 2.108, where the Euphrates, which stands for a large, epic poem, is described as a μέγας ῥόος, 'big stream'. In the same way the Nile here appears on the doors of the temple which represents an epic, and in a proem which rejects the Callimachean rejection of epic; see 1–48n., and 1.509n. for V.'s interest in the end of Callimachus' hymn.

29 nauali surgentis aere columnas: *columnae rostratae*, adorned
with the beaks of captured ships. If, as is likely, V. intends a reference to
the *rostra* taken at Actium (27n.) and incorporated into the Temple of
Divus Julius (29 B.C.), as distinct from the Augustan *rostra* (*rostra uetera*),
then the line gives further evidence of the late date of the proem
(1–48n.).

30 Refers like 31 to Octavian's eastern consolidation after Actium
(1–48n.). V. perhaps alludes to Cat. 66.35–6 (*is haut in tempore longo |
captam Asiam Aegypti finibus addiderat*) on the exploits of Ptolemy III
Euergetes, husband of Berenice; the corresponding lines from Callimachus' *Coma Berenices* (*Aet.* 4, fr. 110 Pf.) do not survive.

pulsumque Niphaten: Niphates is a branch of the Taurus range in
Armenia. Later poets (Luc. 3.245; Sil. 13.765) thought it a river,
perhaps misled by V.'s *pulsum* – normally the conquest of rivers represents the defeat of the region (as, e.g., at *A.* 8.726–8). Possibly V. himself
thought it was a river; but cf. Nisbet–Hubbard on Hor. *Odes* 2.9.20
(*rigidum Niphaten*, which is also ambiguous); Horace is clearly adapting
V.'s lines.

31 The standards lost to the Parthians by Crassus in 53 B.C. were not
recovered until 20, and this has led some to suggest that the line was
added by V. not long before his death in 19. But he refers to a *future*
condition, and must have hoped, as every Roman did, that the disaster
of Carrhae would eventually be righted. When Augustan poets think of
the East, their minds inevitably settle on Parthia, and particularly on
the unconventional mode of warfare waged by its people: Hor. *Odes*
1.19.10–12 *nec patitur* [*Venus*] *Scythas* | *et uersis animosum equis* | *Parthum
dicere*; 2.13.17–18 *sagittas et celerem fugam* | *Parthi*; see 2.125; 4.313–14.

32–3 The references are not to specific victories; V. envisions
successes both in the East and the West, alluding to the areas mentioned
in 25–31. Line 33 merely elaborates 32: 'races from both shores [east
and west] triumphed over [*triumphatas* assumes a transitive *triumpho*]
twice' (i.e. once each). There is a 'mirror' effect between related words
from one line to the next: *et duo* and *bisque* in first place and *diuers*(*o*) and
utroqu(*e*) in the same position. The clear reference to Octavian's triple
triumph again verifies the date of the proem (29); see 1–48n.

34 With mention of statues comes the language of ecphrasis, particularly in the words *spirantia signa*. In ecphrasis it is conventional to
claim that the sculpted object is as lifelike as reality (or more so); cf. the

epigrams on Myron's cow (*Anth. Pal.* 9.713–42, 793–8), the model of
ecphrastic realism (also Prop. 2.31.7–8 *armenta Myronis . . . uiuida signa*),
or Apollonius' description of Jason's cloak at *Arg.* 1.765–7; also *A.*
6.847–8 *spirantia . . . aera | . . . uiuos . . . de marmore uultus*; see 193n.

stabunt: a gloss on the subject-matter (*Parii lapides*, i.e. *statuae*), and
also a feature of Virgilian ecphrasis: twice in *A.* 8 the verb is used
(*stabant*, 641; *stabat*, 653) of scenes on the shield of Aeneas; also in the
ecphrasis on the temple doors at Cumae: *stat ductis sortibus urna*, *A.* 6.22.
Cf. *E.* 7.31–2 (of a statue of Diana) *leui de marmore tota | puniceo stabis suras
euincta coturno* (13n.).

35–6 The characters suggest the *Aeneid*: Tros, great-grandson of
Zeus (*ab Ioue*), is the father of Ilus and Assaracus, the former being the
grandfather of Priam, while Assaracus' grandson is Anchises (see Hom.
Il. 20. 215–40 for the genealogy, recounted by Aeneas); *Assaraci proles* is
therefore a reference to the specific Trojan line which includes Anchises,
Aeneas and Ascanius and through the last of these (Iulus), devolves
upon the *gens Iulia*; see 47–8n. Ennius had adapted the Homeric lines
early in the *Annals* (*Assaraco natus Capys optimus isque pium ex se | Anchisen
generat*, *Ann.* 28–9 Skutsch), a fact relevant to V.'s use of the genealogy
as a representation of his own future epic.

36 Troiae Cynthius auctor: Apollo does not figure in the
Homeric genealogy (35–6n.), but is relevant as one of the builders of the
walls of Troy, and, more important, as the patron of Octavian and
tutelary deity at Actium (*A.* 8.704–5). For the Alexandrians (and
neoteric and Augustan poets after them) he became a favoured literary
deity (see e.g. Callim. *Aet.* 1, fr. 1.21–30 Pf.; *H.* 2.105–12), and V. here
uses the (in effect) exclusively Callimachean epithet, *Cynthius*, which
otherwise occurs only at *E.* 6.3, in the translation and adaptation of the
Aetia preface (Clausen (1976)). One of the three occurrences of the
epithet in Callimachus (it is not in the *Aetia* preface) is at *Aet.* inc. lib.,
fr. 114.8 Pf., on a statue of Apollo, precisely the context here; and V.
refers to Callimachus in what follows (37–9n.).

37–9 These difficult lines do not refer to further statues in the
temple, but to the fate of those who will regard with envy the achieve-
ments and honours of Octavian and, by association, of V. himself. At
Odes 3.4.73–8 Horace assigns the same fate to the giants who assault
Olympus. The treatment of envy is a standard epinician motif, so that
Wilkinson (1970) 289–90, and others, conclude that the influence is

Pindaric. But again 'epinician' does not mean 'Pindaric' (17–22n.), and the context of Pindaric envy (φθόνος) is generally cautionary: in the praise of exploits the poet must guard against incurring envy. The triumph over envy, on the other hand, is a feature of Callimachean programme poetry (at *Epigr.* 21.4 he claimed that 'his poetry surpassed envy', and at *H.* 2.105–12 Apollo, his poetic representative, defeats Envy and perhaps banishes it to the Underworld – precisely as at 37–9). Envy is also a motif of Callimachean epinician (fr. 384.57–8 Pf.), and must surely have figured in the *Victoria Berenices* (1–48, 19–20nn.); if so, the context was not cautionary: in Callimachus' poem to his queen, as here for V. and Octavian, envy will have been powerless. See Thomas (1983b) 99–100.

Envy's fear of the Underworld recalls the vanquishing of that same fear by the man who understands the workings of the universe at 2.490–2 (including V. himself?); the verbal parallels are close: that man was *felix*, Envy will be *infelix*, that man overcame his fear (*metus*), Envy will fear (*metuet*), here the rock which Sisyphus was to push up the mountain for eternity is described as *non exsuperabile*, there fate is *inexorabile* (2.491–2n.).

40–1 interea ... | intactos: a return to the subject at hand, the completion of the *Georgics*; but see 46–8n.

The designation *Dryadum siluas saltusque*, although not appropriate to the entire *Georgics*, obviously fits the theme of the third book.

intactos: Callimachean language returns with the return to the *Georgics*: ἐλᾶν ... κελεύθους | ἀτρίπτους, 'drive on unworn paths', *Aet.* 1, fr. 1.27–8 Pf.; ἀχράαντος ... λιβάς, 'the unsullied spring [is best]', *H.* 2.111–12; *integros* [from *in-* + *tango = intactos] fontes*, Lucr. 1.927; *opus hoc de monte Sororum | detulit intacta pagina nostra uia*, Prop. 3.1.17–18 (8–9n.); *nouosque | Pieridum flores intactaque carmina discens*, Stat. *Silu.* 3.1.66–7.

41 tua, Maecenas, haud mollia iussa: *haud mollia iussa* refers to the difficulty of the task, not to stern directives of Maecenas imposed on a virtually unwilling V.; cf. 289–90; 4.6–7. The patron's involvement in the final stages need not imply pressure; cf. Hor. *Epd.* 14.5–8 *candide Maecenas, occidis saepe rogando* [i.e. 'stop nagging']: | *deus, deus nam me uetat | inceptos, olim promissum carmen, iambos | ad umbilicum adducere.*

Maecenas makes his mandatory appearance, again in line 41 (see 2.41 and 1.2n.).

42   te sine nil altum mens incohat: V. allowed himself a similar fiction at 2.39.

42–3   en age segnis | rumpe moras: the self-address comes rather abruptly on the preceding address to Maecenas; for the sense of urgency cf. 284. V. otherwises uses *en* in the poem only at moments of great emotion (4.326, 495).

For *rumpe moras* see *A.* 4.569; 9.13.

43–4   Cithaeron | Taygetique ... Epidaurus: the Greek localities are appropriate to the pastoral subject of the third book.

Taygetique canes: Spartan hunting-dogs are proverbial; cf. 345 *Amyclaeumque canem*, 405 *uelocis Spartae catulos* – all three instances are in effect formulaic.

On the prosody of *Taygeti* see 2.488n.

Epidaurus: hardly a suitable area for training horses (Wellesley (1985) 35), and though it is possible that V. was merely thinking vaguely of Argos, which is suitable (Hom. *Od.* 4.601–5; Hor. *Odes* 1.7.9; *aptum dicet equis Argos*), Wellesley's conjecture *Epiros* has some merit; cf. 121 *et patriam Epirum referat* [*equus*], and what would be the same line-ending at 1.59 *Epiros equarum*. *Epidaurus* cannot, of course, be ruled out, since V. may have intended an association now unrecoverable.

45   'and the sound rings back, redoubled by the applause of the groves'; an unusual personification. Cf. *A.* 12.722 *gemitu nemus omne remugit.*

46–8   V. returns briefly to the future epic, as *mox tamen* looks back to *interea* (40) and the resumption of the poem at hand (40–5); to exclude reference to the *Aeneid* because it does not treat *pugnas | Caesaris* is literal-minded (1–48n.). In any case the lines merely continue the Trojan genealogy from Zeus to Caesar, begun at 35 (35–6n.).

46–7   mox ... | Caesaris: captures the point of transition from the *Georgics* to the *Aeneid*; see Introduction, pp. 1–3.

accingar dicere: the complementary infinitive after *accingor* is analogous to that with *se parare*, but otherwise occurs only once in Tacitus (*Ann.* 15.51) and a few times in late Latin.

47–8   As the statuary of his temple will represent the line (*nomina*) from Zeus to Caesar (35–6n.), so the poem will transport Octavian's name (*nomen*) as far into posterity 'as Caesar [Octavian] is distant from the far-off birth of Tithonus [brother of Priam; see 1.447n.]'; cf. the prediction of Horace at *Odes* 3.30.7–9 *usque ego postera | crescam laude recens, dum Capitolium | scandet cum tacita uirgine pontifex.*

For the combination *nomen ... origine* see 121–2n.

tot ... quot: otherwise occurs in V. only at *A.* 4.181–3, where, however, there is anaphora of *tot: quot ...* | *tot ...* | *tot ... totidem ... tot.*

49–94   The importance of careful selection

In two sections, each of 23 lines, V. stresses the importance of selecting (*legat*, 51; *dilectus*, 72) the best breeding-stock, treating first cattle (49–71) then horses (72–94). (For this numerical balance cf. 2.1–135n.) V. draws from Varro, *R.R.* 2.5 for cattle, 2.7 for horses, but he has two overriding individual concerns, which set the tone for the book: he does not maintain sharp boundaries between the two types of animals, with the parallel material from one section to the next (51–9n.) giving the sections the appearance almost of dramatic strophe and antistrophe (supported by their equal length); and both animals are treated in human terms (60, 67–8, 81, 92–4nn., *passim*), so that the sufferings and hardships, and ultimately the failure of the animal world, are applicable to man.

The two sections find a grim responsion at the end of the book, as V. spends 17 lines on the death of the horse (498–514; see n.), 16 on that of the bull (515–30), and recalls with irony the present lines as he does so; see 500, 522–4nn.

49–50   Seu ... equos: i.e. in the chariot race. The words would follow very neatly after 1–2, and they may have done so in an earlier draft, before V. fashioned the proem (1.48n.). They perhaps influenced Horace's priamel: *sunt quos curriculo puluerem Olympicum* | *collegisse iuuat, Odes.* 1.1.3–4. *Olympiacae*, the only adjectival form used by V , occurs only here in his works, and seems to be the first instance in Latin, as does Horace's form *Olympicum*; see Stephanus s.v. Ὀλυμπιακός for the debate over which form is 'correct' in Greek.

Seu quis ... equos, seu quis ... iuuencos: cf. 211 *siue boum siue ... equorum.*

50   ad aratra: either with *pascit* or *fortis*, the latter supported by 62 *fortis aratris*; the sense is much the same.

51   corpora praecipue matrum legat: the verb glosses the theme of the passage (*dilectio*), and creates a parallel with 72 (49–94n.). *cura matrum* is the subject of 138–56.

**51–9   The description of the ideal cow is answered by that of the horse (49–94n.): *caput*, 52, 80; *ceruix*, 52, 79; *albo/albis*, 56, 82; *ardua*, 58,

79. For a lengthier description see Varro, *R.R.* 2.5.7–9 and 54–5n.; also Mago *ap.* Colum. 6.1.2, which may have been Varro's source.

51–3 'the best appearance is that of a fierce-looking cow, whose head is ugly, whose neck is thick, [whose] dewlaps hang right down from chin to legs'; cf. 58 *faciem tauro propior.*

53 tenus: only here in V. outside the *Aeneid* where, apart from 10.210 *laterum tenus*, it is with the ablative.

54–5 omnia magna, | pes etiam: in polemical contradiction of Varro, *R.R* 2.5.8 *pedibus non latis* (*etiam* strengthens the polemic); V. may be importing a detail from Mago who, as Columella reports (6.1.2) has the same advice: *ungulis magnis.* Palladius (4.11.2–6) recommends large feet for oxen (*ungulis magnis*), short ones for cows (*ungulis breuibus*), and perhaps this distinction caused the confusion.

56 Varro treats colour at *R.R* 2.5.8 (81–3n.). In this book and the next markings and colour are important *signa*, aids to determining both quality and general condition: at 81–3 (of horses); at 387–90 (of sheep); at 4.91–3 (of bees).

nec mihi displiceat: litotes, 'nor would I be unhappy with …', continuing the description of the best cow (*optima*, 51) – V. does not mean that such markings indicate a second-best type.

maculis … et albo 'with white spots'; hendiadys (1.346n.).

57 interdumque: ἀπὸ κοινοῦ with *aspera* and *propior.*

aspera cornu 'fierce with its horn'.

58 et faciem tauro propior: cf. 51–2.

ardua tota 'tall throughout'; cf. the ideal horse: *ardua ceruix*, 79.

59 A vivid adaptation of Varro's *caudam profusam usque ad calces*, *R.R.* 2.5.8.

60 The use of *Lucinam* (goddess of childbirth) and *hymenaeos* is designed to break down the boundary between animal and man (49–94n.), a feature which continues throughout the book. Cf. 4.340.

aetas … pati: see 2.73n.

iustosque 'lawful': i.e. 'correct'.

pati hymenaeos: for the hiatus (where the unelided syllable is in ictus) see 1.4n.

61 It is hard to know whether V. refers to conception (*hymenaeos*) or birth (*Lucinam*), but in either case he is slightly more conservative than Varro: *non minores oportet inire bimas, ut trimae pariunt, eo melius, si quadrimae* (*R.R.* 2.5.13); on the upper limit he follows Varro, who is, however, flexible: *pleraeque pariunt in decem annos, quaedam etiam plures.*

62 cetera: sc. *aetas* (from 60), 'a cow of any other age'.
fortis aratris: cf. 50 (and n.) *fortis ad aratra iuuencos.*
63 I.e. within the time that the females are fertile.
laeta iuuentas 'the fertility of youth'.

64 solue mares: the urgent tone (an effect strengthened by the strong break in the second foot) reflects the brevity of existence, on which V. dwells at 67-8 (see n.).

64 mitte in Venerem pecuaria primus: cf. 2.329 (and n.), of the herds at the arrival of spring.
pecuaria: for *pecudes*, and only here in V.
primus: see 2.408-10n.

65 generando: ablative of means, 'by breeding provide generation upon generation' (with *prolem* as the result of the breeding), rather than dative, 'Supply young animals one after another for breeding' (Page); cf. 4.201-2 *ipsae regem paruosque Quirites | sufficiunt.*

66 optima quaeque dies ... aeui 'all life's best days'. In 66-8 V. dwells pessimistically and pathetically on the brevity and difficulty of existence, in terms which are now wholly human (*miseris mortalibus*).

miseris mortalibus: Lucretius has the phrase at 5.944, and V. repeats it only at *A.* 11.182, a similarly gloomy context, immediately following Evander's lament for Pallas; cf. *mortalibus aegris* (also Lucretian: 6.1) at 1.237; *A.* 2.268; 10.274; 12.850.

67-8 subeunt ... mortis: theme and movement from sickness to old age and suffering, and finally to death, are very similar at Hor. *Odes* 2.14.1-4 *eheu fugaces, Postume, Postume, | labuntur anni nec pietas moram | rugis et instanti senectae | adferet indomitaeque morti* – though the sequence is not extraordinary, Horace may well be adapting.

morbi: here first in V.'s poetry, and a brief glimpse of what is to come: see 440; also 95-6, where *morbus* is also paired with *senecta* (here *senectus*).

senectus: for the nominative V. only uses *senectus* (eight times), for other cases only *senecta* (nine times), the latter usage only partially dictated by metre.

labor 'suffering', 'distress', as at *A.* 6.277, where it is also coupled with death: *Letumque Labosque*; but *labor* as 'toil', the theme of the poem (1.145-6n.), is also felt.

rapit: frequently used of death: *sed improuisa leti | uis rapuit rapietque gentis,* Hor. *Odes* 2.13.19-20; it is used constantly, in the form *raptus/rapta* (or *ereptus*), of the dead in sepulchral epigrams: e.g. *Anth. Lat.* II 1314.4 Buech. *rapta patri et matri raptaque dulcis auiae*.

69   Not a more tastefully stated treatment of the topic covered at Varro, *R.R.* 2.5.17 *castrare non oportet ante bimum* ..., but (as is clear from 70–1) *quarum* ... *corpora* is merely a periphrasis, *mutari* referring to trading or selling; cf. Varro's exhortations on culling: *dilectus quotannis habendus et reiculae reiciundae*, 2.5.17.

69–70   semper ... | semper: the anaphora conveys great urgency.

70   enim: probably affirming *semper*, as at 2.509 (2.508–10n.), though Page argues, perhaps with excessive complexity, for its normal sense.

ne post amissa requiras 'lest afterwards you regret your losses'.

71   subolem armento '[new] stock for the herd'.

quotannis: cf. Varro, *R.R.* 2.5.17 (69n.); the word appears in the poem in contexts where the farmer must act to prevent reversion: 1.198; 2.398.

72–94   The breeding of stallions; see 49–94n. V. demonstrably borrows from Varro, *R.R.* 2.7, mostly 2.7.5–6, but creates vivid images from his list (Wilkinson (1969) 187–9). The passage ends in the mythical exempla of 89–94 (see n.).

72   pecori ... equino: this looks like a poetic periphrasis, but is in fact taken directly from Varro *R.R.* 2.7.7, 13 *equinum pecus*; the formation is possibly colloquial: Plaut. *Truc.* 269 *clurinum pecus*; cf. Hor. *Odes* 1.2.7–8 *omne cum Proteus pecus egit altos | uisere montis* (i.e. his seals).

dilectus: cf. 51n.

73–4   An antecedent, *eis* (which with *eius*, *ei* (singular and plural), *eorum* and *earum* is completely avoided by V.), must be supplied for *quos*. For the restricted use of the genitive of demonstratives in poetry see Axelson (1945) 70–2.

tu modo: creates a strong didactic flavour.

spem ... gentis: cf. 473, when plague carries off the herds, *spemque gregemque ... cunctamque ... gentem*; also see 4.162 *spem gentis* (of the bees), and *E.* 1.15 *spem gregis*.

summittere 'to rear for stud', as at 159 and *E.* 1.45.

praecipuum ... impende laborem: cf. 124 *impendunt curas* (also at the beginning of its section); also 2.61 *omnibus est labor impendendus*; and see 2.433n. Toil is to be a theme of Book 3, toil which fails before a resurgent nature, as in Book 1 (see Introduction, pp. 17–19).

a teneris impende laborem: see 2.272n. for V.'s use of *tener* in the treatment of plants.

75   continuo: nobility can be detected very early; from Varro, *R.R.* 2.7.5 *qualis futurus sit equus, e pullo coniectari potest.*

76   The description of the ideal stallion begins with the young foal's gait and ends (87–8) with that of the mature specimen. When stricken with plague the horse will proceed very differently: 499–500 *pede terram | crebra ferit* (49–94n.).

ingreditur: the last syllable is lengthened at the point of ictus (1.138n.).

mollia crura reponit: a curious borrowing from Ennius, describing cranes: *perque fabam repunt et mollia crura reponunt* (*Ann.* 570 Skutsch). With *altius ingreditur* V. seems (*pace* Skutsch) to create an opposite image to that in Ennius' *perque fabam repunt*, and he has used *mollia* in a different sense, describing the young feet of the foals, whereas for Ennius it seems to refer to the slowness of the cranes' step (see Skutsch). V.'s much-debated *reponit* probably means 'sets down [after lifting up]' – though *crura reponit* seems rather redundant after *altius ingreditur*. The obscurity perhaps results from the slight inconcinnity of the Ennian reference, but why refer to Ennius here?

77–9   The details and language are developed from Varro, *R.R.* 2.7.6 *equi boni futuri signa, si cum gregalibus in pabulo contendit in currendo aliaue qua re, quo potior sit si, cum flumen trauehendum est gregi, in primis progreditur ac non respectat alios.* A close study of the two versions demonstrates the descriptive powers of great poetry.

79   nec uanos horret strepitus: cf. 83–5n.

ardua ceruix: cf. 52 (and 51–9n.) *plurima ceruix*; in neck and head (80n.) the ideal horse is in contrast to the ideal cow.

80   argutumque caput: cf. 52 *turpe caput* of the cow. *argutum* ('quick-moving', 'alert') is an imaginative development of Varro's *caput ... non magnum* (77–9n.).

breuis aluus obesaque terga 'a short belly and stout back'; the detail seems mainly motivated by the contrast between *breuis* and *obesa*; Varro has *uentre modico*, *R.R.* 2.7.5.

81   luxuriatque toris animosum pectus: more invigoration of Varro's straightforward description: *pectus latum et plenum*, *R.R.* 2.7.5 (77–9n.). V. only uses *luxurio* of horses, here and at *A.* 11. 496–7 *arrectisque fremit ceruicibus alte | luxurians*. With *animosum* the horse is also given a character lacking in Varro's words, and developed at 83–5 (see n.).

81–3 'chestnuts and bays are good, while the worst colour is [that of] whites and duns'; the syntax is rather peculiar, doubtless motivated by V.'s striving for an antithesis between *honesti* and *deterrimi*. Varro makes no mention of the colour of horses; V. includes the topic in order to create a parallel with the description of the cow. Varro did treat the colour of cows, making dun and white (*tertio heluo, quarto albo, R.R.* 2.5.8) the least desirable of a group of four – Virgil has transferred the issue from cows to horses; see 56 and n.

83–5 The focus on the war-horse is V.'s own contribution; Varro merely indicated, towards the end of his treatment, the diverse uses of the horse: *equi quod alii sunt ad rem militarem idonei, alii ad uecturam, alii ad admissuram, alii ad cursuram ..., R.R.* 2.7.15; as in the previous book (2.145–8) it seems characteristic of V.'s practice to bring out the ominous aspects of his subject.

tum, si qua ... 'then again, if ... [sc. this will be a sign of quality]'.

84 micat auribus 'he pricks up his ears'; *auribus* is instrumental: he 'flickers' by means of his ears. The plague-stricken horse is a sorry reversal: *demissae aures*, 500 (49–94n.).

tremit artus: *artus* is accusative of respect; the phrase is borrowed from Lucr. 3.489, from the description of an epileptic fit – an ominous reminiscence, given the fate of the horse at 498–514 (see above).

85 Like the fabulous bulls of 2.140 (see. n.), both lines being based on Lucr. 5.30 *et Diomedis equi spirantes naribus ignem*; the reference prepares the reader for the mythological horses to come at 89–94. Like their ears (84n.), the horses' nostrils are described very differently when plague comes: *it naribus ater | sanguis*, 507–8.

86 A close adaptation of Varro: *iuba crebra ... inplicata in dexteriorem partem ceruicis, R.R.* 2.7.5; but even the change from *inplicata* to *iactata* creates a picture: the mane does not merely 'fall' to the right, it is 'tossed' (77–9n.).

87 at duplex agitur per lumbos spina: after Varro, *R.R.* 2.7.5 *spina maxime duplici*; the spine of course is not 'double'; it just appears to be so. Cf. Xen. *Eq.* 1.11, 'the double one is easier to sit on and nicer to look at than the single one'.

87–8 cauatque | ... cornu: for Varro's *ungulis duris, R.R.* 2.7.5 (77–9n.). Onto that bare detail V. has grafted a reminiscence in rhythm and sense of Enn. *Ann.* 263 Skutsch *summo sonitu quatit ungula terram* – a pattern developed with even more euphony at *A.* 8.596 *quadripedante putrem sonitu quatit ungula campum*; also 11.875; cf. 191–2n.

89–94 The horses of mythology provide a colourful close and serve as examples of high-spiritedness. Of the four horses, or teams of horses, two have strong martial associations (91), and the last serves to eliminate the boundary between man and animal and to suggest that the human condition is identical with that of the animal (92–4n.). The closings at 121–2 and 146–56 have the same function (see nn.).

89–90 Amyclaei ... | Cyllarus: the horse Cyllarus was given to Castor and Pollux by Juno, who had received it from Neptune. V.'s assignation to Pollux is perhaps surprising, since Castor is traditionally the horseman. According to the Berne scholia Alcman stated that Cyllarus was given to Pollux, Xanthus to Castor, but that sounds like problem-solving, for Xanthus is one of the horses of Achilles (91n.), though at Stesich. 1 the two horses are paired – the source of the fragment, however, *Et. Magn.* 544.54, has the lemma Κύλλαρος. ἵππος Κάστορος, 'Cyllarus: the horse of Castor'. The assignation, which comes first in V., may have an Alexandrian source, or it may be V.'s own contribution. Servius' solution (*fratrem pro fratre posuit poetica licentia*) does not satisfy.

Amyclaei: 'Spartan'; cf. 345 *Amyclaeumque canem.*

90 quorum Grai meminere poetae: see 2.16n. on V.'s references to Greek sources, all of which have to do with mythology, and some of which may express slightly polemical *diffidentia*. The primary reference here is to Homer (91n.).

91 The horses of Ares appear at Hom. *Il.* 15.119–20, those of Achilles, Xanthus and Balius, at *Il.* 16.148–9, etc.

currus: i.e. 'horses'.

Achilli: the MSS give all variants of the genitive (*Achilli, Achillei, Achillis*) as well as *Achilles*; *Achillis* is otherwise found in V. only at *A.* 2.476, and where the preceding word ends with an *s* (as here, with *currus*) his preference is clear: *A.* 1.30; 2.275; 3.87; 6.839; 10.581.

92–4 Apollonius relates, in an aetiological account of the island Philyra, how Cronus was discovered by his wife Rhea while making love with Philyra, an Oceanid; to escape he turned himself into a horse, which rather illogically resulted in the nymph's giving birth to the Centaur Chiron (*Arg.* 2.1231–41). V. clearly intends a reference to this

account; cf. 1236–7 ὁ δ' ἐξ εὐνῆς ἀνορούσας | ἔσσυτο χαιτήεντι φυὴν
ἐναλίγκιος ἵππωι, 'he leapt up from the couch and rushed off in the guise
of a horse with flowing mane' – V. adds a whinny (*hinnitu*) for good
measure. The name of Philyra is suppressed in good Alexandrian fashion (1.14–15n.), although V. later refers to her obliquely: *Phillyrides
Chiron*, 550.

The significance of this rather obscure incident (it is otherwise briefly
reported at Apollod. 1.2.4, later in Hyginus) is great. As elsewhere in the
book (with Io at 152–3; see too 115n.), V. selects mythological examples
in which the boundaries between man and animal are crossed; this
contributes to his pervasive suggestion in this book that the two share an
identical fate (see nn. *passim*, but especially 258–63n.). The incident also
foreshadows the theme of the first half of Book 3 – the power and effects
of *amor* (209–83).

effundit ... impleuit: the variation seems to serve no purpose; some
ninth-century MSS have *effudit*.

93   coniugis: Rhea in Apollonius, Ops (with whom, along with
Cybele, the Romans identified Rhea) in Servius. The position of *pernix*
after *coniugis aduentu* creates some humour.

94   Pelion hinnitu ... impleuit acuto: recalling an earlier reference of the same grotesque nature: *Proetides implerunt falsis mugitibus agros*,
E. 6.48.

95–122   *Treatment of the old, training of the young, particularly for racing*

The word *equus* occurs only once (114) as V. speaks of the old and young
in very human terms (89–94, 96, 105–6, 116–17, 118, 121–2nn.). The
subject is only briefly alluded to by Varro (*R.R.* 2.7.15), and the main
literary influence on V. is Homeric (103–12n.), perhaps combined with
that of Sophocles (110–11, 111nn.), Callimachus (111n.) and Lucretius
(103–4, 110nn.).

95   Hunc quoque: transitional (154n.): even the spirited horse will
have to be retired when old.

morbo: as at 67 (67–8n.) the word looks to the plague and apocalypse
to come (440–566).

96   abde domo, nec turpi ignosce senectae 'lock him inside and
have no pity for the disgrace of his old age'. Hor. *Epist.* 1.1.5 *abditus agro*
(Horace too is treating retirement, and the reference may well be direct)

militates against taking *abde domo* 'send him away' (though the Latin obviously allows that). A gerontophile tradition, transmitted by Servius, and not without a following, interprets *nec* as *et non*: 'and pity his not disgraceful old age' – which makes nonsense, since pity hardly suits *abde domo*.

The harsh realities are reminiscent of Cato *Agr.* 2.7 *boues uetulos, armenta delicula, ... seruum senem, seruum morbosum, et siquid aliut supersit, uendat.*

senectae: such terms, although perfectly applicable to animals, have an accumulated effect, when used without qualification, of suggesting the world of man (cf. 118n.).

97–8 Cf. 60–5.

frigidus: with *sine uiribus ignis* (99) strikes an important note. As elsewhere extremes of temperature herald failure, so in Book 3 the destructive forces, *amor* and plague, are attended by imbalance (150–1, 154, 244, 258, 272, 322–38, 441–4, 458–9, 479, 500–1, 554–5, 560, 566nn.).

frustraque laborem | ingratum trahit: the first appearance of *labor* in the third book; here it is unsuccessful, as well as unwelcome, an anticipation perhaps of the final appearance in the book: *quid labor aut benefacta iuuant?*, 525 and n. On *frustra* see 100n.

98 proelia: sc. *amoris*; V. also employs the language of elegy at 127, 130, with the effect, as here, of suggesting a human dimension. Cf. Prop. 2.1.45 *nos contra angusto uersantes proelia lecto*; Hor. *Odes* 1.6.17–19 *nos proelia uirginum | ... cantamus.*

99 An agricultural simile illustrates animal sexuality (cf. 135–7n.) – a neat inversion of the depiction of agricultural fecundity and re-production in human or animal terms at 2.325–35 (see n.). Cf. also the stubble-fire of 1.85.

This 'fire without strength' of sexuality which has passed its prime will be answered by the real fire of love later in the book (cf. 244 *in furias ignemque ruunt*, 271 *subdita flamma medullis*), and by that of plague at the end (cf. 566n.).

100 incassum furit: cf. *frustraque*, 97; for the rhythm cf. 98 *ingratum trahit*. The language returns, without the qualification of *incassum* (99n.), when V. comes to depict the powers of *amor*: 244 *in furias*, 266 *furor ... equarum.* And cf. 511–12 (of the plague) *furiisque refecti | ardebant.*

100–1 ergo animos aeuumque notabis | praecipue: in order to avoid the troubles of having older animals mate. As now, so then the age of the horse was determined from the state of its teeth: *aetas cognoscitur . . . quod equus triginta mensibus primum dentes medios dicitur amittere, duo superiores, totidem inferiores,* Varro, *R.R.* 2.7.2.

animos 'spirit'; cf. 81 *animosum,* 119 *animis.*

praecipue: cf. Varro, *R.R.* 2.7.1 *primum spectare oportet aetatem.*

hinc 'next'.

alias artis 'other merits', probably referring to the two that follow: the horse's pedigree, and its spirit.

prolemque parentum 'the race of their parents'; i.e. their lineage in general; cf. Varro, *R.R.* 2.7.6 *de stirpe magni interest qua sint.* V. returns to pedigree at the end of the section (121–2).

102 A compression of Varro's final criterion, the competitive spirit of the horse (*R.R.* 2.7.6; see 77–9n.). V. also uses the topic to provide a transition to the major theme of the section, that of racing (103–12).

et quis cuique dolor uicto: cf. 2.256n. Varro treats only the attitude of the horse which is superior, but it is in V.'s nature to show the other side; on *uinco,* etc. see 498–9n.

103–12 Didactic recedes as V. produces a vivid adaptation of Hom. *Il.* 23.362–72, a passage of much the same length, describing the chariot-race at the funeral games for Patroclus. In *A.* 5, on the funeral games for Anchises, there is no chariot-race (reasonably it becomes a boat-race), but much of the language of this passage is still incorporated; see 103–4, 105–6, 106–7nn.

103–4 Cf. *A.* 5.144–5 *non tam praecipites biiugo certamine campum | corripuere ruuntque effusi carcere currus* of the boat-race which also recalls the Homeric chariot-race; the allusiveness demands much of the reader (105–6, 106–7n.). Cf. also 1.512.

nonne uides: see 1.56; 3.250nn. The Lucretian flavouring may constitute a direct reference, grafted onto the overall Homeric adaptation: *nonne uides etiam patefactis tempore puncto | carceribus non posse tamen prorumpere equorum | uim cupidam tam de subito quam mens auet ipsa?,* Lucr. 2.263–5.

campum | corripuere: cf. 142 (and n.) *carpere prata.*

105–6 Also reworked in *A.* 5, in the description of the boat-race, a few lines before the simile (103–4n.): *intenti exspectant signum, exsultantiaque haurit | corda pauor pulsans laudumque arrecta cupido,* 137–8.

iuuenum: the drivers, as is demanded by *illi* in the next line, but V. creates a moment of ambiguity: he has just been treating the ages of horses (cf. *senectae/senior*, 96–7 and 100–1), and at 118 *iuuenemque* is a young horse; see 95–122, 116–17, 258nn.

106–7   illi ... axis: begins the Homeric adaptation (103–12n): 'and they all lifted their whips above their horses, and struck with the thongs, and with words urged them on eagerly', *Il.* 23.362–4. The image is again reworked in the simile of *A.* 5 (103–4n.): *non sic immissis aurigae undantia lora | concussere iugis pronique in uerbera pendent*, 146–7.

proni: probably ἀπὸ κοινοῦ with *instant* and *dant*: they lean forward to apply the whip and to give the horse rein; cf. *A.* 5.147 *pronique*.

feruidus axis: cf. Hor. *Odes* 1.1.4–5 *feruidis ... rotis.*

108–9 V.'s rendition of the Homeric picture of the bouncing chariot : 'the chariots now went close to the ground, now leapt up in the air', *Il.* 23.368–9.

iamque ... iamque: reflecting Homeric ἄλλοτε ... ἄλλοτε.

sublime: adverbial, with *elati*: 'raised aloft'.

110   nec mora nec requies: repeated twice in the *Aeneid* (5.458; 12.553), the phrase is Lucretian (2.227; 6.933, where, however, it is the subject of a verb: *nec mora nec requies interdatur ulla fluendi*). Cf. 2.516 *nec requies, quin* (see n.); 4.185 *nusquam mora*; 4.548 *haud mora.*

110–11   at fuluae nimbus harenae | tollitur: Hom. *Il.* 23. 365–6 has ὑπὸ δὲ στέρνοισι κονίη | ἵστατ' ἀειρομένη, 'the dust was stirred up and clung beneath the horses' chests'; Soph. *El.* 714–15 (in a passage clearly adapting that scene) has κόνις δ' ἄνω | φορεῖθ', 'and the dust rose up'.

111   umescunt spumis flatuque sequentum 'they become wet with the foam and breath of those in pursuit'. Hom. *Il.* 23.380–1 has πνοιῆι δ' Εὐμήλοιο μετάφρενον εὐρέε τ' ὤμω | θέρμετ', 'and the back and broad shoulders of Eumelus became warm from the breath [of the horses behind]'; Soph. *El.* 718–19 has ὁμοῦ γὰρ ἀμφὶ νῶτα καὶ τροχῶν βάσεις | ἤφριζον, εἰσέβαλλον ἱππικαὶ πνοαί, 'there was foam all about his back and circling wheels, as the breath of the horses came on' – which may have influenced V., since, unlike the Homeric lines, it treats the flying foam (cf. *spumis*) of the horses. V. may also have had in mind Callim. *SH* fr. 254.16–18, from the *Victoria Berenices* (1–48, 19–20nn.), which appears to say something like 'the horses [of Berenice] warmed the shoulders of none of the charioteers' (i.e. her horses were far in front).

112 A gnomic epigram at the end of the description, as at 2.272 (see n.); the first three words also connect the animals with the themes of Book 2 (*tantus amor terrae*, 301 – plants), and Book 4 (*tantus amor florum et generandi gloria mellis*, 205 – bees).

uictoria: cf. 498–9n.

113   primus: designates Erichthonius as a πρῶτος εὑρετής ('inventor'), in this case of the four-horsed chariot (for which see Eratosth. *Catast.* 13); cf. 1.122–3 (of Jupiter, inventor of toil) *primusque per artem mouit agros*; 1.147–8 (of Ceres, inventor of agriculture) *prima Ceres ... instituit* (1.122, 147–8nn.). Aristaeus has a similar status at 4.283 *Arcadii ... inuenta magistri*.

113–14   currus et quattuor ... | iungere equos: cf. *quadriiugos*, 18.

ausus: the verb is used of 'culture-heroes' and inventors (113n.), with at best a hint of criticism ('to have the nerve to', 'to be so reckless as to'): *Daedalus ... | praepetibus pennis ausus se credere caelo*, *A.* 6.14–15 (the first flyer). Cf. Hor. *Odes* 1.3.9–12 *illi robur et aes triplex | circa pectus erat, qui fragilem truci | commisit pelago ratem | primus* (the first sailor), and at 27 *audax Iapeti genus*.

rapidusque: transferred from *rotis*: 'the flying wheels'.

uictor: ambiguous, with reference to racing, or to battle (115–17n.).

115–17 The race turns to warfare as V. treats the Lapiths, who introduced reins and manoeuvres (*frena ... gyrosque*), and the art of horseback riding (*impositi dorso*) – specifically for battle (*sub armis*).

115   Pelethronii Lapithae: Pelethronium seems to be in Thessaly, is perhaps a part of Mt Pelion, and was mentioned by Callimachus (*ap.* Strabo 7.299). Later tradition (Plin. *N.H.* 7.202 and Hyginus, *Fab.* 274.2) has a Pelethronius as the inventor of the bridle – doubtless a confusion arising from this passage. But the place seems to have more links with the Centaurs, who immediately come to mind anyway with the exclusive mention of the Lapiths; Hesychius and Serv. Auct. both connect it with the education of Achilles by the Centaur Chiron (92–4n.), and at Ov. *M.* 12.452–3 Macareus and Erigdupus are Lapith and Centaur (one of whom is designated *Pelethronius*, depending on the editor's choice between *Pelethronius* and *Pelethronium*) – both appear there as such for the first time, and Ovid may have found them, with the epithet, in a lost model. At Luc. 6.387 *Pelethroniis ... antris* refers to the home of the Centaurs. In any case the connection with Centaurs is sure and partially serves to suggest, once again (92–4n.), the close relationship between man and animal (symbolized by the body of the Centaur); see too 116–17, 121–2nn.

gyrosque 'wheeling' – a military manoeuvre; cf. Ov. *A.A.* 3.384 *sunt illis celeresque pilae iaculumque trochique | armaque et in gyros ire coactus equus*; Tac. *Germ.* 6.2 *nec [equi] uariare gyros in morem nostrum docentur.* At 191 the singular, *gyrum*, refers merely to the 'training-ring'.

116   impositi dorso: responds to 114 *rotis insistere.*

116–17 equitem ... superbos 'taught the horseman to gallop over the ground and round his proud paces'; horse and rider have become completely conflated (95–122, 105–6, 118nn). V. develops and invigorates the language of Varius, *De Morte* fr. 3.3, p. 100 Morel *insultare docet campis* (253–4n.).

sub armis: the horse is now purely military (115–17n.).

118   aequus uterque labor: i.e. *aeque durus*, as at 2.412 *durus uterque labor.* The second syllable of *labor* is treated as long at the point of ictus (1.138n.).

iuuenemque magistri: again deliberate confusion; after *equitem docuere* at 116, and *iuuenum* ('young men') at 105 (105–6, 116–17nn.), the reader cannot avoid the sense 'young man'. The next line brings correction, but the sense of conflation remains (95–122n.).

119   animis: the horse is now high-spirited in a martial sense, a progression from 100–1.

120–2   Past achievements and lineage ultimately count for nothing, as V. brings the passage back to its beginning: *ubi aut morbo grauis aut iam segnior annis | deficit ...* , 95–6. The pathos is close to that of 525 *quid labor aut benefacta iuuant?*

120   ille: i.e. an unspecified *ille alter*, opposed to the young, spirited horse of the preceding lines; ultimately it is the horse of 95–6.

121–2   The two lines give a truly human, and specifically heroic, impression; provenance (*patriam Epirum ... fortisque Mycenas*) and patrilineage (*Neptunique ... origine*) feature in epitaphs from the earliest Greek times, and these proper names place the horse in an epic tradition. For the wording cf. *A* 7.371–2; 10.618–19 (both of the ancestry of Turnus).

Epirum ... Mycenas: Varro singles out Thessalian of Greek breeds, Apulian of Italian (*R.R.* 2.7.6), but see preceding n. On Epirus see 43–4; 1.59nn.

122 Cf. 47–8 *nomen ... origine*; also 1.12–14. This is virtually a golden line, if *Neptuni* is seen as = an epithet.

123–37   Diet and exercise for males prior to mating

Horses and cattle again appear together (49–94n.). The topic, treated openly by Varro (*R.R.* 2.5.12–14, 2.7.7–11) is handled with some delicacy by V., the details mainly conveyed through the important agricultural language of 135–7 (see n.). Though the first half of the book is concerned with the subject of *amor*, this is the only direct treatment of it. The approximation of animal to man continues, through the use of the language of elegy (127, 130nn.).

This section and the next two deal with *cura patrum*, *cura matrum* and *cura uitulorum* [*liberum*], with the key word appearing at the beginning of each (124, 138, 157); see too 286, 384–93nn.

123 **His animaduersis:** only here and at 2.259 (see n.).

sub tempus 'as the time [of mating] draws near'.

123–4 **omnis | impendunt curas:** cf. 73–4n. On *curas* see 123–37n.

impendunt: the subject is *agricolae* or *magistri*, curiously unspecified, although prominent, in the verbs of lines 125, 126, 129, 131, 132, 135, 143, 158.

denso ... pingui 'with a layer of fat' (*pingui* is from *pingue*, the substantive). The terms recall those used in the description of soil types (2.184 n.): the female is to have the opposite treatment (*macie tenuant*, 129, and n.). On *tenuis/pinguis* in a different context, see 1.433n.

distendere: the infinitive is like that following *conor*, etc., since *impendunt curas* implies effort or endeavour.

125 **ducem ... maritum:** the approximation to man continues; Varro used the terms *equus/equa*, *taurus/uacca* or *mas/femina* (on V.'s use of *femina*, see 215–16n.), and it is not sufficient merely to consider V.'s language 'poetical'.

126 **secant herbas fluuiosque ministrant:** cf. 2.213. Cf. the similar instructions on feeding and exercise for the pregnant mare at 143–5.

127 **blando ... labori:** almost an oxymoron, well conveying V.'s view of *amor* (130–1n.); the adjective belongs to the world of elegy: *blandus amator*, Prop. 2.3.16; *blanda tum subit arte Venus*, Ov. *A.A.* 1.362;

blandi praecepta Properti, Trist. 2.465. Cf. also Lucr. 4.1085 *blandaque ...*
uoluptas (cf. *nota uoluptas* at 130, and n.), 1263 *blanda uoluptas*; also 1.19
blandum ... amorem. The word occurs three times in this book (185, 496),
once in the *Eclogues* and twice in the *Aeneid.*

128 'and [lest] the children repeat [i.e. inherit] the leanness of the
fathers'. Columella (having just quoted from a later passage of *G.* 3)
states: *roborandus est largo cibo ... ut ueneri supersit, quantoque fortior inierit,
firmiora semina praebeat futurae stirpi,* 6.27.8.

129 ipsa: indicates a transition from stallions (125 *maritum*) to
mares (*armenta*): 'but as for the mares ...'

macie tenuant: the treatment of the female is opposite to that of the
male (123–4n.); V. is setting the stage for the striking metaphor of
135–7. *macies/macer*, common terms in the agricultural tradition, are not
much used by V. (he prefers *tenuis*, here in the form of *tenuant*): once in
the *Aeneid* (3.590), once elsewhere in the *Georgics* (4.255), and once, also
contrasted with *pinguis*, and in a context close to the present one, in the
Eclogues: *heu heu, quam pingui macer est mihi taurus in eruo!,* 3.100.

uolentes 'deliberately'.

130 concubitus: V. uses the word, which before him is only
applied to humans, only of animals – here of cattle and horses, at 4.198
of the bees, and at *E.*6.49–50 *turpis pecudum ... | concubitus.*

nota uoluptas: cf. Lucr. 4.1085 *blandaque ... uoluptas* (127n.) Like
blandus, uoluptas also has strong erotic and elegiac associations: *o noctem
meminisse mihi iucunda uoluptas,* Prop. 1.10.3. It comes to mean 'sexual
union': *in nemore atque antris, non sub Ioue, iuncta uoluptas,* Ov. *A.A.* 2.623.

130–1 uoluptas | sollicitat: the antithesis, like that in *blando ...
labori* (127n.), anticipates V.'s stance at 209–83.

131 frondesque negant et fontibus arcent: the opposite of 126–
7 (129n.).

-que ... et 'both ... and', as at 223.

132 cursu quatiunt et sole fatigant: the positive advice mirrors
the negative of 131. *cursu quatiunt* marks a return to horses, again with
little distinction between the two animals (49–94, 123–37nn.).

133–4 V. advises pre-conception exercise in the late summer, by
which time, however, mares at any rate will already be pregnant: *initium
admissionis facere oportet ab aequinoctio uerno ad solstitium,* Varro, *R.R.* 2.7.7.
It will not do to claim that the lines go only with *et sole fatigant* (of cows),
but not with *cursu quatiunt* (of horses), or that threshing need not be done

after harvesting, but may wait until the following spring (cf. 1.298). V. is not much concerned with precepts here: the agricultural periphrasis for time provides a transition to the climactic agricultural metaphor at 135–7; see n.

tunsis gemit area frugibus: cf. 1.298 *tostas ... terit area fruges*. For *gemit* cf. 4.173.

Zephyrum: the wind plays a part in the miraculous impregnation of the mare at 273.

paleae ... inanes: cf. 1.192 *pinguis palea ... culmos*, 368 *leuem paleam*.

135–7   nimio ... recondat 'so that the usefulness of the reproductive soil may not be dulled by surfeit and the furrows be clogged and become sluggish, but that it may seize thirstily on the union and store it away within'. At 2.325–35 V. spoke of plant germination as a sexual union between heaven and earth (see n.); here in a brilliant inversion of that striking image he presents the union of animals as the planting of a seed in the earth. For the image cf. Lucr. 4.1106–7 *iam cum praesagit gaudia corpus | atque in eost Venus ut muliebria conserat arua*; for V., however, the metaphor is not casual, but reinforces the unity of his world. He may have been helped by a sentence of Varro: *alternis qui admittant, diutiurniores equas, meliores pullos fieri dicunt, itaque ut restibiles segetes esse exuctiores, sic quotannis quae praegnates fiant*, R.R. 2.7.11 Cf. Servius (ad loc.) *bene rem turpem aperte a Lucretio tractatam uitauit translationibus* – but delicacy was not in this case the sole motive (250–1n.).

135   nimio ... luxu: on the undesirability of such excess in V. cf. 1.191; 2.252–3; see nn. and 1.111, 191nn.

136   genitali: only here and at 2.324, a further indication that the two passages are intended to complement each other (135–7n.).

sulcos oblimet: cf. 1.116, of the excessive richness and moisture of the soil.

inertis: predicative.

137   The final line is powerful, as with *Venerem* the purely agricultural metaphor retreats before the reality of the situation. This reality also looks to 2.329 *et Venerem certis repetunt armenta diebus*; see 135–7n. The impulse, but little more, comes from Lucr. 4.1105–20, 1200, 1270 (cf. also 210n.).

138–56   Cura matrum; *danger of the gadfly*

Care of the pregnant female (on which cf. Varro, *R.R.* 2.7.10) leads into the important aetiological description of the gadfly, whose frenzy-inducing bite is obviously a threat to the female at this stage (146–56; see n.). On the gadfly see Schechter (1975) 360–2; Thomas (1982b); Ross (1987) 157–67.

Horses and cows are again referred to indiscriminately (49–94, 123–37nn.); cows are the subject of 140, and 146–56, horses of 141–2, while 143–5 is general.

138 Rursus: makes the care of or attention to mothers *once again* the focus, and therefore looks back to the passage on selection: *corpora praecipue matrum legat*, 51. Some take it with *cadere* ('fall back'), but that is less satisfactory, given its prominent position – V.'s sections usually open with transitional or connective signposts.

cura: cf. 123–37n.

cura patrum cadere et succedere matrum: elegantly ordered. The verbs suggest the image of celestial succession, though they do not otherwise appear together (rather *cadere/occidere* and *orior/redire*, etc.).

139 exactis … mensibus: i.e. 'when they are in advanced pregnancy'; strictly the phrase should mean 'when the pregnancy is completed'; cf. 190 *tribus exactis* [*aestatibus*]; *A.* 5.46 *exactis … [anni] mensibus*. It may have aoristic aspect: 'with the passing of the months'.

grauidae: cf. the frame with 155 (two lines from the end, as this is from the beginning) *grauido*.

errant: frequently used of the grazing of cattle or flocks in the *Eclogues*, where it is often equivalent to *pascor* (cf. *pascunt*, 143); it is also used of the love-lorn Pasiphae (*E.* 6.52), with reference to Calvus' *Io* – soon to be the focus of attention; see 152–3n.; Thomas (1979) 337–8.

140–1 non illas … quisquam … ducere … sit passus: for *ne quis illas ducere patiatur*. *non* for *ne* occurs in a prohibition where the negation is felt not with the verb or clause as a whole, but with a single word: 'cows in that condition should not be allowed to …' So at 1.456–7; see n., and cf. 2.315–16 (*nec* for *neu*). *sit passus* is a prohibitive ('Let no one …'), rather than a potential ('no one would …') subjunctive.

140 grauibus … iuga … plaustris 'yokes of heavy wagons'. *plaustris* is the same dative found with *iungo*: 'yokes [which are fixed] to wagons'.

141 saltu superare uiam 'go leaping on their way', not 'jump over a road' ('a curious feat' (Page)). Through this and the following details V. almost imperceptibly shifts from cow to mare and provides a contrast with the (recommended) activities of the ideal stallion at 77–8.

142   carpere prata: cf. 103-4 *campum corripuere*, 347 *uiam cum carpit*, where speed is also seen as the 'gathering', 'plucking' or 'seizing' of a plain, road, etc. See also 191 *carpere ... gyrum*, 324-5 *rura | carpamus*.

fluuiosque innare rapacis: cf. 77 *fluuios temptare minacis* (with 141n.), and Lucr. 1.17 *fluuiosque rapacis*.

On *fluuios innare* for *fluuiis innare* see 2.451-2n. (though conceivably the present instance, unlike that at 2.451, could mean 'enter', 'swim into').

143-5   The setting becomes idyllic, a peaceful prelude to the onslaught of the gadfly (146-56); as elsewhere in the poem the georgic reality alternates with the fiction of bucolic tranquillity.

143   saltibus ... | flumina: a reversal of the practice before pregnancy: *frondesque negant et fontibus arcent*, 131.

pascunt: some later MSS and Serv. Auct. have *pascant*, doubtless influenced by the surrounding subjunctives, particularly those in 145, which are however in virtual final clauses (145n.). The indicative, rather than a jussive subjunctive, is supported by Varro, *R.R.* 2.5.11, from which V. is drawing, *pascuntur armenta commodissime in nemoribus, ubi uirgulta et frons multa*; see also 162n.

For the subject of *pascunt* see 123-4n.

144   muscus: there will also be a *musca* present, soon to be the focus of attention (146-56); V., much concerned with variant names for the gadfly (see n.), possibly intends a subtle play (*muscus* is desirable, not so *musca*).

145   tegant ... procubet: the subjunctives are final: *ubi = ut ibi*.

speluncaeque: otherwise in the poem only in the equally pastoral setting of 2.469 *speluncae uiuique lacus*; absent from the *Eclogues* (as is *specus*; both are frequent in the *Aeneid*), where V. preferred *antrum*, once *spelaeum* (*E.* 10.52 – unique in the corpus).

et saxea procubet umbra 'and the shadow of a rock may lie outstretched'. The verb is attested for classical Latin only here. For *saxea ... umbra* and the avoidance of the modifying genitive (*saxi* would have been metrically acceptable) see 1.55n. For the sense cf. 334 *sacra nemus accubet umbra*.

146-56   The threat of the gadfly, which is not related to the present technical context until the didactic resumption at 154-7, provokes an aetiological treatment replete with literary reference (147-8, 149-50, 152-3nn.), and central to the movement and themes of Book 3 (150-1, 152-3nn.).

146–7   est … uolitans: the treatment and the line begin with emphatic *est* ('there is'), with a geographical prepositional phrase (*lucos Silari circa*), and with the subject, in this case a fly, following – all sure signs of an ecphrasis (in its general sense of 'descriptive passage'); cf. 3.425 *est etiam ille malus Calabris in saltibus anguis*; 4.271 *est etiam flos in pratis*; 4.387–8 *est in Carpathio Neptuni gurgite uates | caeruleus Proteus*. These instances all describe animate or living beings or objects, while in the *Aeneid* the device is used to focus attention upon places, islands, groves, or the like: *A.* 1.159, 530; 2.21, 713; 3.163; 5.124; 7.563; 8.597; 11.316, 522. See also 219n.

Silari: an anticipatory gloss on the name of the gadfly (*nomen asīlo*, 147), as if it came from the name of the Lucanian river: *a-Sil(ar)o* (the difference in quantity is not material; cf. 1.75n.); see Schechter (1975) 361. V. does the same, with further play, in the ecphrasis on the curative plant *amellus* (4.271–8), which grows around the river Mella (*a-Mella*). These two aetia are stylistically connected: *est … uolitans, cui nomen asilo*; *est … flos … cui nomen amello*; see Thomas (1982b) 84. On the connections between these aetia and those of 2.126–35 and 3.281–3 see Ross (1987) 166. At 219 V. situates the battle of the bulls in Sila, a forested mountain in Bruttium, while at *A.* 12.715–17 a similar battle takes place (in a simile) there or on Mt Taburnus; together these seem to constitute further etymological play on the names of the gadfly (*tabanus/Taburnus*; *asilus/Sila*). See 150–1, 219nn.

plurimus … uolitans 'a swarming fly'; cf. *A.* 6.239 *uolantes*, 'flying creatures', and 457 *balantum*, 541 *natantum*. It is unusual to find the singular of the participle used as a noun (except in the case of *animans*).

147–8   cui … uocantes: a difficult reference, with a rich literary tradition behind it: Aesch. *Supp.* 307–8 (primary name μύωψ): βοηλάτην μύωπα κινητήριον … | οἶστρον καλοῦσιν αὐτὸν οἱ Νείλου πέλας, 'the ox-tormenting, inciting *myops* … those around the Nile call it the *oistros*'; Callim. *Hec.* fr. 301 Pf. (primary name οἶστρος): [οἶστρον] βουσόον ὄν τε μύωπα βοῶν καλέουσιν ἀμορβοί, 'the ox-driving *oistros*, which herdsmen call the *myops*'; Ap. Rhod. *Arg.* 3.276–7 (likewise) οἶστρος … ὄν τε μύωπα βοῶν κλείουσι νομῆες, 'the *oistros*, which herdsmen call the *myops*'. Discussion of these lines must begin with those references, for V. surely knew them and was adapting them, as is clear from his own statement of primary and secondary names for the gadfly.

There are three possibilities: (1) 'whose Roman name is *asilus*, while the Greeks calling it *oestrus*, made a change [i.e. from *myops* to *oestrus*]';

(2) 'whose Roman name is *asilus*, while the Greeks call it *oestrus*'. This is
the simplest solution, but it does not accommodate *uertere*, which cannot
mean 'call' (which is anyway the force of *uocantes*); (3) 'whose Roman
name is *asilus*, while the Greeks translated (*uolitans* or *asilus*) calling it
oestrus' – the notion of referring to a 'translation' from Latin to Greek
(in the course of specifically pin-pointing classical and Hellenistic versions of the subject) is obvious nonsense. The first alternative, proposed
by Nigidius Figulus (*hic apud Graecos prius* μύωψ *uocabatur, postea* ⟨*a*⟩ *mag-
nitudine incommodi oestrum appellarunt*, ap. Serv. Auct. *ad* 3.146), but rejected until recently (Thomas (1982b)), respects V.'s Latin and makes
it clear that he is describing precisely the process outlined above – the
'change' (from Aeschylus to the Alexandrians) of preferred name from
myops to *oistros*.

In the process V. implies a further, polemical dimension (polemics are
already inherent in the treatments of Callimachus and Apollonius),
consonant with his attitude to Italian poetry: 'I too am making a
change: from *oestrus* to *asilus*' (a passing rejection of the normal Latin
word for the gadfly, *tabanus*, Varro, *R.R.* 2.5.14 – in the very section from
which V. has been adapting); see also 152-3n.

asilo: attracted to the case of *cui*, as in the parallel *cui nomen amello*,
4.271.

149   asper, acerba sonans: from Lucr. 5.33 (of the serpent guarding the apples of the Hesperides) *asper, acerba tuens*. In both cases *acerba*
is adverbial (1.163; 4.122nn.).

149–50   quo ... armenta: recalls Hom. *Od.* 22.299-300, a simile
for the suitors in flight from Odysseus, 'and they fled through the hall
like a herd of cattle, which the darting gadfly has set upon and driven to
terror'. As elsewhere, a Homeric simile becomes Virgilian reality (217-
18; 1.104-10nn.). Cf. also Ap. Rhod. *Arg.* 1.1265-72, where Heracles,
rampaging after the loss of Hylas, is compared to a bull afflicted by the
gadfly.

exterrita ... | diffugiunt: here of the gadfly's effects, at 417 (*exterrita
fugit*) of the snake; cf. also 434 *exterritus*.

150–1   furit mugitibus aether | concussus: cf. the close resem-
blance to Aesch. *Sept.* 155 δοριτίνακτος αἰθὴρ ἐπιμαίνεται, 'struck by
battle the aether goes mad'. V.'s words, and indeed the effects of the
gadfly, anticipate the madness of love: *in furias ignemque ruunt*, 244; see
also 152-3n.

mugitibus: not gentle mooing, but disturbing bellowing. The word appeared in a fictional and idealized context at 2.470 (2.469–71n.), but otherwise occurs in the poem only here and at the end of the book, as the cattle succumb to the final agony of plague, and where, as here, the once pastoral countryside resounds with their cries (554–5).

sicci ripa Tanagri: cf. 555 *arentesque ... ripae* (see preceding n.); in both cases the dryness is associated not only with summer, but with the imbalance of temperature accompanying the two disasters of the book (97–8n.).

The river Tanager ('Tanagrus' Page; not in *OLD*) is, according to Servius, in Lucania – it seems not to be mentioned elsewhere. The concentration in this aition of obscure Lucanian and Bruttian place-names (Silarus, Alburnus, Tanager; also see 145–6n. on Sila and Taburnus) is curious. It is clear from Apollod. 2.1.3 (πολλὴν χέρσον πλανηθεῖσα καὶ πολλὴν διανηξαμένη θάλασσαν Εὐρώπης τε καὶ Ἀσίας, 'wandering over much land and swimming many seas in Europe and Asia') and Ov. *M.* 1.727 (*per totum ... orbem*) that the tour of Io after her affliction by the gadfly was extensive. Perhaps Calvus' version (152–3n.) was geographically expansive (hence Ovid's brevity?), and in-cluded a stop in southern Italy – this would explain V.'s emphasis, and possibly the proper names, which, as so often in him, would then constitute literary references; see 146–7, 219nn.

152–3 The mythological manifestation of the gadfly, which has been lurking behind the previous lines, is treated in a two-line epyllion which is doubtless shot through with reference to the *Io* of C. Licinius Calvus, friend and fellow-neoteric of Catullus, and favoured by V. (Thomas (1979)). Io was a priestess of Juno at Argos, whom Jupiter seduced, then turned into a cow to conceal his affair from Juno. She found out anyway, and set the gadfly on Io.

The second word of 152, *quondam* ('Once upon a time' – though without the triteness of that opening), was also the second word of Catullus' epyllion (*Peliaco quondam ...*, 64.1), and was one of the many trade marks of the genre (cf. 478n.). Lyne (1978) 177 is surely correct in arguing that *horribili oestro* at [Virg.] *Cir.* 184 is plundered directly from the *Io*, and was modified by V. to create the powerful phrase *horribilis ... iras*. With the patronymic *Inachiae* (first *attested* here in Latin) V. suppresses Io's name in good neoteric fashion ((1.14–15n.), and not only is the phrase *Inachiae ... iuuencae* a Callimachean formation (1.138n.), but the very adjective Ἰνάχιος seems to be Callimachean (Aeschylus uses Ἰνάχειος, *Prom.* 590); cf. *H.* 5.140; *Epigr.* 57.1. If Calvus used it, V. must have noticed its special genealogy and hence used it here.

Just as V. ended the section at 72–94 with the story of Saturn and Philyra and referred obliquely to the Centaurs at 115 (see nn.), so here the climax is provided by Io, who similarly occupies a world between man and animal, and so brings those worlds together.

Iuno: only in this book, here inflicting a *pestis* on Io, at 532 in the course of the other *pestis*.

pestem: looks to the real plague at the end of the book; and cf. 1.181n.

154   hunc quoque: otherwise in V. only at 95, where it is similarly transitional and immediately follows the story (parallel to Io's; 152–3n.) of Saturn's transformation into a horse.

nam mediis feruoribus acrior instat: again the association of destructive forces with intense heat. Varro merely says that the gadfly is at its worst in summer: *aestate*, *R.R.* 2.5.14.

155   There is hiatus after *pecori*; cf. 2.144.

arcebis ... pasces: the didactic future for the imperative, as at 176, 320–1; 1.72, 73, 167; 4.105. Cf. 131 *arcent*.

For the dative (*pecori* 'ward it off for [i.e. from] the herd'), cf. *E.* 7.47 *solstitium pecori defendite.*

grauido: see 139n.

156   sole recens orto 'fresh [lit. 'when you are fresh'] from the sunrise'; or possibly *recens* is the adverb.

noctem ducentibus astris: the section closes on a bucolic note; cf. *E.* 1.83; 6.86; 10.77. See 143–5n. Conversely the Day-star is said to 'lead in' the day at *A.* 2.801–2 *surgebat Lucifer ... | ducebatque diem.*

157–78   Cura uitulorum*: the care and education of the young cattle*

The passage, which draws from Varro, *R.R.* 1.20 and 2.5.16–17, is concerned only with calves (the horse's education comes in the next section), and though the language continues to be applicable to man (cf. 163–5n.) V. creates a sort of 'didactic interlude', free of mythological material and little influenced by the more literary traditions which inform the preceding as well as the following sections.

See 49–94, 179–208nn. for the paired treatment of horses and cattle.

157   cura: see 123–37n.

traducitur: just as attention was transferred from father to mother at 138–9.

158   notas et nomina gentis inurunt: cf. 1.263 *aut pecori signum aut numeros impressit aceruis.* 'The first of the two branding-marks (*nota*) was the owner's distinctive symbol which enabled him to trace missing beasts; the second probably provided reference to the dam, giving a rough and ready guide to selection' (White (1970) 287); cf. 71. For the subject of *inurunt* see 123–4n.

159   et quos: there is ellipse of a verb: 'and they set aside those . . .'

pecori . . . habendo 'for keeping up the herd'; cf. 1.3–4 *qui cultus habendo | sit pecori.*

summittere: cf. 73–4 and n.

160   aris seruare sacros '[or those they prefer] to keep sacred for the altars' – the predominant use of animals in the *laudes Italiae* (2.145–8n.), but only briefly mentioned in the reality of the technical treatment. V. perhaps anticipates the failed sacrifice during the plague at 486–93 (see n.).

scindere terram: cf. 2.237n.

161   campum horrentem: proleptic, referring to the result of the ploughing ('the plain with its ridges') rather than to the rugged condition of the ground before ploughing; cf. 198–9 *campique . . . horrescunt,* and see 1.314n. for *horreo/horridus* in similar contexts.

fractis . . . glaebis: the perf. part. is aoristic: 'by breaking the clods'. Cf. 1.94 *glaebas qui frangit;* 2.399–400 *glaebaque . . . frangenda.*

inuertere: cf. 1.65n.

162   Those not destined to share in man's *labor* occupy a pastoral world.

pascuntur: as with *pascunt* as 143, some later MSS have the subjunctive, but the indicative is supported by *traducitur* (157) and *inurunt* – all three verbs state as a matter of fact what is done with the calves, while the precepts for training begin in 163. Cf. also Varro, *R.R.* 2.5.11 *pascuntur armenta commodissime in nemoribus,* where the same verb has virtually jussive force.

163–5   The language is applicable to the education of children, as at 2.362–3 (of the 'training' of young vines); see n.

163   usum . . . agrestem: *usus* specifies the domain of *labor;* cf. 1.133–4 (of Jupiter's imposition of *labor*).

164   uitulos: used rather loosely; Varro states (*R.R.* 1.20.1) that oxen should be acquired unbroken and between the age of three and four, then trained.

hortare: the term applies to education; cf. Cic. *De Or.* 1.234 *studi . . . et hortator et magister*, and Quint. 10.3.23 *studiorum hortator*; cf. 163 *studium*.

uiamque insiste domandi 'and enter the path of training'; cf. 206 (of colts) *domandum*, and 2.62 (of trees) *domandae* (163–5n.). These are the only occurrences in V. of the gerund or gerundive of *domo*. Cf. *domandum* at Varro, *R.R.* 1.20.2 (166–9n.).

165   dum faciles animi iuuenum: the suggestion of a human context is obvious; on the use of *iuuenis* in this connection see 105–6, 118, 258nn.

166–9   The training of the ploughing-ox by using an imitation yoke is taken directly from Varro, *R.R.* 1.20.2 *nouellos cum quis emerit iuuencos, si eorum colla in furcas destitutas incluserit ac dederit cibum, diebus paucis erunt mansueti et ad domandum proni*. As ever, in V.'s words there is a world of difference (167–8n.).

The careful prescriptions will be brought to nothing at 515–30, as the ox drops dead from plague, the yoke still around his neck (see n.).

166–7   circlos | ceruici subnecte: cf. *A.* 10.137–8 *ceruix cui . . . subnectit circulus*. The syncope (for the metrically impossible *circulos*) also occurs at Acc. *Androm.* fr. 100 Ribb.; see *OLD, ThLL* s.v.

167   dehinc: in V. scanned as an iamb (as here) five times, as a monosyllable four times.

167–8   ubi … adsuerint: a vivid and humanizing rendition of Varro's *diebus paucis erunt mansueti et ad domandum proni* (166–9n.).

168–9   ipsis … pares 'join them in pairs fastened together by those same halters' (the *circli* of 166). *aptos* is the perfect participle (in effect the only surviving form) of the obsolete verb *apio*.

169   coge gradum conferre iuuencos 'make the steers keep step with each other'. At 517–18 the union is broken by the plague.

The phrase *conferre gradum* is used of the shades of the Trojan warriors who walk with Aeneas in the Underworld (*A.* 6.488). See 191–2n.

170–1   atque … terram: the subject is now the draught ox, which in Varro also immediately follows the ploughing ox: *quod ad uecturas, item instituendum ut inania primum ducant plaustra et, si possis, per uicum aut oppidum*, *R.R.* 1.20.3.

illis: dative of agent, somewhat rare when not with the perfect passive, though cf. *E.* 4.16 *uidebitur illis*; 6.72 *tibi ... dicatur.* As in these cases it is most common with pronouns, though Cicero extended the usage to substantives (K–S I 324).

171 summo uestigia puluere signent: a visual detail arising from *inania*: the empty wagon barely leaves a mark on the surface. V. draws a parallel with the young horse, which moves so quickly it too barely leaves a track (195).

172–3 post ... | instrepat: a clear adaptation of Hom. *Il.* 5.838–9 'and the oaken axle groaned greatly under the weight'. Though *faginus axis* is virtually a transliteration of φήγινος ἄξων, Latin *fagus* = beech, not oak.

post: adverbial: 'later'; parallel to *dehinc*, 167.

instrepat: the enjambment is perhaps intended to reflect that of Homer: βριθοσύνηι.

173 iunctos temo trahat aereus orbis: the elegant word-order (A–n–V–a–N) normally extends over the whole line; see 2.531n.

temo ... aereus: not 'made of bronze', but 'encased' or 'reinforced' with it.

174–6 At 205–6 the diet of the colt is treated in the same position relative to the section in which it appears.

174 interea: V. now returns to the period before their training begins (*indomitae*), i.e. the first three years.

pubi: apparently the first instance in Latin of the word referring to animals (105–6, 118, 130, 165, 215–16nn.).

175 uescas 'small', 'attenuated', therefore 'inadequate'; cf. 4.131 *uescumque papauer.*

176 frumenta manu carpes sata 'but feed them on growing corn, picked by hand'; cf. 394–5.

For the didactic future for imperative see 155n.

176–7 nec ... uaccae: so Varro, *R.R.* 2.2.17 (on ewes after they have given birth) *interea matres eorum iis temporibus non mulgent quidam.* Varro's *quidam* shows that the *mos patrum* had not been entirely abandoned. At *E.* 3.30 this advice is not followed: *bis uenit [uitula] ad mulctram, binos alit ubere fetus* – but the speaker, Damoetas, is advertising the production of his cow, so the line need not reflect agricultural reality. Young goats are treated at 398; see also 309–10n.

178   The passage ends elegantly, with a golden line (1.117n.), and with the subject returning to its beginning (*natos* looks to *post partum ... uitulos*, 157); the same happens in the next section (202–4n.).

*179–208   The care and education of the young horse,
specifically for war and games*

Based on Varro, *R.R.* 2.7.11–14, but the departures are radical. V. stresses only the military aspect of the horse (and the quasi-military—chariot-racing), and makes only passing reference to its only agricultural function, the pulling of carriages (183–4n.). In fact from an agricultural point of view it is the donkey and the mule (passed over by V.) which merit treatment (White (1970) 288). V. presents a vivid picture, full of literary allusion, of the spirited horse, and, on a broader level, sets the scene for the return of the animal at 498–514, where its agonizing death from plague (like that of the ploughing ox at 515–30) negates the *cura* which is the subject of the present passage (49–94n.).

179   Sin ad bella magis studium turmasque ferocis: cf. 2.195 *sin armenta magis studium uitulosque tueri.*

180   Alphea ... flumina Pisae: the periphrasis for Olympia (cf. 202–3n.) recalls the reference to Olympia and Nemea at 19 *Alpheum ... lucosque Molorchi*, as well as the opening of the 'technical' part of the book at 49–50 *seu quis Olympiacae miratus praemia palmae | pascit equos.*

praelabi: like *agitare* in 181, a complementary infinitive dependent (as is the prepositional purpose phrase, *ad bella ... turmasque*) on *studium.* The use of *praelabi* is somewhat unusual, and is perhaps transferred from the river.

181   Iouis in luco: for Olympia, as *lucosque Molorchi* at 19 stood for Nemea.

currus agitare uolantis: cf. 194 *uolans*, 201 *uolat*; also 18 *centum quadriiugos agitabo ad flumina currus*; cf. too 287n.

182–4   Expanded from Varro, *R.R.* 2.7.12 *eademque causa ibi frenos suspendendum, ut eculi consuescant et uidere eorum faciem et e motu audire crepitus.* Only the final words of V. (184 *et stabulo frenos audire sonantis*) are paralleled in Varro; V. introduces the need for the young horse to look upon the arms and endure the din of battle.

182   primus equi labor: unlike the plants and trees of Books 1 and 2, which are the object of man's *labor*, the horse and the ox (163n.)

actually share in the toil of man, and in the failure of that toil (525–30n.).

Cf. 193 *sitque laboranti similis*.

182–3   animos ... | bellantum: 'to endure the sight of the bravery and the weapons of the warriors'; cf. 83 (the description of the ideal war-horse).

183–4   tractuque ... rotam 'and to endure [the noise of] the groaning wheel as it is dragged'; this may refer to the chariot wheel (again the intrusion of military reference), or (less likely) to the wheel of a carriage (*qui uectorios [equos] facere uult ... ad raedam*, Varro, *R.R.* 2.7.15).

184   stabulo ... sonantis: cf. Varro, *R.R.* 2.7.12 (182–4n.).

185–6   magis atque magis: otherwise in V. only at *A.* 2.299; 12.239; cf. also 12.406 *magis ac magis*.

blandis: here 'caressing', distinct in sense from 127 (see n.); cf. also 496 *canibus blandis*, 'fawning hounds'.

gaudere ... amare: still dependent on *labor est*, 182.

plausae ... amare 'to love the sound of its neck being patted'; cf. *A.* 12.85–6 *circumstant properi aurigae manibusque lacessunt | pectora plausa cauis*.

187–208   The stages in the colt's training: 187 *primo*, 188 *inque uicem*, 190 *tribus exactis ubi quarta successerit aestas*, 205 *tum demum*. Cf. the training of the vine at 2.362–70 (see n.): 362 *prima ... aetas*, 363–4 *dum se laetus ad auras | palmes agit*, 367–9 *inde ubi iam ... tum ... tum ... tum denique*; and cf. 163–5n.

187   haec: i.e. the things mentioned in 182–6.

iam ... matris 'as soon as he is removed from the teat of his mother'; final weaning ideally occurs after two years (*neque prius biennio confecto a lacte remouendum*, Varro, *R.R.* 2.7.12), but the process begins well before that.

188   inque uicem: for *et inuicem* 'and in turns', 'now and then' (i.e. 'gradually'); cf. Varro, *R.R.* 2.7.12–13 *eosque, cum stent cum matribus, interdum tractandum ... cum iam ad manus accedere consuerint, interdum imponere iis puerum.*

det mollibus ora capistris: cf. 399 – the only other instance of *capistrum* in V.

189   inualidus: the final syllable is scanned long at the point of ictus (1.138n.).

etiamque ... etiam: i.e. *etiamnunc*; cf. *A.* 6.485 *Idaeumque etiam currus, etiam arma tenentem.*

inscius aeui 'ignorant of life'; *aeui* is an objective genitive; cf. *A.* 8.627 *uenturique inscius aeui*.

190   Cf. Varro, *R.R.* 2.7.13 (on first setting a rider on the horse) *haec facere cum sit trimus.*

tribus exactis [sc. aestatibus]: cf. 139 *exactis … mensibus.*

191   carpere … gyrum 'to pace the training-ring'; cf. 115. On *carpere*, see 142n.

191–2   gradibusque sonare | compositis: cf. the war-horse of 88 (87–8n.). *gradibus compositis* describes the orderly arrangement of the canter (192n.); cf. the (somewhat different) harmony of the bullocks' step at 169.

192   sinuetque alterna uolumina crurum: lit. 'and let him curve the alternate bendings of his legs' – a fine description of the mechanics of the canter. *sinuo* is otherwise used by Virgil (also with *uolumen*) only of the serpents at *A.* 2.208 – also a vivid description.

193   sitque laboranti similis: perhaps conveys the notion of rehearsal: 'let him be as if [really] toiling'. *laboro* in part describes the awkwardness of the canter, but V. seems to strain after the suggestion of *labor*.

193–4   tum … | tum: emphatic anaphora, picked up by *tum demum* at 205; cf. 2.368–70 (and n.) *tum … tum … tum denique*; also 187–208n.

cursibus auras | … uocet 'challenge the winds to a race'; cf. 20; *A.* 5.291 *rapido contendere cursu*, which suggest that *cursibus* is an instrumental ablative rather than dative (= *ad cursus*). Cf. also *A.* 11.442 'solum [*Turnum*] *Aeneas uocat'*.

uolans: cf. 181 *currus uolantis*, 201 *uolat*.

liber habenis: cf. 1.514 *neque audit currus habenas* (of the chariot out of control); 2.364 *laxis … habenis* (of the vine-shoot; cf. 187–208n.; preceding n.).

195   uix … harena: cf. 171.

196–201   As at 103–12, the horse leads V. to Homer and the world of heroic war, this time to the storm-similes of *Il.* 2.144–8. But the similarities are fairly slight, as V. adapts the model to create his own emphasis – on the conflict of elements. In Homer there are two similes, with two storms – one at sea ('the assembly was shaken as are the big waves of the sea', 2.144), the other on land ('as when the West wind comes and shakes the deep crops', 2.147). In V.'s single simile the effects of the single storm are felt by sea and land, with the two carefully arranged and reiterated, so as to reflect but elaborate on the Homeric original. At the same time the North wind sweeps down Scythia's cold and dry storms. V. adds his own characteristic literary dimension by conflating Catullus and Lucretius with the transformed Homeric original (197–8, 201nn.).

The storm, which immediately precedes the treatment of the destructive powers of *amor*, recalls those other storms of the poem, the one which devastated the works of the farmer at 1.311–50, and the one which swept fire through the olive trees at 2.303–14 (see nn. and 196, 197, 199–200).

196 Hyperboreis ... oris: cf. 1.333 *ingeminant Austri et densissimus imber*; here, however, *densus* means 'in its power', not 'thick [with rain]', which applies to the South wind, but not to the North (cf. *arida ... nubila*).

197 incubuit: cf. the storm at 2.311 *tempestas ... | incubuit* (196–201n.). Both are influenced by Lucr. 6.1142–3 *mortifer aestus ... | incubuit*, a description of the plague, from which a detail is adapted in the very next line (198n.).

197–8 arida differt | nubila: taken from Lucr. 1.272 (also of a storm) *nubila differt*, where, however, the sense of *differt* is the normal 'disperses', while here it must mean 'marshals'.

198 segetes ... campique: see 196–201n.

campique natantes: a Lucretian periphrasis for the sea (5.488; 6.405, 1142 (197n.); also 6.267 *camposque natare* – of the flooded land). Heyne and others take it as = 'billowing' fields of grain, but *natantes* is not the same as *undantes* or *fluctuantes*, and such a reading (merely repeating *segetes*) would destroy the alternation between land and sea (196–201n.); at *A.* 6.724 *camposque liquentis* = the sea.

199 lenibus horrescunt flabris: the verb is appropriate to the rippling surface both of the sea and of a field of grain (1.314n.). *flabra* is another Lucretian touch (2.293n.).

199–200 summaeque sonorem | dant siluae: noise is also stressed in the storm at 1.334 and the fire-storm at 2.306.

siluae ... fluctus: land and sea are again paired (196–201n.).

urgent: the intransitive is rare; cf. 1.443–4 (also of a storm) *urget ab alto ... Notus.*

201 The line (the last of the simile) refers to the North wind, though used somewhat ambiguously, being applicable to the horse itself; cf.

120 *quamuis saepe fuga uersos ille egerit hostis*, and see 194 (of the horse) *uolans*.

The purely dactylic rhythm gives the line a vigorous speed which supports the sense.

arua ... aequora: cf. 196–201n.

uolat ... aequora uerrens: perhaps a reference to the opening of Catullus 64, where the rowers of the Argo (*uolitantem flamine currum*, 9) are also said to 'sweep the sea': *uerrentes aequora*, 7.

202–4 Such a horse will be good for the games or (with chariot) in battle: a return to the theme of the beginning (179–84), as in the previous section (178n.).

202 hic: *hinc* also has good MS support, but though Mynors and Geymonat both read it, the argument of Forbiger, Page and Williams ('a reiteration of the subject of the narrative is needed after the long simile') is compelling.

202–3 ad Elei ... spatia 'will sweat [his course] towards the turning-posts of Elis and the great laps of the plain'. The periphrasis for Olympia (situated in the state of Elis) creates a frame with 180 (see n.). For *spatia* cf. 1.513 (and n.); 2.541.

sudabit: before death the cold sweat of plague will infect both horse (500–1) and man (564–5); see following n.

spumas aget ore cruentas: from the bit, but the image is ominous; cf. the picture of the dying horse: *it naribus ater | sanguis*, 507–8. Cf., too, of the racehorse at 111 *umescunt spumis flatuque sequentum*.

204 Belgica ... esseda: the *essedum* is strictly the chariot of the Gauls and Britons, but *Belgica* is an acceptable poeticism, and the bland variant *bellica* (a word not used by V.) is to be rejected; the phrase is ethnographical and colourful. Though the chariot was used for transport in Rome, this reference is without doubt to military use.

205–6 The colt's diet is treated in the same relative position as that of the ox in the previous section (174–6).

tum demum: otherwise used four times in the *Aeneid*; cf. 2.369 *tum denique* (187–208n.). The words go closely with *domitis*: 'then at last, when they have been broken'.

crassa ... farragine 'with fattening forage' – *farrago* is a mixture of grains. V. is adapting directly from Varro, who prescribes this diet after the horse has been broken, usually at the age of three: *a quo tempore farrago*

dari solet, *R.R.* 2.7.13; he changes Varro's reason: *haec enim purgatio maxime necessaria equino pecori.*
  For the force of *crassa* cf. 406 (and n.) *pasce sero pingui.*
  magnum: proleptic: 'let their bodies grow big'.
  sinito: see 2.408–13n. for imperatives in -*to*.
  206 ante domandum 'before the breaking'; with *E.* 9.24 *inter agendum*, this is the only instance of a preposition with the gerund in V. Much more common is the quasi-prepositional instrumental ablative, e.g. 2.36 *colendo*, 239 *arando*, 250 *habendo*, 407 *putando*; 3.215 *uidendo*, 454 *legendo*.
  207 ingentis tollent animos: like the plants at 2.350. *ingentis* = 'natural', 'unrestrained [by breaking]'; see Mackail (1912).
  prensique: cf. 1.285 *prensos domitare boues.*
  208 An elegantly ordered closing: n – a – v *et* a – v – n; see 2.216n.
  lenta 'pliant'.
  duris ... lupatis: the first instance of *lupatus* ('with jagged teeth') used as a noun (*lupata, -orum*, 'jagged-toothed bit'); for the adj. cf. Hor. *Odes* 1.8.6–7 *lupatis | ... frenis.* So called from the similarity to a wolf's teeth – λύκος is so used in Greek, *lupus* (first attested after V.) in Latin: *et placido duros* [cf. V.'s *duris*] *accipit ore lupos*, Ov. *Trist.* 4.6.4.

209–41   Guard against the destructive powers of amor *and sexual passion. Battle of the rival bulls*

The section begins on a didactic note and serves as a transition to the treatment of *amor* (242–83; see n.). It is dominated by the superb lines on the battle for the herd, relating the expulsion and return of the defeated rival (219–41). V. here intensifies his use of language suggesting a human context – the connection is made specifically in the next passage – but completely avoids the grotesquerie which such a suggestion could have produced. Varro had treated the topic briefly (*R.R.* 2.1.18; 2.5.12; 2.7.8–9), but the technical tradition is not really an influence on this, or the next, section. In that tradition, moreover, the stress is not so much on the separation of male and female as on the importance of bringing about conception – the very opposite of V.'s focus. Lucretius' diatribe against love (4.1037–1287) has some influence on the diction, but V.'s emphasis and intentions are very different.

209–10   Sed non ulla magis uiris industria firmat | quam ...:
cf. 452–3 (a parallel context, treatment against plague) *non tamen ulla magis praesens fortuna laborum est | quam ...*; the toil fails in both cases. Cf. 215 *carpit ... uiris*; also 229, 235nn.

210   Venerem 'sexual desire'; cf. 64, 137; 2.329, with a slightly different shade of meaning in each case.

caeci stimulos ... amoris: *caeci* is best taken as 'concealed', 'hidden'; cf. Lucr. 4.1120 (of those afflicted by love) *incerti tabescunt uolnere caeco*, and 215, 271 (and n.) *subdita flamma medullis*. V. developed the idea in his treatment of the passion inflicted on Dido: *at regina graui iamdudum saucia cura | uulnus alit uenis et caeco carpitur igni*, A. 4.1–2.

211   'whether a person prefers dealing with cattle or horses'; cf. 49–50 *Seu quis ... equos, seu quis ... iuuencos*. As throughout, V. is careful to merge cattle and horses (49–94n.) – the powers of *amor* make no distinction, not only among animals, but among all living creatures (242–4).

cui: for *alicui* after *si(ue)*.

212–13   in sola ... | pascua: the language of elegy begins; this is typically the resort of the unrequited or frustrated lover: *E.* 10.14 *illum* [sc. *Gallum*] *etiam sola sub rupe iacentem*; *G.* 4.465–6 *te solo in litore secum ... canebat*; Prop. 1.18.4 *sola ... saxa*.

relegant: here of the farmer's banishment of the bull. *relegatio* (the fate suffered by Ovid) is a technical term for a geographically specified banishment without loss of civil rights, and V.'s use of the word here anticipates the major banishment of the passage, that of the defeated bull; cf. 225 *exsulat*.

213   post ... lata: the first of a complex of references to the separating of male and female by mountains and bodies of water, the barriers of nature – the measure fails: 253–4, 269–70 (see nn.). The idea is expressed on a higher, openly human, level at 258–63, through the figure of Leander (258n.).

montem oppositum: cf. 373 *oppositum ... montem.*

214   As was done when the storm threatened: *quid saepe uidentes | agricolae propius stabulis armenta tenerent*, 1.354–5. This is a permanent condition in Scythia: *illic clausa tenent stabulis armenta*, 352.

215–16   'the sight of the female [lit. 'the female, by his seeing her'] gradually drains his strength and inflames him'; perhaps something of a hysteron-proteron.

carpit ... uiris: the opposite of the desired effect: *uiris ...firmat*, 209; cf. also 229, 235nn. For the use of *carpo*, and the sense of the whole line, cf. *A.* 4.2 (210n.).

femina: emphatic, and only here in the *Georgics*, never in the *Eclogues* (it is only possible in hexameters in the nom. and voc. sing.). When applied before V. to animals, the usage is specific: it is either a virtual adjective *(canis femina*, etc.; cf. the use of *senex*), or it is consistently found in the close company of *mas* (once with *aries*, once with *taurus* – in the sole exception, at *R.R.* 2.9.5, Varro has been treating *catuli*, then turns to *feminae*, with *canes* understood); see *ThLL* VI. 462.30–78. The effect of the word in the present line is unmistakable: if only momentarily, the boundary between man and animal is once again broken (95–122n.).

216 nec nemorum patitur meminisse nec herbae: forget-fulness of normal functions with passion or grief is as old as the Homeric poems; so Thetis asks Achilles how long he will continue grieving, μεμνημένος οὔτε τι σίτου | οὔτ' εὐνῆς, 'remembering neither food nor sex', *Il.* 24.129–30 (the Homeric world, very different from V.'s, sees sex as an everyday function). At 245 *amor* causes the lioness to forget her cubs, and the effects of plague are precisely the same (498–9 and n.); see also 236n. The poetry of Damon and Alphesiboeus has the same effect on a heifer at *E.* 8.2–3 *immemor herbarum quos est mirata iuuenca | certantis*. Cf. also 4.490–1n.

217 dulcibus ... inlecebris 'with soft enchantments'; the noun comes from the world of the prostitute *(istam in uicinitatem te meretriciam | cur contulisti? cur inlecebris cognitis | non ... refugisti*, Caecil. *com.* 234–6 Ribb.); here for the first time of an animal.

illa ... quidem: Page's note is worth citing: 'serves to point out and draw marked attention to the thing or person spoken of, as here where special attention is drawn to the charm and beauty of the animal'; he compares 501; cf. also 2.125; 4.457 (see n.), 506.

217–18 et saepe ... amantis: the transition to the battle (219–41). The theme of bulls fighting over a heifer exists elsewhere in litera-ture as a simile: Ap. Rhod. *Arg.* 2.88–9 'again they rushed back against each other, as two bulls vie in anger for a grazing heifer'; *A.* 12.715–17; Ov. *M.* 9.46–8 (Achelous in his fight with Hercules appropriately takes on the form of a bull, 80–8). For V.'s conversion of simile to reality see 1.104–10n.; his own simile exemplifying this reality comes at 237–41;

cf. also 149–50n. The reader who is aware of the tradition will recognize the human dimension exemplified by those other treatments, and will apply it to the present version.

superbos: cf. 226 *superbi*.

amantis 'lover'; a word from the human, specifically elegiac, world (215–16, 217, 227nn.).

219   The account proper begins with an arresting and vivid line, in the style of an ecphrasis, and with *pascitur* placed emphatically at the beginning (146–7n.). Sila, a mountain in Bruttium (146–7n.) is also the site of a battle between rival bulls at *A.* 12.715 (217–18n.) – most of the MSS have the bland *silua*, but Servius also preserves the truth.

The rhythm and word-order of the line are unusual. While the cadence in *magna Sila* occurs elsewhere in V. (e.g. *A.* 1.569 *Hesperiam magnam* ; see Forbiger for further examples), the repeated juxtaposition of noun and adjective of the same declension (*formosa iuuenca*), with the resulting double rhyme (the enclitic at *A.* 1.569 distinguishes that line) is distinctly un-Virgilian. Horace is clearly borrowing rhythm and language at *Epist.* 1.3.36 *pascitur in uestrum reditum uotiua iuuenca.* This, together with the location in Bruttium, could perhaps suggest that V. is borrowing – specifically from the *Io* of Calvus a line describing Io as a heifer (150–1n.); its very oddity may have appealed to him. *formosa iuuenca* points in the same direction; the adjective *formosus* is otherwise found exclusively in the *Eclogues* (17 times), and Ovid, drawing heavily on Calvus for his account of Io, writes *inque nitentem | Inachidos uultus mutauerat ille iuuencam | (bos quoque formosa est)*, *M.* 1.610–12.

220   Cf. *A.* 12.720 *illi inter sese multa ui uulnera miscent* (217–18, 221nn.); also 4.174; *A.* 8.452, and cf. 2.282–3 *necdum horrida miscent | proelia.*

illi: a return to the *amantes* of 218; neither *taurus* nor any other such word is used in the rest of the passage.

221   lauit ater corpora sanguis: cf. 507–8 (the effects of the plague) *it naribus ater | sanguis*; *A.* 12.721–2 *sanguine largo | colla armosque lauant* (217–18, 220nn.); *A.* 10.727–8 (of the lion to which Mezentius is compared) *lauit improba taeter | ora cruor.*

lauit: for this inflection V. uses exclusively the third conjugation (359; *A.* 3.663; 7.663; 10.727), while for all other forms where two systems exist (i.e. excluding those based on the perfect, *laui*), he uses the first (*lauant, A.* 6.219; 12.722; *lauabo, E.* 3.97; *lauabat, A.* 7.489; *lauandi,* 1.387).

222-3 'with a great bellow their horns are levelled and pressed against the butting enemy'; cf. 233 *obnixus.*

gemitu: otherwise in the poem once in Book 4 (353), and twice at the end of this book, of the dying horse (*gemitu grauis,* 506), and the dying bullock (*extremosque ciet gemitus,* 517); cf. also 226 *multa gemens.*

223   reboant siluaeque et longus Olympus 'the woods and the sky, from end to end, re-echo' – as when the gadfly struck (150-1); and cf. the sounds of the animals during the plague (554-5).

reboant: aptly used here (and nowhere else in V.), reflecting the etymology (mentioned by Varro, *L.L.* 7.104) of *boo* '*a boue*'. Ennius (quoted by Varro), seems to have been responsible (*bouantes, Ann.* 585 Skutsch), '[inserting] *u* in order to reveal the etymology which is later given by Varro', Skutsch ad loc. Its real connections, of course, are to βοάω, 'shout'.

-que ... et: cf. 131n.

224   bellantis ... stabulare: the acc. and infin. with *mos (est)* is found in Plautus, otherwise only rarely in Cicero and Livy.

una stabulare 'to share the same dwelling [i.e. herd]'; *stabulare* usually means 'to house', and the deponent is normally used for V.'s sense. He seems to be the first to use the active intransitively – the only way he uses it: cf. *A.* 6.286 *Centauri in foribus stabulant.*

224-5   sed alter | ... oris: this application of *exsulo* to an animal is unique in Latin, and creates a pathos and personification of great intensity. Cf. 212 (and 212-13n.) *relegant;* 2.511-12 – lines which help to reinforce the human application here. See also 228n.

uictus: cf. 227 *uictoris.*

226   multa gemens ignominiam plagasque: Page notes the rarity of internal accusative (*multa*), here adverbial, along with a direct object (*ignominiam plagasque*).
For the lack of a third-foot caesura, see 1.350n.

226-7   superbi | uictoris: once they were both proud: 217-18 *superbos ... amantis;* cf. 225 *uictus.*

227   tum quos amisit inultus amores: still the object of *gemens.*
The language of elegy and love poetry, and with it the personification, continues; cf. 127, 130nn.

228   stabula aspectans: cf. 224 *stabulare;* a vivid and pathetic picture.

regnis excessit auitis: a rhythmic variation on the parallel words at 225 *ignotis exsulat oris.*

229　ergo omni cura uiris exercet: the defeated bull goes into training to recover the strength lost in the fight and sapped by *amor*; cf. 215–16; also 209–10, 235nn.

229–31　inter | ... acuta: V. employs the language and ideas used by observers of the *duritia* of primitive societies (Thomas (1982a) 47, 95–100), who invariably specify unsophisticated diet and sleeping on the ground: *Africam initio habuere Gaetuli et Libyes, asperi incultique, quis cibus erat caro ferina atque humi pabulum uti pecoribus,* Sall. *B.J.* 18.1; cf. also *A.* 8.314–18. Livy's description of Hannibal draws from the same tradition: *cibi potionis desiderio naturali ... multi saepe militari sagulo opertum humi iacentem ... conspexerunt,* 21.4.6–7. The effect of V.'s language is to humanize the bull.

229–30　inter | dura ... saxa: *dura* suggests that the result of this hardship will be acquisition of *duritia*; cf. Lucr. 5.925–6 (on primitive early man) *at genus humanum multo fuit illud in aruis | durius, ut decuit, tellus quod dura creasset*; cf. 257n.

pernox: not in the MSS, but known to Serv. Auct., and clearly correct as against *pernix*, which cannot mean 'persistent' and which may have been imported from 93 *pernix Saturnus,* describing Saturn's flight as a horse.

instrato ... cubili: a good instance of V.'s linguistic audacity (4.565–6n.); the phrase is taken from Lucr. 5.987 (of early man's bedding) *instrata cubilia.* But there the words are followed by *fronde*: 'leaf-strewn beds'; i.e. the *in-* of *instrata* is affirmative, while here, and only here in Latin, it is privative ('uncovered'). Neither *ThLL* (which takes V.'s phrase with *frondibus* in 231 – thus making that line virtually impossible to construe), nor *OLD* (which defines this instance 'covered with a rug, cloth, etc.' – where did the bull get a rug (the presence of which would make nonsense of his hardy training)?) recognizes a privative sense for *insterno.* See 4.341–2n. for a similar redefinition of the force of a prefix.

231 'feeding on prickly leaves and sharp sedge'; so of the pre-Saturnian Italian: *rami atque asper uictu uenatus alebat, A.* 8.318 (229–31n.).

232–4　irasci ... | ictibus: V. draws on disparate literary sources. For the rather odd expression *irasci in cornua discit* ('learns to throw his anger into his horns'), he is indebted to Eur. *Bacch.* 743 ταῦροι δ' ὑβρισταὶ κὰς κέρας θυμούμενοι, 'arrogant bulls which put their anger into their horns' (see Dodds ad loc.); and the idea of butting against the air looks to Callim. *frag. inc. auct.* 743 Pf. (πολλὰ μάτην κεράεσσιν ἐς ἠέρα θυμήναντα, 'with his horns vainly expending great anger on the air') and to Catullus' adaptation, *nequiquam uanis iactantem cornua uentis,* 64.111. V. reworks the lines at *A.* 5.377 (of Dares) *uerberat ictibus auras,* and at *A.* 12.104–6 (105–6 = 233–4); cf. 217–18n.

   arboris obnixus trunco: cf. 222 *obnixos;* see 256 [*sus*] *fricat arbore costas.*

   234   sparsa … harena 'he paws the sand in prelude for the battle'; cf. *E.* 3.86–7 *pascite taurum, | iam cornu petat et pedibus qui spargat harenam.* The world of man is again suggested, since the image suggests the sanding of the oiled body in wrestling.

   235   post, ubi …: adverbial *post,* with *ubi,* is a favoured means of temporal transition in V.: 4.189, 544, 552; *A.* 4.80; 5.362.

   uiresque refectae: sc. *sunt;* the strength lost to the powers of *amor* in 215 (*carpit … uiris*) has now been recovered through separation and toil; see also 209–10, 229 and nn.

   236   The battle has become a human one (237–41n.).

   oblitum: the obvious meaning is that the *uictor* of 226 no longer has any concern for the enemy he once defeated and sent into exile; but implicitly the *obliuium* is induced by *amor.* The defeated bull, on the other hand, has recovered (*uiresque refectae*) through isolation. V. moves to the concluding simile, perhaps partly because to recount the triumph of the regenerated bull would muddy this antithesis.

   237–41   The simile is adapted from Hom. *Il.* 4.422–6 (but see 241n.). Both versions focus on the gathering strength of the breaker, the sound as it comes in, and its impact on the shore, and Page has noted that V. carefully arranges the syntax to reflect these three movements. Recollection of the outer context of the Homeric simile (an attack by the Greeks) strengthens the human application in V.'s adaptation. The simile is reworked, with less detail, at *A.* 7.528–30, in a conventional battle scene. As at 1.201–3 the simile in effect replaces the narrative: 236n.

   237   albescere: similarly of the tail of the comet at 1.367.

   238   longius … trahit 'draws its wave from further back and from the deep sea'.

239   ad terras immane sonat per saxa: sound is accommodated to sense in a close adaptation of the Homeric model: χέρσωι ῥηγνύμενον μεγάλα βρέμει, 'breaking on dry land it gives a great boom', *Il.* 4.425.

239–40   neque ipso | monte minor procumbit: so when Cyrene parts the waters to admit Aristaeus (*in montis faciem*, 4.361); cf. *A.* 1.105 (of the storm) *insequitur cumulo praeruptus aquae mons*.

ipso 'an actual'.

240–1   at ima exaestuat unda | uerticibus 'but [explaining *neque ... minor*] the wave boils up in eddies from the bottom'.

241   nigramque ... harenam 'and tosses black sand up from the bottom'; cf. *A.* 1.107 *furit aestus harenis.* V. perhaps recalls the reality of 234 (*sparsa ... harena*), thus providing a harmony between outer context and simile. As at 95–122 (see n.), Homeric reference is conflated with Sophoclean, for 'black sand' does not occur in Homer's simile, but is found in Sophocles' adaptation at *Ant.* 590 κελαινὰν θῖνα.

242–83   omnia uincit amor: *the powers and destruction of love affect all living beings; impregnation of mares by the West wind; hippomanes*

The stance is no longer didactic, as V. advances the theme of the previous section and finally implicates man openly in the discussion (*hominum*, 242; 258–63nn.). The passage ends with a discussion of the unbridled lust of mares, and of their impregnation by the West wind (266–79), a theme adapted from Aristotle (*H.A.* 572a8–30), and with an aition on *hippomanes* (280–3). V. also recalls Lucretius' opening prayer to Venus. As with the storm and the civil war of Book 1, and the plague at the end of this book, so here the *cura* and *labor* expended by man in the preceding lines is impugned by a natural power outside his control.

242–3   Excerpted from Lucr. 1.1–20, the prayer to Venus which, like the present lines, places all living creatures under her sway: 4 *genus omne animantum,* 12 *aerii ... uolucres,* 14 *inde ferae* [(?) sc. *et*] *pecudes.* Cf. also Lucr. 2.342–4, specifically including the *genus humanum* and *aequoreum: praeterea genus humanum mutaeque natantes | squamigerum pecudes et laeta armenta feraeque | et uariae uolucres.* V.'s last group, *pecudes pictaeque uolucres,* reappears at *A.* 4.525, perhaps significantly in the context of Dido's *amor.* Cf. 480, 541nn. on connections with the plague. Cf. 4.222–3 for a similar style.

genus aequoreum: cf. 541 *genus omne natantum*.

242 The line is hypermetric; see 1.295–6n.

adeo: gives a prominence to the word it follows; see 1.24n.

244 in furias ignemque ruunt: a powerful mingling of the two ideas of *amor* as a madness and a fire; cf. 100 *incassum furit*; 150 (of the effects of the gadfly, which foreshadow those of love) *furit mugitibus aether*; 266 *furor . . . equarum*; 258–9 *magnum cui uersat in ossibus ignem | durus amor*; 271 *subdita flamma medullis*; see also 97–8, 99, 210nn. The same combination of fire and madness characterizes the plague; cf. 511–12 (and n.) *furiisque refecti | ardebant*.

amor omnibus idem: see 1.145–6n. on the parallel appearances, in such epigrammatic statements, of *amor* and *labor* (cf. 4.184 *labor omnibus unus*).

245–9 The passage begins vividly, with examples of *ferae* (242); both sexes are affected: *leaena, ursi, aper, tigris*.

245 tempore non alio: cf. 1.487n. on such temporal phrases; for this one cf. 531, in a parallel context, as plague destroys the ploughing-oxen.

catulorum oblita leaena: cf. 216 (and n.); now children, not merely favourite haunts and grazing, are forgotten.

leaena: twice in the *Georgics* (here and at 4.408 – for λέων, 'lion', of the Homeric model; see n.), and once in the *Eclogues* (2.63 – where the female is not required by the context), while in the *Aeneid leo* is used exclusively (17 times – also twice in the *Eclogues* and once in the *Georgics*); V.'s early predilection for the feminine may owe something to Catullus, who used it twice, at 60.1 and 64.154 – though, of course, the reference to *catuli* more or less necessitates the fem. here.

246–7 errauit ... dedere: gnomic perfects: 'at no other time does the lioness roam more savagely, nor bears deliver such great death and destruction'.

stragemque dedere: also of the plague (the only other use of *strages* in the poem): [*Tisiphone*] *dat stragem*, 556.

248 saeuus ... pessima: emphatic: 'then is the boar savage (cf. *saeuior*, 246), then the tigress most baneful'.

249 Cf. 1.448 and n.; there is a similar, even stronger, authorial interjection at 435–6.

erratur: impersonal, 'wandering [then is bad]'.

250 nonne uides: see 103–4; 1.56nn.

250–1 ut ... corpora: the effects on stallions; this looks to 266–83, the effect on mares (*equarum*, 266). At 506–7 the plague-ridden horse behaves somewhat similarly.

si tantum notas odor attulit auras: Varro tells you how to deal with bashful stallions: *ab locis equae nares equi tangunt*, *R.R.* 2.7.8. Forbiger, with the support of Orelli on Hor. *Odes* 2.8.23–4 (*tua ne retardet | aura maritos*), has an interesting comment: *talia non ad nostrum sensum esse diiudicanda, ab huiusmodi enim imaginibus ex ipsa rerum natura petitis minus abhorruisse Graecos et Romanos*; V. however did show some sensibility: compared with Varro, who is very explicit, he rarely talks openly of such matters; see 135–7; 2.130nn; also 253–4n.

notas: cf. 130 *nota uoluptas*.

252–3 neque ... neque ... | non ... atque: the change from regular *neque ... neque* to *non ... atque* creates a vivid rhetorical heightening; cf. 2.136–9 *neque ... nec ... atque ... non ... neque ...-que.*

252 neque ... frena ... neque uerbera: cf. 208 *uerbera ... et ... lupatis.* The effect of *amor* is to negate the training that has been lavished on the horse (179–208).

253–4 non scopuli ... | flumina: Macrobius (*Sat.* 6.2.20) preserves a six-line fragment of the *De Morte* of Varius Rufus, describing the relentlessness of a hunting-dog on the scent of a deer, and containing the line *non amnes illam medii, non ardua tardant* (fr. 4.5, p.100 Morel). He quotes the lines against *E.* 8.88, which is identical to *De Morte* fr. 4.4 *perdita nec serae meminit decedere nocti* (260n.), a line which V. reworks at 467 *serae solam decedere nocti* (of the plague's effects – again love and plague are bound together). The line immediately preceding in Varius' poem refers to the scent of the deer (*tenues ... odores*), which V. transferred to the scent of the mare (*odor*, 251, see 250–1n.). Richter thinks that the whole passage of Varius is derived from Virgil, but it seems less likely that the disparate versions (i.e. different lines in the *Eclogues* and *Georgics*) would precede the single one (i.e. the lines of the *De Morte*), and such borrowing is perfectly in V.'s manner. Moreover, 2.506–7 and 3.116–17 (on which Richter has no comment) are clearly expansions of Varius, *De Morte* frr. 2 and 3 respective (see nn.).

On the attempt to separate the sexes with natural barriers see 213 and n. These lines show the failure of such measures – recapitulated at 260 and 269–70.

scopuli: cf. 261n.

254   correptosque unda torquentia montis 'and which uproot and sweep away mountains with their wave'; the clause is parallel to *obiecta*.

255   ruit...sus: as at 1.313 (*ruit...uer*; see n.) and *A.* 2.250 (*ruit... nox*), the abruptness of the monosyllabic line-ending reinforces the sense of the verb. Four of the five instances of *sus* in V. are at line-end (*A.* 3.390; 8.43, 83); cf. also Hor. *Epist.* 2.2.75 *ruit sus* | .

dentesque ... exacuit: so of the bees at 4.74 (see n.) *spiculaque exacuunt rostris*; also at 1.264.

Sabellicus: the form is extremely rare, and seems to occur here first.

256   prosubigit 'digs up in front'; the only double pre-verbal compound in *prosub-* in Latin, clearly coined by V. in imitation of the Greek, where the phenomenon in general and this instance in particular (προὔπο-) are common.

fricat arbore costas: the boar uses a tree, as did the exiled bull: *arboris obnixus trunco*, 233.

257   hinc atque illinc: only here in V. (he prefers *hinc atque hinc*, which occurs six times in the *Aeneid*); in fact *illinc* itself is rare, otherwise occurring (in the asyndetic formula *hinc ... illinc*) only at 1.509 and *A.* 4.442.

durat: physically, but perhaps with the ethical overtones implied by *dura ... saxa* at 230; see 229-30n.

258-63   A human *exemplum* for the destructive power of *amor* is inserted in the middle of the examples concerning animals. Leander of Abydos, in love with Hero of hostile Sestos (a familiar pattern), swims across the Hellespont each night, until (inevitably) he drowns after the lamp which guides him is extinguished. The girl's suicide follows. These lines once constituted the first reference to the story (for which see Ov. *Her.* 18, 19; Musaeus, *Hero and Leander*), but it was obviously treated by an Alexandrian poet, as is clear from V.'s manner of reference (1.14-15n.), and there are now papyrus fragments which may come from that original (cf. *SH* adesp. pap. 901A, 951). Serv. Auct. claims *Leandri nomen occultauit, quia cognita erat fabula* – which looks like anachronism; the story had probably had a single prominent treatment, to which V.'s suppression is perhaps intended to point; but see 258n.

258   quid iuuenis ...?: the reader who has seen human terms applied to animals throughout the first half of the book, who has seen *iuuenis* applied at one moment to animals, the next to men (105–6, 118, 165nn.), and who has just read (253–4) that opposing crags and rivers will not keep out the animal affected by *amor*, will initially be unsure not of the identity of the youth, but of the nature of the animal. The uncertainty is resolved partially with *parentes* at 262 but not finally until the last word of the passage at 263, *uirgo*. The ambiguity is reinforced by the resumption of the subject of animal passion at 264, where the words *quid lynces . . . ?* eliminate any distinction between Hero and Leander and the animals.

Leander (*iuuenis*) and Hero (*uirgo*) stand at the beginning and end of the passage, providing a frame, and perhaps suggesting the real separation to which they were subject.

magnum ... in ossibus ignem: cf. 244n. Leander's 'love' is no gentle, elegiac romance (as it may have been in V.'s source), but the same sexual passion shared by the rest of the animal world; cf. the passion of Dido: *donisque furentem | incendat reginam atque ossibus implicet ignem*, *A.* 1.659–60; also the effects of plague: *ima dolor balantum lapsus ad ossa | cum furit . . .*, 457–8.

259   durus amor: so in the Underworld, of the region in which Aeneas meets the suicide Dido (also the fate of Hero): *hic quos durus amor crudeli tabe peredit*, *A.* 6.442.

nempe: only here in V.; it answers and elaborates the preceding question: 'What does the passion-struck *iuuenis* do? Why, he swims stormy straits, etc.'

259–60   The nouns and their modifiers are arranged in a triple interlocking structure: *abruptis . . . procellis/turbata . . . freta/nocte . . . caeca.*

abruptis: for *abrumpentibus* 'bursting'.

260   The line resembles 2.503 *sollicitant alii remis freta caeca*, where *caeca*, however, modifies *freta*; both suggest the audacity of the undertaking.

nocte ... caeca serus: perhaps developed from Varius, *De Morte* fr. 4.6, p.100 Morel *nec serae meminit decedere nocti* (253–4n.).

natat: the transitive use of *natare* is normal, unlike that of *innatare* (2.451–2n.).

freta: as for impassioned animals, so for Leander, barriers are of no avail (253–4, 258nn.).

261   porta tonat caeli: from Homer (*Il.* 5.749 = 8.393 πύλαι μύκον οὐρανοῦ, 'the gates of heaven groaned'), perhaps by way of Ennius (*mi* *soli caeli maxima porta patet, Var.* 24 V.), but V.'s words *quem ... caeli* are surely not (*pace* Sen. *Epist.* 108.34) directly from Ennius; see Skutsch 788–9.

scopulis: though not barriers to Leander's *amor*, they recall the *scopuli* of 253, which do so function (253–4, 260, 276nn.).

reclamant: following *tonat*, this surely means 'cry back', 're-echo', rather than 'cry out against his daring' (Martyn, Conington).

263 She jumped off the tower at Sestos. Dido uses similar words in her attempt to keep Aeneas from leaving: *nec moritura tenet crudeli funere Dido?, A.* 4.308 (258, 259nn.).

super: adverbial: 'in addition [to his own death]'; some take *super ... funere = super corpore* (in Musaeus she landed on his corpse), and though *A.* 4.308 (see preceding n.) and *E.* 5.20 (*exstinctum ... crudeli funere*) suggest otherwise, V. may have intended a secondary sense, 'on his cruelly-slain corpse'.

uirgo: not strictly true, since Leander had successfully made the crossing a number of times. Musaeus described Hero through a nice conceit: παρθένος ἡματίη, νυχίη γυνή, 'a maiden by day, by night a wife', 287. Perhaps the point was treated in the Alexandrian original (258–63n.), and V.'s choice of *uirgo* is somehow a reference to it. *uirgo* looks back to *iuuenis* (258n.).

264   quid lynces ...?: as if continuing the series from 258 (see n.) *quid iuuenis ...?*

264–5   genus acre luporum | atque canum: *genus acre* is otherwise used by V. only in the *laudes Italiae* (*genus acre uirum*, 2.167 and n.). Cf. perhaps Lucr. 5.862 *genus acre leonum*.

At 537–40, in the grim return to a sort of golden age, as wolves and dogs become harmless through disease, V. plays on the word *acris: acrior illum* [sc. *lupum*] | *cura domat*, 538–9.

265   quid ... cerui 'what of the battles which [even] peaceful stags fight?' The construction with *quid* has changed since 258–9, where *facit* (*uel sim.*) was in ellipse.

266 The rest of the section is concerned with the sexuality and airborne impregnation of mares, and with the phenomenon *hippomanes.* The first of these becomes a topos: cf. Hor. *Odes* 1.25.14 *quae solet matres furiare equorum.* V. is adapting Aristot. *H.A.* 572a8–30, which begins exactly as he does: 'of female animals mares are the most eager for sexual intercourse'.

furor ... equarum: a gloss on ἱππομανέω ('to be horse-mad'), which occurs in Aristotle immediately following the sentence quoted above. V.'s words look to the treatment of *hippomanes* (with more complex etymologizing) at 280–3 (see n.), and thus provide a characteristic frame for the treatment of the mare.

267 mentem Venus ipsa dedit 'Venus herself gave them this passion'; cf. 4.149–50 *naturas apibus quas Iuppiter ipse | addidit expediam.*

267–8 quo tempore ... quadrigae 'at the time the chariot-horses of Potniae devoured with their jaws the limbs of Glaucus'. Mythology again provides elaboration (258–63n.), this time the story of Glaucus, son of Sisyphus, who kept mares for racing at Potniae, and who was killed by them, either because he had fed them on human flesh (and his supply became exhausted; see Probus), or because he kept them away from stallions (in order to preserve their strength for racing), and thus incurred the wrath of Aphrodite (cf. *Venus*, 267; see Servius); the latter version obviously suited V.'s purposes. The incident is not mentioned by Aristotle (the only detail in the passage which is not), and V. may have in mind Varro, *R.R.* 2.7.9, a bizarre anecdote about a groom who tried to induce an unwilling stallion to perform its duty: *tametsi incredibile, quod usu uenit, memoriae mandandum. equus matrem salire cum adduci non posset, cum eum capite obuoluto auriga adduxisset et coegisset matrem inire, cum descendenti dempsisset ab oculis, ille impetum fecit in eum ac mordicus interfecit.* V.'s scenario is the exact reverse of this (mare deprived, rather than stallion compelled), but the fate of the groom (down to specifics; *mordicus*) is the same, and V. knew the passage, having adapted the sentence preceding it at 250–1 (see n.). He returns to the theme at 514, providing yet another connection between *amor* and plague, as the plague-ridden horse turns on itself with its own teeth (*dentibus*).

Potniades ... quadrigae: V. seems to be adapting Eur. *Phoen.* 1124–5, a description of a scene on the shield of Polynices: Ποτνιάδες ... πῶλοι δρομάδες, 'the racing-steeds of Potniae'; their madness is also referred to: ὥστε μαίνεσθαι δοκεῖν, 'so that they seemed to be mad', 1127; cf. *furor ... equarum*, 266.

269–70 Gargara ...| Ascanium; ... montis et flumina: the general follows the specific: Gargara (or Gargarus) is a mountain in the Troad (cf. 1.103), Ascanius a river, 200 miles away in Bithynia. Servius claims that the two stand for any mountain and any river, but there is something curious about the location and the specificity; the river appeared in Callimachus (*frag. gram.* 407.105 Pf.) and Euphorion (fr. 46 Powell), and also at Prop. 1.20.4, in a poem indebted to Cornelius Gallus (cf. Ross (1975) 74–84).

The wording of 270 is a specific exposure of the futility of the 'technical' advice of 212–13; see 213n.

flumina tranant: cf. Lucr. 1.14–15 (as Venus and spring arrive) *pecudes ... rapidos tranant amnis.*

271 auidis ubi subdita flamma medullis: cf. 244 (and n.), and *A.* 4.66 (the effects on Dido) *est mollis flamma medullas* (258, 259nn). Venus has the same effect on Vulcan at *A.* 8.388–90. The image is taken from Ap. Rhod. *Arg.* 3.286–7 'and the arrow [of Eros] burnt deep down in the maiden's heart, like a flame'.

272 uere magis, quia uere calor redit ossibus: cf. 258 (and n.) *in ossibus ignem*; also *A.* 3.308 *calor ossa reliquit.* Spring is most conducive to such fire of passion, because the bones are already heated by the growing warmth. The line, particularly with the anaphora of *uere ... uere* (2.323–4n.) looks directly back to the praises of spring at 2.323–45, where animal sexuality was briefly hinted at: *et Venerem certis repetunt armenta diebus*, 329, and where V. presented the fertility of the earth in terms of human or animal sexuality (2.325–35n.). The reader who has observed the progress and effects of *amor* in Book 3 will readjust his view of those 'praises' (2.323–45n.).

273–9 Servius refers to Varro's discussion (*R.R.* 2.1.19) of the mares of Mt Tagrus in Spain, which are impregnated by the wind, but V. is also looking directly to Aristotle's treatment of the mares of Crete (*H.A.* 572a8–30) – and he adds Homeric colouring; see 266, 273, 277–9nn.

273 ore ... uersae in Zephyrum stant: neither Aristotle nor Varro specifies the impregnating wind, and V. perhaps refers to Hom. *Il.* 16.150 on Achilles' horses 'which Podarge the Whirlwind bore to the West wind'. The West wind, the wind of spring, is here appropriately the instrument of conception (272n.).

274 saepe: used, as at 2.32 (see n.), precisely at a point where credibility is strained (275n.). Aristotle says it occurs περὶ τὸν καιρὸν τοῦτον, 'at this season', *H.A.* 572a13; Varro, *certo tempore, R.R.* 2.1.19.

275 uento grauidae: the Greeks had a verb for it: ἐξανεμοῦσθαι, 'to be impregnated by the wind' (Aristot. *H.A.* 572a13); cf. Varro, *R.R.* 2.1.19 *e uento concipiunt.*

(mirabile dictu): Varro has *res incredibilis est ... sed est uera*, and Aristotle merely reported the phenomenon (λέγονται, 'they are said to ...'). V. indicates a θαῦμα (*miraculum*), and implies *diffidentia*, as at 4.309, 554-5 (see nn.).

276 A line with curious rhythm: the opening dactyls convey the speed of the horse, which is then arrested, with no apparent reason, by the fifth-foot spondee (very rare in the poem; see 1.221n.).

scopulos: again no barrier (261n.).

277-9 Aristotle situates the event in Crete, with the horses running north or south – until they reach the sea (the detail suits the geography): 'they run away neither to the east nor the west, but towards the north or the south', *H.A.* 572a16–17. V. repeats the detail, though its function is less clear in that Crete does not figure in his version; but merely to have echoed Aristotle (Page) would be uncharacteristic (277n.).

277 'they flee not to your rising, East wind, nor to the sun's' – which is to say the same thing twice. The structure of the line (*non ... neque*) creates the expectation that the sun's setting will balance its rising ('not to the west or east, but to the north or south'), and the expectation is strengthened by Aristotle's words (277-9n.). The answer may be quite simple; V. already had the mares facing the west (273), so when they flee (*diffugiunt*) it will not be in that direction.

The apostrophe (*non, Eure, tuos*) seems somewhat dramatic, and is perhaps intended to invigorate Aristotle's technical information.

278 in Borean Caurumque: strictly 'to the north and north-west', but probably little more than a poeticism for 'to the north' (cf. Aristotle's πρὸς ἄρκτον, 277-9n.).

nigerrimus Auster: the superlative otherwise in V. only at *A.* 5.696.

279 pluuio contristat frigore caelum: with *nigerrimus* in the previous line, and with these words, V. dwells on the cold and wet nature of the South wind (Aristotle merely says ἢ νότον, see 277-9n.), creating a contrast with the heat which has characterized the actual impregnation (271-3). Cf. *A.* 10.275 (where Aeneas' coming is likened to the dry and pestilent heat of the Dog-star) [*Sirius ardor*] *nascitur et laeuo contristat lumine caelum*; he does not otherwise use *contristo*.

280-3 The section, and the first half of the book, ends with an aition, parallel to that concerning the *asilus* at 146-56 (see particularly 147-8n.). Aristotle notes that when the mares have reached the sea (cf.

hic demum, 280) they produce a discharge called ἱππομανές (= *hippomanes*), and that this stuff is much sought after by 'women who deal in drugs' (αἱ περὶ τὰς φαρμακείας, *H.A.* 572a22). This is merely the impulse for V.'s aition. Aristotle had drawn no parallel between the madness of mares (ἱππομανοῦσιν, 'they become horse-mad') and the secretion; V. begins his treatment with a gloss on Aristotle's verb (*furor* ... *equarum*), treats the madness of Glaucus' mares (*mentem*, 267), and ends with an aition on *hippomanes*, which he refers to in aetiological fashion (147–8n.). He clearly suggests an etymological parallel (not in Aristotle) between horse-madness and *hippomanes*. The connection is obvious, but it is strengthened by Theocr. 2.48–9 '*hippomanes* is an Arcadian plant, for which all the foals and swift mares run mad in the hills' – V.'s *pastores* may constitute an acknowledgement of Theocritus (and see 283n.). This is the force of *uero* ... *nomine*: 'they call it horse-madness by a true name' (Page notes that *uero* = τὸ ἔτυμον, 'etymology'). Some have seen in that phrase a reference to and rejection of yet another *hippomanes*, the growth on the forehead of the young colt (see *A.* 4.515), but this seems not to figure in the present lines. At 281 V. elaborates: *lentum destillat ab inguine uirus*. In a brief note Jacobson (1982) draws attention to a gloss *destillat* = *manat:* in other words *furor equarum* joined by *manatio equarum*, a hybrid etymology, which restores the Aristotelian connection. The difference in quantity between μᾰνία and *māno* does not prevent the association (cf. 1.75n.). This is V. at his most Alexandrian, subsuming and reshaping the tradition. See also Schechter (1975) 363–5; Ross (1987) 157–67.

282–3   quod ... uerba: an expansion and ominous development of Aristotle's 'and it is particularly sought after by women who deal in drugs' (280–3n.).

Mention of *nouercae*, and the parallel subject-matter, doubtless motivated the interpolation of 283 after 2.128 (see 2.129n.).

283   herbas: perhaps a reference to Theocritus' *hippomanes* (φυτόν); see 280–3n.

284–94   The second proem

The proem to the second half of the book (treating smaller animals) balances that at 1–48; see 292–3, 294nn. The passage also looks to the opening of Book 4 (286, 289–90nn.). This proem helps to underscore the bipartite nature of the book, and ultimately to emphasize the two great crescendos which in each half follow the technical or didactic parts – the twin devastations brought by *amor* and by the plague. On the poetic programme of these lines see Introduction, pp. 1–3.

284 V. seems to have felt (or gives the impression of having felt) the pressures of both space and time in this poem; cf. 4.147–8. The anaphora of *fugit* reinforces this sense.

Cf. the words of Jupiter to Hercules at *A*. 10.467–8 *stat sua cuique dies, breue et inreparabile tempus | omnibus est uitae.* The compound adjective appears first in V., and after him almost invariably modifies *dies, tempus,* etc.

285 singula 'details', as at *A*. 6.723 *Anchises ... ordine singula pandit.*

capti ... amore: a brilliantly ambiguous phrase. The natural interpretation is 'possessed by love of our theme', as at *E*. 6.9–10 *haec quoque si quis | captus amore leget.* But the theme by which V. has been proccupied is *amor* itself, and to that extent he has been 'possessed by love'; the effect cannot be translated. V. continues to play on the word, and thereby provides a frame for the proem, at 291–2 *me ... raptat amor.* Cf. also 2.476 *ingenti percussus amore.*

286 The transition from large to smaller animals. *cura armentorum* has been the topic of the first half (123–37n.), and *cura* figures prominently in the early sections of the second (384–93n.). But man's *cura* has failed in the first half, under the resurgent powers of *amor*, and the words *hoc satis armentis* carry a certain irony (almost 'so much for herds'). The reference to a second *cura* is perhaps ominous.

pars altera: recalled at the beginning of the next book: *hanc etiam, Maecenas, aspice partem,* 4.2.

287 lanigeros: only here in the *Georgics*, the word occurs five times in Lucretius, and is by nature an epicism (*A*. 3.642, 660; 7.93; 8.664); the elevation is appropriate in an invocation; cf. 290.

agitare: the poet equates his art with that of the shepherd (329n.); cf. 18 *agitabo*; see also 181, 372, 409, 415. The verb is also felt in its sense 'to be concerned with', 'to treat'.

288 On *hic labor, hinc...,* see 2.514n. On V.'s limited acknowledgement of his didactic addressees (here elevated by the epithet *fortes*), see 2.36n.

The *labor* will fail (*quid labor aut benefacta iuuant?*, 525), the hope be frustrated and lost (473).

289–90   nec ... sit 'nor am I unaware how difficult it is to be victorious with words in these matters'. A Lucretian conflation: *nec me animi fallit Graiorum obscura reperta | difficile inlustrare Latinis uersibus esse*, 1.136–7; *nec me animi fallit ... quam difficile id mihi sit peruincere dictis*, 5.97–9; *difficilest ratione docere et uincere uerbis*, 5.735; see 292–3n.

uincere: so in the proem to the book, V. twice refers to himself (in the future) as *uictor* (9, 17).

290   angustis hunc addere rebus honorem: the theme is lowly, but the glory is to be great; see 294n. This is an important component of the poem's development of Callimachean programmatic ideas; cf. 4.6 *in tenui labor; at tenuis non gloria* (see n. and Introduction, pp. 1–3).

291   Parnasi: the inspirational mountain has already appeared in a programmatic context at *E.* 6.29 *nec tantum Phoebo gaudet Parnasia rupes*; also *E.* 10.11 *Parnasi ... iuga*; and see 292–3n. on *Castaliam*. Cf. Horace's transportation into the Sabine hills: *uester, Camenae, uester in arduos | tollor Sabinos*, *Odes* 3.4.21–2.

292   amor: cf. 285n.

292–3   qua ... cliuo 'where no forerunner's wheel-track winds with a gentle slope down to Castalia'. The commentators all note the similarity to Lucr. 1.926–7 *auia Pieridum peragro loca nullius ante | trita solo*. Certainly V. has recalled Lucretius in the proem (cf. 287, 289–90 and nn.), and particularly at the end of this book he draws from him; but in programmatic terms Lucretius is not the chief source of influence. He speaks of paths 'trodden by the *foot* of nobody' (*nullius .... | trita solo*), V. of *wheel-tracks* (*orbita* does not and cannot mean *uestigium*), drawing directly from Callimachus: πρὸς δέ σε] καὶ τόδ' ἄνωγα, τὰ μὴ πατέουσιν ἅμαξαι | τὰ στείβειν, ἑτέρων ἴχνια μὴ καθ' ὁμά | δίφρον ἐλ]ᾶν, 'and I tell you this too: tread where wagons do not travel, do not drive your chariot in the common tracks of others' (*Aetia* I, fr. 1.25–7 Pf.). As always in the programmatic statements of the *Georgics*, it is to Callimachus that V. is responding (3–8, 294nn.; Introduction, pp. 1–3).

Castaliam: perhaps the spring had a programmatic importance for the Alexandrians (Callimachus?), which cannot be entirely recovered; cf. the 'puzzling intrusion' (Gow) of the Castalian nymphs on the Coan landscape in the highly allusive *Idyll* 7 of Theocritus ('Castalian Nymphs who hold the steeps of Parnassus', 148).

molli deuertitur ... cliuo: cf. *E.* 9.7–8 *qua se subducere colles | incipiunt mollique iugum demittere cliuo.*

294   The last line of the second proem recalls the first of the first: *te quoque, magna Pales, et te memorande canemus* . . . , 1 (1–2n.). V. compensates for the attenuated nature of his theme (*angustis . . . rebus*, 290) with elevation of style: *magno . . . ore* (the use of *os* with the appropriate adjective (e.g. *grauis, animosus, contractus*) becomes in Latin a standard means of stylistic definition; see Thomas (1978) 448–9). A similar antithesis occurs at the opening of Book 4 (4.1–7n.); both passages define the transitional status of V.'s programme in the poem (Introduction, pp. 1–3). Page and others see a comic element in the line and in the antithesis between low subject matter and high style; this antithesis, however, is at the heart of V.'s programme.

295–321   The winter steading, feeding and general care of sheep and goats

Varro had treated sheep and goats at *R.R.* 2.2–3, and V. does take details from him, but he chiefly lays the foundations for connections later made between the technical material and the onset of plague (295, 298–9, 300–1nn.). Cf. 4.8–50, on the care of bees – who will themselves succumb to disease later in that book (295, 300–1, 302–3), and who, at 4.10, are threatened, ironically, by sheep and goats. As the preceding proem has connections with the proem to Book 4 so the entire second half of Book 3 is resumed (with greater complexity) by the first half of the fourth book: in both cases technical material on the care of smaller animals and bees, and on the fragility of their existence, leads into the devastation of plague and extinction.

See 322–38n. on the connections between this passage and the next (summer care) and the treatments of Libya and Scythia (339–83).

295   Incipiens stabulis . . . : cf., immediately following the proem in Book 4, *principio sedes* . . . , 4.8. The priority is perhaps determined by the ethnographical tradition, in which *situs* is the first category treated (Thomas (1982a) 1–3). The transitional passage between technical material and onset of the plague (414–39) also begins with a discussion of *stabula* (414). *incipiens . . . edico* is picked up by *post hinc digressus iubeo*, 330. Cf. also 2.9 (in the same position relative to the proem of Book 2) *principio*.

edico: a formal word, from the realm of the magistrate: cf. 300 *iubeo*.

296–8   carpere ouis . . . | sternere: the subject of the infinitives changes from *ouis* to *te* (understood): 'I proclaim that the sheep should eat grass ... and that you should spread ...'; for the irregular syntax cf. perhaps 331 (see n.).

296   dum mox frondosa reducitur aestas – which occurs in the next section: *at uero Zephyris cum laeta uocantibus aestas* | ... *mittet*, 322-3.

297-8   multa ... humum: cf. Varro, *R.R.* 2.2.8 *subicere oportet uirgulta alia, quo mollius requiescant purioresque sint.*

298-9   glacies ... podagras: a clear foreshadowing of the disease which will become plague at 441-2. These are the only instances of *scabies* in this sense in V. The lines strangely recall the fears of Gallus for his roaming Lycoris at *E.* 10.48-9 *a, te ne frigora laedant!* | *a, tibi ne teneras glacies secet aspera plantas!*

300   post hinc digressus: looks to *incipiens*, 295. As Conington notes, *digressus* may be intended in both its senses: 'moving on [to the next topic]', and 'moving on [around the farm]'.

300-1   iubeo ... recentis: a like prescription, not represented in Varro, is given for the bees (4.18-24); cf. 4.62 *iussos asperge sapores.*

302-3 'and to position their stalls away from the winds towards the winter sun, directed to the south': cf. 318-20 *glaciem uentosque niualis ... auertes;* so Varro, *R.R.* 2.3.6 *stabulatur pecus* [sc. *caprinum*] *melius, ad hibernos exortos si spectat, quod est alsiosum.* Cf. 4.8-9 on the establishment of the beehive.

303-4   cum ... anno 'as often as chilly Aquarius is already setting and bringing its rain down on the year's end'; i.e. 'in February'. The temporal clause is similar in tone, diction and content to 2.403-4. *inrorat* functions as a gloss on *Aquarius* (the Water-bearer); cf. 1.217-18 (and n.), where *aperit* glosses the unstated *Aprilis*.

305   hae 'these she-goats'; cf. 300 *capris* (from *capra*). V. is talking of milking; other uses follow (312-13; cf. *hirci*).

non cura ... leuiore: on *cura* cf. 123-37, 286, 384-93nn.

306   nec minor usus erit: profit (*usus*), in reality the end of agricultural activity, appears in the *Georgics* only here (with *magno ... mutentur* in the next line). Varro naturally begins his treatment of goats (as of most topics) with profit uppermost in his mind: *quae* [*aetas*] *iam ferre possit fructum; ... nouella enim quam uetus utilior* ('more profitable'), *R.R.* 2.3.1. See also 313n.

306-7   quamuis ... rubores: though fine wool (referring to 295-9) is sold at a high price (*magno* | ... *mutentur*), the profit from goats' milk is not to be despised.

Milesia ... | uellera: cf. 4.334–5. The softness, and therefore costliness, of Milesian wool is proverbial, at least from the fifth century: 'Xanthias, a slave, flat on his back on Milesian rugs', Aristoph. *Frogs* 543–5; also *Lys.* 729; Theocr. 15.126.

magno | ... mutentur 'are sold [lit. 'exchanged', 'traded'] for a high price'; cf. *E.* 4.38–9 *nec nautica pinus | mutabit merces* (where the sense of 'trading' is more prominent).

Tyrios incocta rubores '[fleeces] steeped in Tyrian purple'; cf. 2.506–7n. The accusative is retained with the passive *incocta*, as in Greek: 'fleeces which have been given a purple colour'; cf. *E.* 1.53–4 *saepes | Hyblaeis apibus florem depasta salicti,* 'the hedge which has had its willow blossom sipped by Hyblaean bees'. See also 4.337, 357.

308   densior hinc suboles: *hinc* refers to goats, as opposed to sheep; cf. Columella 7.6.7 *parit autem, si est generosa proles, frequenter duos, nonnumquam trigeminos.*

largi copia lactis: cf. *E.* 1.81 *pressi copia lactis.*

309–10   The couplet has a somewhat miraculous ring to it (316–17, 319nn.); cf. *E.* 3.30 (Damoetas, of his prize cow) *bis uenit ad mulctram, binos alit ubere fetus,* and see 176–7, 394–403nn. For a similar expression, cf. 4.248–9.

310   A golden line serves as a clausula (1.117n.).

311   nec minus interea: a transitional phrase (here moving the subject from *caprae* to *hirci*); cf. 2.429; *A.* 1.633; 6.212; 7.572; 12.107.

barbas incanaque menta: cf. *A.* 6.809 (of Numa (!)) *crinis incanaque menta.*

312   Cinyphii ... hirci: the Cinyps, a Libyan river forming the western boundary of the Ptolemaic territory, was mentioned by Callimachus (*ep. et eleg. min.* 384.24 Pf.); V. is perhaps anticipating his treatment of the *pastores Libyae* (339–48).

313   This 'hair-cloth' seems to have been used for sailors' jackets, tents, and similar products; cf. Varro, *R.R.* 2.11.11 *fructum* [cf. 306n.] ... *capra e pilis ministrat ad usum nauticum et ad bella tormenta*; also Sil. Ital. 3.276–7. *miseris* adds a characteristic touch of colour and pathos.

314–17   The goats, situated in Arcadia (*Lycaei*), are depicted in clear pastoral terms, and ultimately in ways which place them in the golden age (316–17; see n. and 319, 322–38nn.).

314   pascuntur: the emphatic initial placement shows that a technical subcategory of *pastus* is being treated: 'as for grazing, they do that in the woods . . .'; cf. Varro, *R.R.* 2.5.11 *pascuntur armenta commodissime in nemoribus*; also 2.3.6 *stabulatur pecus melius, ad hibernos exortos si spectat.*

The verb is normally intransitive, and regularly occurs with an instrumental ablative (*herbis pasceris amaris*, Calvus, p. 85 Morel), but V. uses it with the accusative here and elsewhere (458 *depascitur*; 4.181; also *A.* 2.471 *mala gramina pastus*).

siluas et summa Lycaei: cf. 2 *siluae amnesque Lycaei*; also 4.539 *uiridis depascunt summa Lycaei.*

315 amantis ardua dumos: cf. 4.124 *amantis litora myrtos*, and 2.113n.

316-17 Regardless of the realities of the goats' behaviour, V. specifically sets them in a golden-age context; cf. *E.* 4.21-2 *ipsae lacte domum referent distenta capellae | ubera*; also 2.520 *glande sues laeti redeunt*, with the same implications (see n.). On *ipse* in such contexts see 1.127-8; 2.10-11nn. See also 319n.

317 ducunt: V. rarely allows a spondaic word to occupy the first foot, and then almost always for special effect; here it portrays the slowness of the goats' return; see 375n.

318 ergo omni studio: cf. 229 *ergo omni cura.*

glaciem uentosque niualis: cf. 4.517 *Hyperboreas glacies Tanaimque niualem.*

319 Since the goats have just been depicted (316-17) as creatures of the golden age, it seems best to take *mortalis egestas* together as nom., *curae* as dat. of purpose: 'to the extent that [as members of a Saturnian age] they are less involved in the dire want [which is man's lot in the age of Jupiter] – to that extent you should all the more protect them against [the features of the age of Jupiter,] the ice and snowy winds of winter'. *ergo* can then have its full force: you should protect them *precisely because they have Saturnian qualities.* The more usual reading is to take *curae mortalis* as a gen. dependent on *egestas*: 'to the extent that their need for man's care is less' ('because the goats ask so little, we should all the more give what they do ask', Williams). This gives rather weak sense, and the use of *egestas = necessitas* would be unique in classical Latin. In its two other occurrences in V. *egestas* has the conventional meaning ('extreme want', 'destitution'), and is an important concept: at *A.* 6.276 *turpis Egestas* is one of the nightmarish abstractions of the Underworld, and at *G.* 1.145-6 it is coupled with *labor* as one of the burdens to which man is subject in the age of Jupiter.

320–1   feres ... nec ... claudes: on these futures cf. 155n.

uirgea ... pabula: poetic for *uirgarum pabula* 'meals of twigs' (cf. 1.55n.).

feres ... laetus 'bring cheerfully'; i.e. in abundance, unstintingly; cf. 394–5 *frequentis ... ferat*.

321   tota ... bruma 'all winter long'.

322–38   The summer care of sheep and goats

Summer follows winter, a process reflected in the next two sections, the 'digressions' on torrid Libya and cold Scythia. As in the first half of the book (97–8n.), so throughout the second, extremes of temperature are the catalysts of disaster: love and plague are both characterized by imbalance, and in technical passages such as this and the preceding one V. focuses on the extremes. The pastoral element is heightened, with specific reference to the *Eclogues* (326, 328, 331–4, 338nn.), partly as a prelude to the treatment of the Libyan herdsman, but partly as an evocative but ultimately ominous prelude to the plague, which will destroy the pastoral existence and set the notion of a pastoral golden age on its head (476–7, 537–45nn.).

The technical impulse for the lines may be found at Varro, *R.R.* 2.2.10–11, whose content V. faithfully transmits: pasture the flocks in the early morning (five lines), give them water in mid-morning (four lines), rest and shade in the heat of midday (four lines), and again give them food and water as evening comes on (four lines). The passage is carefully structured to reflect the herdsman's day, with the Morning Star (*Luciferi*, 324) and the (identical) Evening Star (*Vesper*, 336) framing the whole (three lines from the beginning and three from the end); see also 337n. For V.'s stylistic transformation of Varronian material, cf. Introduction, pp. 25–6.

322–6   This joyful and exuberant tone is very much like that at 1.43–4, also on the coming of spring; cf. also 4.51–3, as the bees emerge at the end of winter. The parallels become darker in tone as the heat of summer turns to the plague of summer (472, 479nn.), a fate shared by the bees (414–15; 4.251–80, 281–2nn.).

323   utrumque gregem: sheep and goats alike.

324–5   Luciferi ... | carpamus: sc. *pedibus*: 'let us cross the chilly fields with the Day-star's first appearance' (cf. 142n. on *carpo*); or

possibly 'let us graze [our flocks] on ...' The first person contributes to
the exuberance.

Luciferi: cf. 336 *Vesper*, and 322–38n.

325 dum gramina canent: i.e. with dew; cf. 2.376 (of extreme
frost, and not desirable) *frigora ... cana concreta pruina.*

326 A strong pastoral touch (322–38, 328n.); cf. *E.* 8.15 *cum ros in
tenera pecori gratissimus herba.* On this and the previous lines cf. Varro,
R.R. 2.2.10 *... aestate quod cum prima luce exeunt pastum, propterea quod
tunc herba roscida meridianam, quae est aridior, iucunditate praestat.* See 337
and n.

327 inde: marking the next stage of the day; cf. 331 *aestibus at mediis,*
335 *tum.*

sitim ... collegerit 'has built up their thirst'; cf. Hor. *Odes* 4.12.13
adduxere sitim tempora. It is also taken as 'when the fourth hour has
become thirsty' (cf. Ov. *M.* 5.446; 6.3410), but it seems preferable to
have the heat of mid-morning cause the effect, rather than suffer it.

The effects of the plague are very similar (482–3).

328 Another careful evocation of the pastoral world (cf. 322–38,
326nn.); cf. *E.* 2.13 *sole sub ardenti resonant arbusta cicadis* (338n.). It also
recalls the croaking of the frogs at 1.378.

The word-order is artful (330, 338nn.).

329 iubebo: cf. 300 *iubeo*; for the future see 4.264 *suadebo.* Here the
word is not so much part of the didactic apparatus (as at 300; 4.264), but
refers rather to V.'s presentation of himself *as herdsman*: 'I shall bid the
flocks ...' (287n.).

330 A golden line, as often, closing the subsection (1.117n.).

currentem ... canalibus undam: the reference should be to
troughs; so Conington, '[water] poured into troughs'. But *currentem*
suggests that V. is thinking of channels, used to transport the water.
This, however, makes rather unsatisfactory sense in that the channels
are right next to (*ad*) wells and pools. V. perhaps strains after the point,
that the animals are not to muddy the pools or wells.

ilignis: the more common form in V.'s time is *iligneus.*

331–4 The midday heat brings thoughts of shade, a natural connection in the Italian landscape, and an important bucolic component.
V. adapts Varro: *circiter meridianos aestus, dum deferuescant, sub umbriferas
rupes et arbores patulas subigunt, quaad refrigeratur, R.R.* 2.2.11 (immediately
following the sentence cited at 326n.).

331 aestibus at mediis: cf. 327n.; also see 1.297–8 (and n.) *medio . . . aestu | et medio . . . aestu.*

exquirere: dependent on *iubebo.* Some see a change of subject from the flocks at 330 (*potare*) to the shepherd; while this is quite possible, and would find a neat parallel at 296–8 (see n.), it is easier to take the flocks as the subject of both infinitives.

332–3 sicubi . . . aut sicubi 'if anywhere . . . or if anywhere'.

magna Iouis antiquo robore quercus: cf. 2.14–16 (and n.) *nemorumque Ioui quae maxima frondet | aesculus.* With *antiquo robore* ('with the ancient strength [of its trunk]') V. surely intends a gloss (*robur = quercus*); cf. *A.* 4.441 *annoso ualidam cum robore quercum.* The second syllable of *Iouis* is 'lengthened' in ictus.

ingentis tendat ramos: cf. 2.287 *poterunt se extendere rami,* 296 (also an oak) *ramos et bracchia tendens* (2.296–7n.).

334 ilicibus crebris: dependent on *nigrum*: '[a grove] dark with many holm-oaks'.

sacra . . . accubet umbra 'reclines with hallowed shade'; i.e. 'throws its shadow', as at 145 *saxea procubet umbra.* The subjunctive *accubet,* like *tendat,* is indefinite.

sacra: groves are numinous.

335 tum: cf. 327n.

335–6 tenuis . . . occasum: repeating (*rursus*) the activities of the early and late morning (323, 330). V.'s words are again close to those of Varro: *ab occasu paruo interuallo interposito ad bibendum appellunt et rursus pascunt, quaad contenebrauit, R.R.* 2.2.11.

tenuis: probably 'thin', 'trickling', rather than 'clear' (Williams) or 'penetrating' (Conington) – which suits a misty rain (1.92) but hardly a stream.

336–7 frigidus aëra Vesper | temperat: the only specific reference to *temperatio* or *temperies* in the poem (1.237–8; 2.343–5nn.). Here briefly, just before the 'digressions' on the intemperate extremes of Libya and Scythia, a temporary balance is achieved. Cf. 1.110, where irrigation has a similar effect (*temperat*).

Vesper: cf. 324 *Luciferi,* and see 322–38n.

337 et saltus reficit iam roscida luna: the desirable conditions of the early morning are restored: *et ros in tenera pecori gratissimus herba.* Varro, whose section also began with the dew of morning (326n.), here provides a structural, as well as dictional, model: *iterum enim tum iucunditas in herba redintegrabit, R.R.* 2.2.11.

338 As at 2.328 (see n.), the sound patterns of the words enclosing *resonant* reflect the verb's meaning: *alcyonen resonant acalanthida*. This again looks to the *Eclogues*, to a line which has just been recalled (328n.): *sole sub ardenti resonant arbusta cicadis*. On *alcyones* see 1.398–9n.

This elegant line, with its complex sound-patterns, the enclosure by *litora* and *dumique*, and the ellipse between the two clauses, reflects and reinforces the beauty of the entire passage (322–38n.).

acalanthida: for the regular *acanthida*, V.'s form (designed to match *alcyonen* in sound; see n. above) being the only instance in Latin. The bird, probably the goldfinch, is for V. Theocritean: ἄειδον κόρυδοι καὶ ἀκανθίδες, 'larks and goldfinches sang', *Id.* 7.141.

339–83   The herdsmen of Libya and the ethnography of Scythia

Taken together, these two 'digressions' elaborate the themes of the technical passages which precede, the winter (295–321) and summer care (322–38) of flocks, as V. presents two environments which permanently exhibit those two seasons. The pastoral motivation seems to come from Theocr. 7.109–14 (338, 351nn.), where Simichidas says to Pan: 'If you do not consent ... in mid-winter may you be on the mountain of the Edonians, turned to the river Hebrus near the pole, and in summer may you shepherd among the furthest Ethiopians, beneath the rock of the Blemyes, whence the Nile is no longer visible.' V. had already adapted the antithesis, at the end of *Eclogue* 10, where Gallus sings of the implacability of Amor in the frigid north or the torrid south (64–8). It is in part a pastoral one, with the two extremes representative of pastoral hardship and failure, and, given V.'s focus on extremes of temperature and their consequences in Book 3, that is the setting evoked here. The contrast is also a motif in the ethnographical tradition, going back to the Hippocratic *Airs, Waters, Places* (Thomas (1982a) 36–60); in which context it has already appeared in the poem (1.240–1n.). The descriptions, particularly that of Scythia, look outside the present book to the *laudes Italiae*, with which a contrast is inevitably established (349–83n.).

339–48 On the abbreviated nature of the Libyan sequence (compared with the Scythian), see 349–83n.

339–40   Quid ..., quid ... | prosequar: cf. 40 *Dryadum siluas saltusque sequamur*.

pastores Libyae: parallel with *Scythiae gentes*, 349.

pastores ... pascua: pastoral emphasis.

raris ... tectis 'camps inhabited by sparse huts'; a somewhat poetical way of putting it. *mapalia* are specifically Libyan settlements, apparently a sort of mobile farmyard ('perhaps something like gypsy encampments', Page) mentioned by Sallust in his Libyan ethnography (*B.J.* 18.8 *aedificia Numidarum agrestium, quae mapalia illi uocant*), and appearing at *A.* 1.421 as *magalia*, which seem to be distinguished only in the spelling and quantity of the first syllable. The word establishes the ethnographical connection.

341–3 The unbroken flow of the sentence, with its two strong enjambments, reinforces the unrelenting monotony of the Libyan shepherd's existence, as reflected in the diction. There is an immediate contrast with the Italian farmer and shepherd, for whom night and day, and the days of the month, bring distinct labours and duties. The constant activity of these lines is also in contrast to the constant inactivity of the Scythian landscape (352–3 and 356).

341   totum ex ordine mensem: cf. 4.507 (of the wandering Orpheus) *totos ... ex ordine mensis.*

342   deserta: cf. 462 (of the *northern* nomads) *deserta Getarum.*

342–3   sine ullis | hospitiis: by contrast the Scythian animals never leave their shelters (352).

343   tantum campi iacet: cf. 354–5 (of Scythia) *sed iacet ... terra.*

344–6   armentarius...|armaque...armis: Ross (1987) 173–4 notes that V. uses word-play to connect the African herdsman with the Roman soldier, at the expense of correct usage (cf. Servius: *ARMENTARIVS AFER: abusiue* ['loosely']: *nam de gregibus loquitur*). *armentarius*, the correct and official term for a herdsman (*alius enim opilio et arator, nec, si possunt in agro pasci armenta, armentarius non aliut ac bubulcus*, Varro, *R.R.* 2, *Praef.* 4), is not otherwise used by V. (2.529n.), a fact which confirms the word-play.

344–5 The accumulation of the enclitic -*que* (used five times) is striking and conveys a sense of the Libyan's burden.

344   laremque: while V. is not slow to apply terms from Roman life to non-Roman peoples, and even to animals (cf. 4.43 *sub terra fouere* [*apes*] *larem*, and see Thomas (1982a) 73), the word perhaps prepares for the simile at 346–8.

345   Amyclaeumque canem Cressamque pharetram: 'unseasonable reminiscences ... the Numidian was not likely to be thus equipped' (Conington). The usual explanation, 'ornamental', makes them no more seasonable, Richter suggests a source in Nicander, *Ther.* 670 σκυλάκεσσιν Ἀμυκλαίηισι κελεύων, 'calling to his Amyclaean whelps', but that would only explain one of the pair, and Nicander's context has no relevance to V.'s. In the Scythian excursus the detail suggests that in spite of the harshness of climate all is not completely bleak, that the Scythians even enjoy a sort of Saturnian existence (376–7, 379, 381nn.). Similar qualification might be expected for the Libyans. Sparta and Crete (and it is the places, not the hound and the quiver, that are the real focus of this line) are regarded in the ethnographical tradition as the two morally exemplary states, disdaining organized agriculture and the use of gold and silver (cf. Schroeder (1921) 51–2); at *Dial.* 40.3 Tacitus has Maternus say *quem enim oratorem Lacedaemonium, quem Cretensem accepimus?* – such states do not need oratory. Perhaps V.'s line has a moral dimension; the assignation to the Libyan of Spartan and Cretan trappings, absurd if taken literally, implies a moral strength which contrasts with the miserable conditions of Libya and ultimately with the suspect morality of the *laudes Italiae* (346; 2.136–76n.).

Amyclaeumque canem: cf. 44 *Taygetique canes*, 405 *Spartae catulos.* **Cressamque:** the adjective is never found in the masculine.

346   patriis ... armis: recalls *armaque* in the previous line (and cf. 344–6n.); *patriis* contrasts with the foreign accoutrements of 345.

acer Romanus: cf. the warriors of Italy in the *laudes Italiae: haec genus acre uirum*, 2.167; also the farmer who does battle with the vines at 2.405–6 *acer ... rusticus*, and 461 *acerque Gelonus.*

347   iniusto sub fasce: cf. 1.164 (the farmer's *arma*) *iniquo pondere rastri*; also 3.515, of the dying bull, *duro ... sub uomere. iniustus* is otherwise used by V. only once: *iniusta nouerca, E.* 3.33. *fascis*, strictly a bundle (of sticks, etc.) to be carried, here = simply 'load', 'burden'.

uiam cum carpit: cf. 142n.

hosti: dative with *stat* 'takes his stand against'.

348   ante exspectatum: for the neuter of the perfect participle used as a noun see 2.398n.

positis stat in agmine castris: cf. 2.280 (also in a simile) *[legio] campo stetit agmen aperto.*

349–83 Like the *laudes Italiae* (2.136–76; see n.), the description of
Scythia, which balances the account of the Libyan herdsman, conforms
exactly to the ethnographical format, in which treatment of *situs*, climate and produce is generally followed by discussion of the origin and
institutions of the people in question (Thomas (1982a) 37, 51–6). The
contrasts with the Italian landscape of Book 2 are pointed and pervasive (349, 350, 352–3, 356, 368, 382nn.), but Scythia does not always
suffer from the comparison; its harsh cold rules out organized agriculture, but there are redeeming features (376–7, 379, 381nn.).

The episode is given considerably more space than the description of
Libya, partly because Virgil creates a contrast not only between Scythia
and Libya, but also between Scythia and Italy (Thomas (1982a) 35–
36). See Richter for V.'s sources for the details.

349–51 These lines effectively define the *situs* of Scythia (349–
83n.).

349 At non qua 'But the situation is very different where . . .'; cf.
the beginning of the *laudes Italiae*: *sed neque* . . . . The use of *at non* with
ellipse occurs at 4.530 *at non Cyrene*, and *A.* 4.529 *at non infelix animi
Phoenissa*, but here the material in ellipse is to be recovered from the
entire preceding paragraph.

Scythiae gentes: cf. 339 *pastores Libyae*.

Maeotiaque unda: cf. *A.* 6.799 *Maeotia tellus.*

350 turbidus et torquens flauentis Hister harenas: the sub-
ject matter, the sound pattern (*t*, *t*, *f*, *H*, *h*), and *harenas*, connect the line
to 2.139 *totaque turiferis Panchaia pinguis harenis* – the fourth line of the
laudes Italiae; cf. also 2.137 *turbidus Hermus* – the only other instance of
turbidus in the poem; see nn. and cf. 4.126 (and n.).

351 'and where Rhodope stretched out towards the central pole
comes back [south] again' – referring to the north–south situation of the
mountain range. Cf. Theocr. 7.112 Ἕβρον πὰρ ποταμὸν τετραμμένος
ἐγγύθεν Ἄρκτω, 'turned to the river Hebrus, near the pole' (339–83n.).

porrecta sub axem: provides a frame with 381 (three lines from the
end of the description) *Septem subiecta trioni.*

352–3 For the virtually formulaic couplet treating the three agro-
nomical divisions (the subjects of *Georgics* 1–3), see 2.143–4n. The
situation here is in contrast to that in the *laudes Italiae*: herds do not
graze, there are no crops and no trees, while in Italy all three exist in
abundance: 2.143–4. The use of *tenent* in both couplets strengthens the

parallel. See also 4.127–8 (and n.), where ethnographical influence is also at work, and cf. Thomas (1982a) 39–40.

352   clausa tenent stabulis armenta: looks to the plague, where *stabula* will give no protection (*ipsis | in stabulis*, 556–7; see n. and 1.355n.).

353   The word-order is artful:

$$\overbrace{\textit{aut herbae campo}}\ (\text{verb})\ \overbrace{\textit{aut arbore frondes}}$$

campo ... arbore: locative ablatives without prepositions, as with *appareo* at 1.484.

354–5   sed iacet ... | terra: cf. 343 *tantum campi iacet*.
As with *concrescunt*, 360 and *intereunt*, 368, the emphatic initial placement of the verb helps to create a vivid picture.

354   aggeribus niueis informis: cf. Hor. *Odes* 2.10.15 *informis hiemes*.

355   septemque adsurgit in ulnas 'and rises to a height of seven cubits'; i.e. about 12 feet.

356   In contrast to the climate of Italy (2.149).
spirantes frigora Cauri: cf. 2.316 *Borea ... spirante*; the Caurus, the North-west wind, is mentioned at 278. *frigora* is an internal accusative.

357–9   V. adapts Hom. *Od.* 11.15–18, a description of the land of the Cimmerians: 'nor does shining Helios look down on them with his rays, neither when he climbs up to the starry heaven, nor when he turns to return again from heaven to earth'. His version is very close, but he omits the next Homeric line, the climax which relates weather to the human condition: 'but baneful night is spread over wretched mortals'. V.'s Scythians, in spite of their climate, are not so wretched (376–83).

357   tum: introduces a further item: 'and the Sun, moreover, ...'
pallentis ... discutit umbras: cf. Lucr. 4.341 *nigras discutit umbras*.

358   nec cum ... nec cum: cf. Hom. *Od.* 11.17–18 (cf. 357–9n.) οὔθ' ὁπότ' ... | οὔθ' ὅτ'. V. gives variety to the repetition and places greater emphasis on the negation by having the second conjunction in the sixth foot, with the two framing the line.

359   Cf. 1.246 *Arctos Oceani metuentis aequore tingi*. Only *Oceani* prevents the line from being golden.
rubro 'red', from the sunset.

360 concrescunt ... crustae: similar sounds (with *currenti* in the middle) frame the line; cf. Lucr. 6.626 (of the effect of mud drying) *concrescere crustas*. On the emphatic placement of *concrescunt* see 354–5n.

361 An ethnographical θαῦμα ('marvel'), already in Herodotus' ethnography of Scythia: 'the sea and the whole Cimmerian Bosporus freezes over, and they drive their wagons on the ice right across to the land of the Sindi', Herod. 4.28. See 362n.

ferratos ... orbis: cf. Lucr. 6.551 *ferratos ... rotarum ... orbis*.

362 The θαῦμα continues with a brilliantly phrased paradox: the sea which once welcomed ships now welcomes wagons. Ovid, exiled to the same region, made much of the conceit: *quaque rates ierant, pedibus nunc itur, et undas | frigore concretas ungula pulsat equi*, etc., *Trist.* 3.10.31–2.

363 aeraque dissiliunt uulgo 'brass vessels burst everywhere'. Eratosthenes (*ap.* Strabo 2.74), tells of a bronze vessel which burst 'through the water's freezing' (διὰ τὸν πάγον) in the temple of Asclepius at Panticapaeum (on the Bosporus; cf. 361n. and 349 *Maeotiaque unda* – Lake Maeotis is just to the north). Cf. 4.135–6.

364 indutae: i.e. 'on the back'.

umida '[which is elsewhere] fluid' – a somewhat bold usage. Ovid developed the picture: *Trist.* 3.10.23–4 (362n.) *nudaque consistunt, formam seruantia testae, | uina, nec hausta meri, sed data frusta bibunt*. On wine cf. 379–80n.

365 It has been objected that the subject has already been treated at 360 and that it does not proceed well from 364; hence *lagenae* has been suggested for *lacunae*, but there does seem to be a satisfactory progression and expansion from 364: 'not only does wine in jars turn to ice, but entire lakes [and the drinking water they contain] freeze solid'.

uertere: sc. *se*. For this intransitive use of *uerto*, cf. Lucr. 5.831 *omnia commutat natura et uertere cogit*. Like *induruit* in the next line, the verb is a gnomic perfect: 'have been known to'; see also 377–8n.

366 Cf. *A.* 4.251 (of Atlas) *glacie riget horrida barba*. Ovid again developed the image (362, 364nn.): *Trist.* 3.10.21–2 *saepe sonant moti glacie pendente capilli, | et nitet inducto candida barba gelu*. On the force of *horrida*, cf. 442–3 *horrida cano | bruma gelu*.

While not quite golden, the line is just as artfully ordered (2.531n.), and serves, like the golden line, to close the period; cf. 1.117n.

induruit: though *induresco* ('harden', 'set') is reasonably common, this is the first attestation.

367   interea: i.e., along with the intense cold, the snow keeps on (which is *not* usually the case, and therefore remarkable).

toto ... aëre ningit 'snow fills the sky'; *in* is regularly omitted with *totus*; cf. 1.474–5 (and n.) *toto ... caelo.*

non setius: cf. 2.277 *nec setius.*

368   intereunt pecudes: recalls in rhythm and (opposed) sense the herds of the *laudes Italiae: bis grauidae pecudes,* 2.150; also cf. 1.152 (of the fate of the crops if *labor* fails) *intereunt segetes.* The words foreshadow the death from plague which will shortly occupy V. (*intereo* occurs in him only here, at 1.152, and at 3.544 – where even the snake dies from the plague).

intereunt creates an unusual rhythmic repetition of *interea* in the preceding line.

368–9   stant ... boum: the inconsistency with 352 is motivated by V.'s foreshadowing of the peculiar method of hunting animals immobilized by the snow (371–5).

370   mole noua: sc. *niuis; nouus* ('strange', 'unaccustomed') suggests another ethnographical θαῦμα ('marvel'). Cf. 2.82 (and n.) *miratastque nouas frondes et non sua poma.*

summis uix cornibus exstant: cf. *A.* 6.667–8 (of Musaeus) *medium nam plurima turba | hunc habet atque umeris exstantem suspicit altis.*

371–5   In the ethnographical tradition primitive societies are generally hunters rather than farmers, and this normally implies a higher moral status: cf. *A.* 8.316–18 (of the original inhabitants of Latium) *nec iungere tauros | aut componere opes norant aut parcere prato, | sed rami atque asper uictu uenatus alebat;* also *A.* 9.605 (of the hardy Latins) *uenatu inuigilant pueri siluasque fatigant.* The same is implied here (cf. 376–7, 381nn.), though the emphasis is mainly on the marvellous nature of Scythian hunting, distinct from conventional practice (371n.).

371–2   A tricolon abundans, describing the absence of the usual methods of hunting, and setting up the θαῦμα of 373–5.

371   non immissis canibus: hunting-dogs will shortly be V.'s subject (404–13); during the plague, for different reasons, the deer will also be immune from any threat from dogs (539–40).

372   puniceaeue ... pauidos formidine pennae 'terrified by the device of the purple feather'. The *formido* was a rope with bright feathers attached used to direct the prey in hunting; cf. *A.* 12.750 *ceruum ... puniceae saeptum formidine pennae.* V. also exploits the normal meaning, as does Ovid at *Fast.* 5.173–4 *pauidos formidine ceruos* | *terret* (where *terret* acts as a gloss).

373   frustra ... trudentis pectore 'trying vainly to breast'.

oppositum ... montem: cf. the relegation of the bull at 213 (and n.) *post montem oppositum*.

374   comminus obtruncant ferro: a brutal combination, expressing the defencelessness of the 'hunted' animal.

rudentis: properly applied to the braying of asses, thus well capturing the distress of the dying stag.

375   caedunt: very emphatic; cf. 317n.

laeti: so in their drinking (379–80).

376–7   ipsi in defossis specubus secura sub alta | otia agunt terra: in spite of the conditions, the Scythians enjoy a leisure which approximates them to the happy 'rustic' at the end of Book 2: *secura ... otia ... speluncae*, 2.467–9. This peaceful existence is also in contrast with the toilsome and military lifestyle of the *laudes Italiae* (cf. Thomas (1982a) 52–3).

in defossis specubus: so of the bees at 4.42–3 *effossis ... latebris* | *sub terra fouere larem.* Cave-dwelling is a recurrent ethnographical detail; cf. Xen. *Anab.* 4.5.25; Mela 2.1; Tac. *Germ.* 16.3.

377   A hypermetric line (1.295–6n.).

377–8   totasque | ... ulmos: the exaggeration strengthens the sense of cold.

aduoluere ... dedere: gnomic perfects (365n.).

379   hic noctem ludo ducunt: all is not miserable, in spite of the climatic hardship; cf. 376–7, and see 2.527–31, where the rustic and his *familia* sit around the fire, also engaged in play.

ducunt: best taken = 'spend', rather than either 'protract' or 'speed on'; cf. Lucr. 2.996–7 *pabula ... quibus omnes corpora pascunt* | *et dulcem ducunt uitam*; Prop. 4.6.85 *sic noctem patera, sic ducam carmine.*

379–80   pocula ... sorbis 'and through the fermentation of [lit. 'and'] sour service-berries they imitate wine-drinking [draughts of the vine]' – taking *fermento ... atque acidis ... sorbis* as a sort of hendiadys; some see two distinct products ('beer and sour service-juice').

pocula laeti ...: the cadence occurs at 2.383 (*inter pocula laeti ...*), where early Athenians are involved in similar celebrations; cf. also 2.528, of the rustic family, *socii cratera coronant.*

380   Hyperboreo Septem subiecta trioni 'lying beneath the Hyperborean north'. A cultural, as well as geographical, designation, since *Hyperboreo* also suggests the Hyperboreans, the mythical northern race whose Utopian society was treated by Hecataeus of Abdera, Herodotus (4.32–6), Pindar (*Pyth.* 10.29–46), and Callimachus (*Aet.* fr. 186 Pf.); see Thomas (1982a) 53. There is therefore a further contrast with the close of the *laudes Italiae* where *Saturnia tellus* also equated Italy with a golden age, but in conflict with the details of the description (2.173n.).

The metrically necessary tmesis *Septem . . . trioni* reflects the derivation of *Septentrio(nes)*: the seven stars of Ursa Major, or the Wain.

381 gens effrena uirum: the adjective, properly applied to horses (*effreno equo*, Livy 4.33.7), implies that the Scythian belongs outside civilization (cf. 352–3 and n.); again there is a contrast with the inhabitant of Italy in the *laudes Italiae*, described in a parallel but different way: 2.167 *haec genus acre uirum* – where *acre* implied military prowess (cf. 346 (and n.) *acer Romanus*). Cf. also Sallust's Libyan ethnography (*B.J.* 17.6 *genus hominum salubri corpore, uelox, patiens laborum*), and *A.* 8.315, of the Italian aboriginals, *gensque uirum truncis et duro robore nata.*

382 Riphaeo . . . Euro: cf. 1.240 *Riphaeasque . . . arces.* The adjective ˊΡιπαῖος seems to be essentially Hellenistic (1.240–1n.), and its appearance at Callim. *Aet.* 186.9 Pf. ('The Hyperboreans', cf. 380n.) makes it possible that V. is specifically recalling that context. *Riphaeus* does not modify a wind before V., and it is possible that he is thinking of the specific Callimachean instance ˊΡιπαίου . . . οὔρεος ('Rhipaean mountain'): the epic form of ὄρος (οὔρος, -εος, 'mountain') is close to the word for 'wind' (οὖρος, -ου; cf. *Euro* here). Servius connects *Riphaeus* with ῥιφή (i.e. ὁρμή, 'blast of wind'), *a perpetuo uentorum flatu nominati*, which may explain the aspirate in Latin.

383 pecudum fuluis . . . saetis 'with the tawny skins [lit. 'hair'] of animals'; the reference to clothing provides a neat transition to the subject and opening of the next section.

uelatur corpora: the accusative is best seen as the object of a verb with middle force ('cover their bodies'), rather than a retained accusative ('have their bodies covered'); see 306–7n.

384–93 Sheep's wool

Ten lines on the best way to ensure superior wool production are followed by ten on goat's milk (394–403), and a further ten on the value of dogs (404–13); cf. 2.1–135n. The three sections provide a 'didactic interlude' between the accounts of Libya and Scythia on the one hand, and the precautions against snakes on the other (414–39) – a passage which clearly serves as a proem for the plague (see n.). As in the first half of the book (123–37n.), the key word *cura* is repeated at the beginning of two of these sections (*si* ... *lanitium curae*, 383; *cura canum*, 404), and is implicit in the other (*lactis amor*, 394). Each section ends with a graphic vignette, designed to enliven the material.

384   Si tibi lanitium curae: cf. 383n.; also 384–93n. on *curae*, here a dative of purpose (with *tibi*, forming the so-called 'double dative').

lanitium (wool as a product) appears here and rarely elsewhere (and not until Pliny the Younger).

384–5   aspera ... absint: a strong evocation of the necessity of *labor*; cf. 1.152–3.

Such undergrowth damages the wool and creates the danger of disease in the sheep – hence the jacketed sheep of Tarentum (Varro, *R.R.* 2.2.18 *ouibus pellitis*; Hor. *Odes* 2.6.10 *pellitis ouibus*). The present injunction looks to the plague: *hirsuti secuerunt corpora uepres*, 444.

absint: cf. 4.13–19 *absint ... lacerti*, etc. (also *adsint*, 4.19); the form appears nowhere else in V. and is perhaps used to equate the dangers to animals and bees (cf. 322–6, 387–90nn.).

385   fuge pabula laeta: cf. 1.277 *quintam* [*diem*] *fuge*. Luxuriant pasture (tall grasses) will harm the sheep; Columella allows such pasture for tall sheep: *pinguis et campestris situs proceras oues tolerat*, 7.2.3.

386   'and start out by picking flocks with white, soft fleeces' (lit. 'white flocks with soft fleeces'). Colour was likewise important in the selection (cf. *lege*) of cattle (56; see n. and cf. *legat*, 51), horses (81–3; cf. *dilectus*, 72), and figures with the bees as well (see 4.91–6, and cf. 387–90, 389nn.).

387–90   The exhortation to reject a ram which will taint the flock is very similar to the attitude towards the 'king'-bees at 4.89–90; see 389n.

388–9   nigra ... lingua ... maculis ... pullis: Aristotle states (*H.A.* 574a5–8) that the colour of the offspring will be the same as that of the veins beneath the ram's tongue, and Varro concurs (*R.R.* 2.2.4). V.'s claim that a black tongue produces speckled offspring perhaps results from his characteristic abbreviating of Varro.

389   reice: scanned as a dactyl here, as a trochee in its only other appearance in V. (*E.* 3.96). In emphasis and tone there are strong parallels with the advice on the rejection of the inferior bee: 4.90 | *dede neci*, 107 [*alas*] | *eripe*. Cf. also 422 | *deice* (and see 1.109n.).

maculis: also used of a desirable cow (56), and of the better bee (4.91); see 386n.

390 plenoque ... campo: i.e. *toto grege*: 'look around for another [ram] from your whole flock'.

391–3 A mythological *exemplum* closes the section (as does a vivid scene from everyday life at 400–3; see n., and 72–94n.): it was with fine wool that Pan was able to charm the Moon (the effort is therefore worthwhile). The story is very obscure (according to Macrobius (*Sat.* 5.22.9–10) Valerius Probus, *uir perfectissimus*, confessed he was unaware of its details or provenance). Macrobius attributes it to Nicander, to whom V. refers closely at 414–39 (see n.). Pan either turned himself into a handsome-fleeced ram and so attracted the Moon, or did so merely with the beauty of a fleece (so Servius, who also thinks V. has confused Pan with Endymion); the latter variant better suits the wording *munere ... niueo lanae*, but the former is more consistent with 392 *captam te ... fefellit* 'charmed and deceived you'. Perhaps it was a false metamorphosis: cf. Serv. Auct. *ut illi* [i.e. *Lunae*] *formosus uideretur, niueis uelleribus se circumdedit.*

391 si credere dignum est: expresses *diffidentia*, perhaps of a specific literary source: for such expressions, cf. Norden on *A.* 6.14; Stinton (1976) esp. 66. The phrase otherwise occurs in V. at *A.* 6.173.

392–3 With the double epanalepsis *te ... tu, uocans ... uocantem*, the apostrophe to *Luna*, and the progression from [*te*] *uocans* to *nec tu aspernata uocantem*, the lines have an appealingly whimsical tone, evident in much Alexandrian poetry.

Pan deus Arcadiae: so called at *E.* 10.26.

uocans ... uocantem 'calling' to an assignation, but also referring to the 'invoking' of a deity (1.42; 4.6–7nn.).

394–403   Goat's milk

See 384–93n. The subject is treated by Varro at *R.R.* 2.3, and is one of great importance in the ancient world.

394 At cui lactis amor: looks back to *si tibi lanitium curae*, 384 (384–93n.).

cytisum: a favourite with goats; cf. 2.431 *tondentur cytisi* (and see n.).

394–5 ... frequentis | ipse manu ... ferat praesepibus: the supply is to be abundant, as at 320–1 (see n.), cf. *feres*; also 4.112 (of the bee-keeper) *ipse ... ferens.*

salsasque 'salted'.

396 hinc: as a result of eating salted fodder.

magis ubera tendunt: cf. 317 *grauido ... ubere*; *E.* 4.21-2 *lacte ... distenta ... | ubera*; Hor. *Epd.* 16.50 *tenta ubera*.

397 'and their milk retains [lit. 'they retain in their milk'] the lurking flavour of the salt' – presumably a desirable trait.

398 Contrast what is recommended for cows (176-8 and 176-7n.).
multi: cf. 1.193 *semina uidi equidem multos medicare serentis*.

excretos: from *excerno* ('separate them and keep them from the mothers'), rather than *excresco* ('keep them from the mothers when they have grown up'), V.'s point being that the kids are separated *soon* after birth; Varro says they should be turned out three months after birth (*R.R.* 2.3.8).

399 A golden line (1.117n.).

primaque: modifies *ora*, but in effect adverbial: 'from the first' (i.e. 'when young'). Page and others understand 'the point of their nose'.

praefigunt ora capistris: cf. 188 *det ... ora capistris*; *capistrum* does not otherwise occur in V.

400-3 The making and marketing of cheese. There are two pressings, tied to the two milkings: the morning milk is pressed at night, the evening milk before dawn the next morning. The product is then either taken to market (if of the perishable type) or salted and stored for the winter. These two uses have no particular relationship to the two pressings, though earlier editors created one by having no colon after *lucem*: the evening's milk, pressed immediately, is taken to market before dawn.

400 horisque diurnis: repeats the sense of *surgente die*, as does *sole cadente* of *tenebris* in 401.

402 calathis: here wicker baskets for holding curd-cheese (through which the whey would run off: Colum. 7.8.3 *confestim cum concreuit liquor, in fiscellas aut in calathos uel formas transferendus est*), at *E.* 2.46 flower baskets, at *E.* 5.71 goblets, at *A.* 7.805 wool baskets.

(adit oppida pastor): the parenthesis contains an important antithesis *oppida/pastor*. *oppida*, in fact closely tied to agricultural existence, are mentioned elsewhere in the poem only in the *laudes Italiae* (2.155-6, 176) and at 4.178, of the bees' 'town'. Cf. however the vignette at 1.273-5 (see n.).

403 parco sale contingunt: cf. Colum. 7.8.4 *torrido sale contingitur [caseus]*.

hiemique reponunt: like the bees of 4.156–7 and the ants of *A.* 4.402–3 (*hiemis memores ... reponunt* in both cases).

404–13   cura canum

Cf. 384–93n. Dogs are treated at Varro, *R.R.* 2.9, and are clearly important both as guardians of the flock and farm (406–8) and for hunting (409–13) – in both of which capacities the plague will render them ineffective (539–40); see 406–8, 409–13nn. In the second half of the book dogs present a paradigm for success and failure: here they perform their correct function, at 371 (an abnormal situation) they were not necessary for hunting, and at 539–40 they are powerless to hunt.

404   **Nec tibi cura canum fuerit postrema:** recapitulates 384 *si tibi lanitium curae* and 394 *at cui lactis amor*. There is some irony in *nec ... postrema*, in that this is precisely that – the final *cura* of the book. On *nec* for *neu* in a prohibition, cf. 2.252–3n.; also 1.456–7n. on *non* for *ne.*

405   The two types of dog are paradigmatic; cf. Hor. *Epd.* 6.5 *nam qualis aut Molossus aut fuluus Lacon.* The former appeared at 44 and 345 (and n.). Molossian hounds are mentioned at Lucr. 5.1063, and serve as the watchdogs which terrify the two mice at Hor. *Sat.* 2.6.114–15.

406   **pasce sero pingui** 'feed them on fattening whey'; for the force of *pingui* cf. 205 *crassa farragine* and 205–6n. V. is perhaps drawing from Hes. *W.D.* 604 μὴ φείδεο σίτου, 'do not grudge him his food' (406–8n.).

406–8   **numquam ... Hiberos:** here, as in Hesiod, the value of the dog as a protector immediately follows the exhortation to keep it well fed (406n.): 'lest some Day-sleeper steal your property', *W.D.* 605 (*nocturnum ... furem* here translates and explains the colourful ἡμερόκοιτος).

The obvious connection between correct feeding and the dog's performance is also made by Varro: *diligenter ut habeat cibaria prouidendum. fames enim hos ad quaerendum cibum ducet, si non praebebitur, et a pecore abducet, R.R.* 2.9.8.

incursusque luporum: here a threat, but no longer so when plague comes (537–8).

408   Brigands seem to have been something of a problem in Spain: cf. Varro, *R.R.* 1.16.2 *multos enim agros egregios colere non expedit propter latrocinia uicinorum, ut ... in Hispania prope Lusitaniam.* But since V. is writing for Italians his *Hiberi* may be generic. As for the problem in general, Varro even considers it in determining the ideal site for a farmhouse; lowlands are undesirable, not only because of the threat of flooding: *et repentinae praedonum manus quod improuisos facilius opprimere possunt*, *R.R.* 1.12.4.

impacatos: the only instance of the word in V.; perhaps an indication that Augustus' pacification of Spain (beginning in 27) was already in the air. Cf. *Res Gestae Div. Aug.* 26.2 *Gallias et Hispanias prouincias ... pacaui.*

409–13 Varro mentions the hunting-dog in passing (*R.R.* 2.9.2), but dismisses it as inappropriate to a work on agriculture. V. devotes half of this section to the hunting-dog in order to set up the powerful image of 539–40, where deer, the traditional prey of the plague-stricken dogs, wander immune among their hunters (see n.).

409   cursu ... agitabis: cf. *A.* 7.478 (of Ascanius) *insidiis cursuque feras agitabat Iulus. agitare*, with no qualification, is a technical term for hunting (cf. 372 *agitant pauidos*; *A.* 11.686 *feras agitare*), and given the speed of the quarry in the present line, as at *A.* 7.478, *cursu* suggests hunting with horses. Nor does it sit well with *incursus* two lines earlier (normally the simplex, when repeated soon after the compound, has the meaning of the compound – which is not possible here). What is needed rhetorically is an emphatic reference to dogs: dogs are good for guarding the fold and the farmhouse (406–8); with dogs you can also hunt. Did V. write *canibus* where the text has *cursu*? This would give a tricolon with anaphora of the key word, a familiar feature in the poem (1.266–7, 289–90nn.), and the type tricolon decrescens (with anaphora) is paralleled by 2.221–2. Though the repeated word is not usually in the same inflexion, cf. 4.525–7. *cursu* could have come from a gloss on the subject of the lines or from knowledge of *A.* 7.486.

onagros: the wild ass is not found in Italy: *[asinorum] genera duo: unum ferum, quos uocant onagros, ut in Phrygia et Lycaonia sunt greges multi; alterum mansuetum, ut sunt in Italia omnes*, Varro, *R.R.* 2.6.3.

410   Cf. 1.308 *auritosque sequi lepores, tum figere dammas.*

411   uolutabris 'haunts of boars' (i.e. place where they wallow, *uolutari*); the word occurs only here and in late Latin.

412   latratu: i.e. *canibus latrantibus.*

montisque per altos: otherwise in V. only at 535.

413   ingentem ... ad retia ceruum: cf. 1.307 *retia ponere ceruis*. Cf. the fateful stag hunted by Ascanius: *ceruus ... cornibus ingens*, *A.* 7.483; but see following n.

clamore: cf. 43–4 *uocat ingenti clamore Cithaeron | Taygetique canes*; 375 [*ceruos*] *magno laeti clamore reportant.* Should *ingenti* be read in the present line (for *ingens clamor* cf. also *A.* 9.38; 12.268)?

414–39   Fumigate against the snake

One of the most chilling and powerful passages in V., ostensibly didactic (*disce* . . .), serves as a transition to the plague, of which the snake itself is emblematic (*pestis acerba boum,* 419 and n.). The images were reworked in the *Aeneid*, particularly at *A.* 2.471–5 (437–9n.; also 421n.); in fact almost every subsequent reference to snakes in V. looks back to this passage. His model is Nicander's *Theriaca*, a typical product of the Alexandrian mind, a poem dealing with poisonous creatures and remedies. Though his borrowing is at times close (414–15, 421, 425–34nn.), the passage becomes an integrated part of his poem and of the progression towards the calamity of plague. This is particularly true in the lines on the Calabrian water-snake (425–34), whose appearance is attended by the scorching heat which also marks the onset of the plague, and in the authorial interjection of 435–6 (see nn.).

414   Disce: the imperative of this verb occurs only here in the poem, and obviously creates a strong didactic tone; cf. 558 *discunt.·*

414–15   odoratam . . . nidore: adapted from Nic. *Ther.* 51–4: 'and again, let the heavy-scented juice of all-heal [= *galbanum*] stimulated over a fire, and stinging nettle, and cedar cut with saws . . . produce in their burning a smoky and repellent smell'.

Just before sickness kills the ailing hive in Book 4, V. recommends similar fumigation: 4.264 *hic iam galbaneos suadebo incendere odores*; forms of *galbanum* ('all-heal'; the resinous gum of various species of *Ferula*) do not otherwise occur in V., who is here setting up a parallel fate for beast and bee alike (322–6n.).

odoratam . . . cedrum: cf. *A.* 7.13 (of Circe) *urit odoratam . . . cedrum.*

grauis . . . chelydros: an amphibious snake (which anticipates the more extensively treated *chersydrus* at 425–34; see n.) whose deadly plague-like effects are described by Nicander at *Ther.* 411–37. It apparently has a very unpleasant smell (*grauis*; cf. 4.49 *odor caeni grauis*): *Ther.* 421 τὸ δ' ἀπὸ χροὸς ἐχθρὸν ἄηται, 'it gives off a hateful breath from its skin'. Cf. 2.214–15 *nigris exesa chelydris | creta.*

416   immotis: i.e. 'uncleaned', 'neglected'.

416–17   mala tactu | uipera 'the viper, deadly to the touch'.

417 caelumque exterrita fugit: cf. the parched *chersydrus* at 434 *exterritus aestu*; also of the gadfly's effect on cattle at 149–50 (see n.) *exterrita* ... | *diffugiunt armenta*; and the effect of plague on the snakes at 545 *attoniti ... hydri*. Cf. *A.* 12.660 (the death of Amata) *occidit ... lucemque exterrita fugit*.

418 tecto ... umbrae: hendiadys: 'a snake accustomed to getting underneath the shelter of a thatch'. Cf. 464 *molli succedere ... umbrae*.

419 (pestis acerba boum): cf. 1.181n. on the limited and important occurrences of *pestis* in the poem; they all look to 471 – the real *pestis*.

pecorique aspergere uirus: from its position under the roof – a fanciful notion.

420 fouit humum 'hugs the ground'. It is generally (*adsuetus*, 418) found in the roof, but is particularly dangerous when it comes down. For *foueo*, cf. 4.43 *fouere larem*; *A.* 9.57 *castra fouere*.

cape saxa manu, cape robora, pastor: as he addresses his didactic audience of shepherds, V. adopts a simple but powerful and urgent asyndetic style, reminiscent of Hesiod; cf. 1.299 (and n.) *nudus ara, sere nudus*.

421 Adapted from Nic. *Ther.* 179–80, 'and its dust-coloured neck swells as it hisses continuously'. V. reworked the line at *A.* 2.381, where the Greek Androgeos, suddenly finding himself in the midst of the enemy, is likened to a man who comes upon a snake [*anguem*] *attollentem iras et caerula colla tumentem*.

colla: accusative of respect.

422 deice!: cf. 389n. (*reice*) for the emphatic position; *iamque* underscores the urgency.

422–4 Again in a simile (cf. 421n.) at *A.* 5.276–9 V. describes in similar terms (though there is little in the way of shared diction) the death throes of a snake which has been run over: *nequiquam longos fugiens dat corpore tortus* | ... *pars uulnere clauda retentat* | *nexantem nodis seque in sua membra plicantem*.

423–4 cum ... | soluuntur 'while the coils of its middle and the end of its gliding tail [lit. 'the glidings of the end of its tail'] are untwining' (so as to follow the head into the hole); V.'s style and syntax seem particularly convoluted whenever he describes the movement of snakes (cf. 422–4, 424nn.; *A.* 2.202–11).

The scene is made more vivid by the change from exhortation to indicative (*soluuntur, trahit*), reinforced by *iamque*.

424 tardosque ... orbis: the 'last curve' (*sinus ultimus*) is seen as doing what the snake does ('slowly drags its coils').

425-34 Of the numerous snakes described in detail by Nicander (*Ther.* 98–482), V. selects just one for full treatment, and his selection is significant. Though the snake is not named (425n.), it is readily identifiable as the *chersydrus* (*Ther.* 359–71), whose name defines its amphibious nature (χέρσος, 'dry land'; ὕδωρ, 'water'). V. closely follows Nicander (428–31, 432–4nn.), who relates that it stays in the water during the wet seasons, but emerges in high summer when ponds dry up. The symbolic potential of this creature is enormous: the intense heat which characterizes its baleful emergence will also attend the onset of plague (479 and n.) – which it clearly symbolizes. And ultimately the snake itself will be carried off by that plague (544–5n.).

425 est etiam ille malus Calabris in saltibus anguis: an ecphrasis is announced, its tone identical to that on the gadfly (145–6n.), with which the snake shares destructive powers (both are *pestes*; see 419n.).

Calabris in saltibus: Solinus' claim (2.33) that this snake is common in Calabria may be mere parroting; it is significant that V. places the snake in the torrid south of Italy (425–34n.), along with the gadfly.

anguis: V. expects his reader to recover the name from the close similarities to Nicander. The manner is Alexandrian (1.14–15n.), and the suppression in fact conveys emphasis, much as with the *praeteritio* (425–34n.). In what follows he glosses the name of the snake (428–9 *amnes, udo, pluuialibus* = ὕδωρ, 'water'; 432–3 *exusta ... ardore, siccum* = χέρσος, 'dry land').

426 'coiling its scaly back, with breast erect'. Cf. *A.* 2.474 *lubrica conuoluit sublato pectore terga* (437–9n.); the two images are separately applied to the serpents set upon Laocoon: *A.* 2.206 *pectora ... arrecta*, 218–19 *squamea ... | terga.*

427 notis ... maculosus: cf. *A.* 5.87–8 [*anguis*] *caeruleae cui terga notae maculosus et auro | squamam incendebat fulgor.*

428-31 In the wet seasons the snake stays in the water and feeds on fish and frogs; adapted from Nic. *Ther.* 366–7 'at first beneath some shallow lake he wreaks implacable malice on the frogs'. V. expands on the model: he stresses the connection between this stage of the snake's activity and the moisture of spring (428–9; only implicit in Nicander), an emphasis further realized with the arrival of the hot, dry summer (432–4); and he constructs a more specific image of the snake's feast (430–1), characterizing the frogs (*loquacibus*) and thereby intensifying the sense of horror.

428   ulli: V. otherwise uses *ullus* only with negatives, questions and conditionals (which indeed is in effect the force of *dum*).

429 In spring and winter (the wet seasons); V. is establishing a contrast with the coming summer (432–4).

pluuialibus Austris: cf. *A.* 9.668 *pluuialibus Haedis*.

430–1   atram | ... ingluuiem 'his black and deadly maw'. *ater* suggests both blackness and a poisonous or lethal quality; cf. 1.129 (and n.) *ille malum uirum serpentibus addidit atris*; 2.130 *atra uenena*.

improbus: renders Nicander's ἄσπειστον ... κότον, 'implacable malice'; on *improbus* in the *Georgics* see 1.119, 145–6nn.

ingluuiem ranisque loquacibus implet: developed from Nicander (428–31n.), but also perhaps with an eye to Arat. *Phaen.* 946 ἢ μᾶλλον δειλαὶ γενεαί, ὕδροισιν ὄνειαρ, 'or more wretched tribes [i.e. frogs], a boon for water-snakes' – already adapted at 1.378 (see n.).

432–4 Even closer to Nicander: 'but when the Dog-star dries up the water, and the lake-bottom is parched, then dusty and colourless he comes onto dry land ...' (*Ther.* 367–9). V. lays yet greater stress on the heat and its maddening effect.

432   exusta ... dehiscunt: cf. 1.479 (one of the omens of civil war) *sistunt amnes terraeque dehiscunt*; also 2.353.

433   in siccum = ἐν χέρσωι (432–4n.), for V. as for Nicander a gloss on the name of the snake (*chersydrus*; cf. 425n.).

flammantia lumina torquens: cf. the eyes of Charon in the Underworld, *A.* 6.300 *stant lumina flamma*; also the serpents of *A.* 2.210 *ardentisque oculos suffecti sanguine et igni*; cf. the eyes of the dying horse at 505 (and see n.) *ardentes oculi*.

434   saeuit: like Tisiphone, instrument of plague (551), and Mars at 1.511 (see n.); cf. also 438n.

asperque siti: plague has the same effect on the animals at 482–3.

exterritus aestu: cf. 417 (and n.) *uipera ... exterrita fugit*.

435–6 Cf. 1.456–7; 2.252–3nn. on such authorial intrusions, and most immediately see 249 (and n.) *heu male tum Libyae solis erratur in agris*.

The impulse comes from Nic. *Ther.* 21–7, 55–6 (those with knowledge of venomous creatures will be able to sleep safely outside). Characteristically, V. develops this, turning it into a personal, apotropaic wish.

435 mollis ... somnos: cf. 2.470 *mollesque sub arbore somni* (and see 436n.); also *E.* 7.45 *somno mollior herba*, a figure taken from Theocritus: εἴρια ... ὕπνω μαλακώτερα, 'fleeces softer than sleep', 5.50–1. The evocation and dismissal of this pastoral image perhaps looks to the upsetting of the pastoral world by the plague (cf. 476–7, 537–45nn.).

sub diuo 'under the open sky' (= αἴθριος, Nic. *Ther.* 25).

436 neu ... libeat iacuisse per herbas: these realities contrast with the idealization at 2.470 (435n.), 527 *ipse dies agitat festos fususque per herbam* ...; see 2.469–71n.

437–9 This brilliant image is repeated at *A.* 2.473–5, with 438, no longer appropriate, replaced by *lubrica conuoluit sublato pectore terga* (*A.* 2.474), which is in turn developed from 426 here. In *Aeneid* 2 the image is as chilling as its prototype: it occurs in the simile likening Pyrrhus to a snake, just before his destruction of Priam and his house.

437 positis ... iuuenta 'fresh and gleaming in its youth, having doffed its slough'. The image is taken from yet another section of the *Theriaca* (cf. 414–39n.): 'nor when the viper, having doffed his shrivelled old age, again proceeds exulting in his new youth', 137–8.

438 aut catulos ... aut oua relinquens: the drought causes the snake to desert its young, as *amor* did the lioness (245–6), with no less dangerous results.

439 arduus ad solem: cf. Nic. *Ther.* 370 θάλπων ἡελίωι βλοσυρὸν δέμας, 'warming his fearful body in the sunshine'.

linguis micat ore trisulcis: *linguis ... trisulcis* is an instrumental, *ore* a source ablative: 'flickers from his mouth with three-forked tongue'.

440–77   Causes, signs and treatment of disease

V. leads gradually into the plague, which forms the climax of the book (478–566), as he first treats, for the moment still in the manner of the didactic poet, the causes and indications of disease (440n.). This is a legitimate part of the technical tradition (*de sanitate*; Varro, *R.R.* 2.1.21–3; see 440n.), but by 470 the emphasis begins to change as the prescriptions against disease give way to the account of the plague, and by the end of the section desolation has set in. The sequence is very much like that of Book 1, where the real storm, and the storm of civil war, come in spite of the *signa* which precede them and which are therefore of limited value. Precisely the same progression occurs in V.'s treatment of the bees (4.251–2, 281–2nn.).

440   Varro wrote *fere morborum causae erunt, quod laborant propter aestus aut propter frigora . . . signa autem sunt . . .* ; *item ad alios morbos aliae causae et alia signa,* R.R. 2.1.22. The phrase *morbi causa* is important in *Georgics* 4 as Aristaeus, after losing his hive to disease, seeks the cause (4.396–7, 532). But causes and signs will not necessarily lead to remedies, either here at the end of the third book, or in the first, or the fourth.

   signa: regularly precede disaster in the *Georgics*; cf. 1.351n.; see also 503n.

   docebo: V. uses a first person of *doceo* only here in the poem; cf. 414 *disce.*

   441   turpis ouis temptat scabies: cf. Cato, *Agr.* 96 *oues ne scabrae fiant.* The subject was anticipated at 298–9 *glacies ne frigida laedat | molle pecus scabiemque ferat turpisque podagras* (see n.). *scabies* only occurs in the *Georgics* – in these two places of the disease, at 1.495 (*scabra*) and 2.220 of the detritus from rusting weapons, at 2.214 (*scaber*) of rough soil.

   temptat 'attacks'; cf. *E.* 1.49 *non insueta grauis temptabunt pabula fetas.*

   441–4   ubi frigidus imber | ... persedit ... uel cum ... adhaesit | sudor: extremes of cold and heat are seen as the cause, as by Varro (*propter aestus aut propter frigora,* see 440n.). The sweat is that of summer (*aestiuum sudorem,* Colum. 7.5.5), which afflicts the sheep after shearing (*tonsis*). V. establishes at the very outset that disease is caused by extremes of temperature (not in fact true of scab). Such extremes have been destructive throughout the technical parts of the book, have been stressed on a different level in the accounts of Libya and Scythia (339–83) and in the description of the *chersydrus* (425–34), and receive particular emphasis when the actual plague comes (97–8n.).

   441   frigidus imber: cf. 1.259 *frigidus . . . imber.*

   442   altius ad uiuum persedit 'has sunk deep into the quick'; the first reference to the hidden and internal effects of disease; cf. 454 *alitur uitium uiuitque tegendo,* 457–8 *dolor . . . lapsus ad ossa | . . . atque artus depascitur arida febris,* 484–5 *omniaque in se | ossa . . . morbo conlapsa,* 566 *artus sacer ignis edebat.* Cf. also 457–8n. (on *ima*).

   443–51   The disease comes from the dirt in the sweat, introduced into the body when the skin is cut by brambles after shearing. Cato has the following recommendation: *amurcam condito, puram bene facito, aquam in qua lupinus deferuerit et faecem de uino bono, inter se omnia commisceto pariter. postea cum detonderis, unguito totas, sinito biduum aut triduum consudent. deinde lauito in mari; si aquam marinam non habebis, facito aquam salsam, ea lauito,*

Agr. 96. V. recommends washing *before* shearing (446) and only applying ointments afterwards (448); since the sheep's body is vulnerable after shearing, Cato's scheme seems the more reasonable – perhaps a Virgilian lapse. Columella, though quoting liberally from V., agrees with Cato: *uel post tonsuram, si remedium praedicti medicaminis non adhibeas, si aestiuum sudorem mari uel flumine non abluas,* 7.5.5

443–4 inlotus adhaesit | sudor: here the sweat of summer (441– 4n.), later, a symptom of plague, a cold sweat: *incertus ibidem | sudor et ille quidem morituris frigidus,* 500–1; and finally the sweat of plague which infects man himself: *immundus* [= *inlotus*] *olentia sudor | membra sequebatur,* 564–5.

444 hirsuti secuerunt corpora uepres: one reason for the advice at 384–5 (see n.).

445–7 Dipping sheep was one of the activities important enough to be permitted on sacred days: 1.272 *balantumque gregem fluuio mersare salubri.* mersare occurs in V. only there and at 447.

fluuiis ... gurgite ... amni: Cato recommends sea- or at least salt-water, Columella (perhaps influenced by V.) salt or fresh (443–51n.); V. seems to speak only of fresh water.

447 missusque secundo defluit amni: a vivid image; cf. 2.451– 2 *leuis ... alnus | missa Pado;* also 1.203 *illum in praeceps prono rapit alueus amni.*

448–51 V.'s concoction is partly of his own devising. Cato (443– 51n.) suggests the ubiquitous oil-lees (*amurca;* 1.194n.), with equal parts of lupin broth and wine dregs, while Columella (7.4.7, 7.5.7–8) follows Cato, but adds crushed hellebore (as in V.), and, as an optional ingredient, hemlock. Six of V.'s items are therefore not traditional, and he is perhaps just striving for a colourful recipe (in any case of little functional use, since he gives no proportions – a breach of the real tradition).

448 A golden line (1.117n.).

449 spumas ... argenti: the healing properties of silver slag are mentioned by Pliny (*N.H.* 33.105), though scab is not included.

uiuaque sulpura: hypermetric (1.295–6n.), with 1.295 and 2.69 the only instance in the poem not involving *-que;* the truth is recovered from scholiasts and grammarians, since in the MSS the difficulty has been removed (*et sulpura uiua*), as was attempted at 2.69 (see n.).

450 Recalled apropos of the beehive (4.38–41; cf. 440–77n.).

451   scillamque elleborosque grauis nigrumque bitumen:
none of these items is elsewhere associated with curing scab. The line has
the look of an adaptation from Greek, which need not however imply
that there was ever such a line in Greek (1.138n.).

grauis 'strong'.

452   non tamen ulla magis ... | quam ...: 'and yet no help for
their ills is more timely than ...' Cf. 209–10 *sed non ulla magis uiris
industria firmat | quam ...* (see n.). In both cases the *industria* or *labores* are
destined to fail. This is the first of a number of references connecting the
symptoms and effects of *amor* with disease or plague (the twin calamities
of Book 3); cf. 454, 457–8, 464–7, 467, 498, 514, 520–1, 554–5, 566nn.).

453–4   ferro ... rescindere summum | ulceris os: a more
radical procedure; cf. 468 *culpam ferro compesce* (see n.; the reference is not
merely to surgery). Finally this and all medical arts will be of no avail:
quaesitaeque nocent artes; cessere magistri ..., 549 (see n.).

os: *os (uenae)* is a technical term for the source of any haemorrhage;
cf. Cels. 4.11.2.

454   alitur uitium uiuitque tegendo: a chilling line, adapted
from Lucr. 4.1068 *ulcus enim uiuescit et inueterascit alendo*. With *tegendo* V.
retains the rare syntax of Lucretius' *alendo* (see n. below), with *alitur* the
actual verb. The allusion is subtle, for Lucretius' line comes not from
the account of the plague in Book 6, but from the discussion of the
power of *amor*, which he treats as an illness. V. thus presents disease
in terms of Lucretius' *amor*, equating the two afflictions, as throughout
(452n.).

uitium: cf. 1.88n. on the restricted use of this grim word.

tegendo: impersonal: 'by concealment'; cf. 2.250 *habendo*, and the
source of this instance, Lucretius' *alendo*.

455–6   medicas ... poscens: the shepherd's failure is a failure of
knowledge, brought about by a relaxation of *labor* and by inactivity
combined with a misguided reliance on religion, the inappropriateness
of which will be demonstrated when the real plague comes (486–93n.).
Cf. also 1.335–50n. on the words *in primis uenerare deos*, which had little
to do with averting the destruction of the storm.

deos ... omina: a double accusative after *poscens*. Of the older MSS
only the Medicean has *omina*, but it is clearly correct against the too
general *omnia*.

457   quin etiam 'and what is more'.

457-8 ima ... furit: the symptoms of love and disease are again parallel: 258-9 *quid iuuenis, magnum cui uersat in ossibus ignem | durus amor,* 271-2 *ubi subdita flamma medullis | (uere magis, quia uere calor redit ossibus).*

ima: used also at 506 and 522, suggesting the deep-seated nature of the infection (cf. 442n.).

balantum 'bleaters'. The colourful phrase *balantum pecudes* is Ennian (*Ann.* 169 Skutsch), and is reproduced by Lucretius (2.369) and varied by V. (*balantumque gregem*, 1.272; *greges ... balantum*, *A.* 7.538). The plain substantive *balantes* occurs only here, at Lucr. 6.1132 *uenit ... pigris balantibus aegror* (whence V. took it), and in late Latin. Cf. 541n. on *genus natantum.*

458 artus depascitur arida febris: so at *A.* 2.215 the serpents 'feed on' the limbs of Laocoon's sons: *miseros morsu depascitur artus*; again the association between snakes and disease (414-39n.).

458-9 arida febris, | ... incensos aestus: plague as fire again (441-4n.).

459-63 The age-old panacea, bleeding, is also recommended, as a last resort, by Varro: *si hoc genus rebus non proficitur, demittitur sanguis, maxime e capite, R.R.* 2.1.23. Columella (7.5.10) first recommends bleeding from the hoof (but he may be merely parroting V., whom he cites: *subicit [Vergilius] aeque prudenter ...*), then concurs with Varro: *nos etiam sub oculis et de auribus sanguinem detrahimus.*

Lines 461-3 say little more than *ut faciunt Scythae*, and there is no indication elsewhere that blood-letting was necessarily a northern practice. V. perhaps intends some connection with the description of Scythia (349-83): the inhabitants of the frigid north are associated with a practice which repels the burning heat of disease (*incensos aestus auertere*, 459).

459 profuit: cf. 509 *profuit* where, as is clear from what follows, the sense is 'it has *seemed* [wrongly] to be helpful'. The same scepticism may be implicit here.

459-60 inter | ... uenam: either 'to lance the vein which throbs with blood in the middle of the bottom of the hoof', or 'to lance a vein which [then] spurts with blood ...' For the construction *ima pedis* cf. 4.321-2n.

461-2 Bisaltae ... Gelonus ... Rhodopen ... deserta Getarum: a pastiche of northerners and northern regions, giving ethnographical colour (cf. 459-63n.). The Bisaltae are in fact

Macedonian, the Geloni (cf. 2.115) Scythians, while Rhodope is in Thrace (see 351), and the Getans are neighbours of the Dacians on the western shore of the Black Sea.

461   acerque Gelonus: cf. 346 (and n.) *acer Romanus*.

462   fugit: i.e. they are nomadic.

deserta: cf. 342, of the regions used by the Libyan nomads.

463   Somewhat different from the simple drinking of mare's milk, attributed to various peoples: e.g. Hom. *Il.* 13.5–6 (of a Scythian tribe) Ἱππημολγῶν | γλακτοφάγων, 'the milk-drinking Hippomolgi [Mare-milkers – the epithet glosses the name]'. References to the drinking of the blood seem to be later; Hor. *Odes* 3.4.34 (of the Spaniards): *et laetum equino sanguine Concanum*; and for the same combination as in V., cf. Stat. *Achill.* 1.307–8 (the Massagetae) *lactea Massagetae ueluti cum pocula fuscant | sanguine puniceo*. In suggesting that the blood drawn from the hoof is then used to curdle the milk, V. seems to be conflating.

464–7   V. creates a strong pastoral image, but it is pastoral gone wrong: sheep staying in the shade, listlessly nibbling the grass, lagging behind, falling forward while grazing, and returning late at night. Cf. *E.* 8.86–8, where two of these signs are, once again, symptoms of love (452n.): *bucula ... | propter aquae riuum uiridi procumbit in ulua | perdita, nec serae meminit decedere nocti*, 86–8. On listlessness as betokening both love and disease, cf. 498–9n.

464   molli succedere ... umbrae: cf. 418.

465   summas carpentem ignauius herbas: see 498–9 and n.

466   procumbere: see 464–7n. So of the ox killed by Entellus at *A.* 5.481 *procumbit humi bos*.

467   et serae solam decedere nocti 'and retire alone as the late night advances'; cf. *E.* 8.89 (464–7n.); also see 4.23 *decedere ... calori* 'go into the shade'. This line, like *E.* 8.89, is adapted from Varius, fr. 4 Morel, a passage already used by V. in his discussion of the power of *amor* (253–4n.) – another allusive linking of the two themes.

Page well notes the pathos of the two balanced and emphatic spondees *serae* and *solam*.

468   continuo culpam ferro compesce: cf. 453–4 (and n.) *ferro ... rescindere summum | ulceris os*. The surgery has now become extreme; though the wording is ambiguous, *culpam*, as the next line shows, refers to the infected animal which must be killed to preserve the rest of the flock. Some take the words as a further reference to the removal of the sores.

compesco denotes vigorous and violent suppression, as at 2.369–70, the only other instance in V.

469 A golden line ends the movement (1.117n.).

incautum: an important word in the poem; see 303n.

serpant: given the importance of 414–39 as a prelude and emblem for plague (see n.), V. doubtless intends a reference to substantival *serpens*.

contagia: cf. 566 *contactos ... artus*.

470–566 Some editors see the final section as beginning at 470, rather than 478, and Harrison (1979) 40–1 has detected a peculiar pattern of line-arrangement predicated on such a division.

470–1 non ... pestes: almost imperceptibly V. shifts from disease to plague, the focus of the rest of the book (478–566n.). Through the comparison with a storm he also brings the plague into a close connection with the calamity of Book 1, the unseasonable storm; cf. 1.320–1 (*turbo* occurs in the poem only in these two places, see 1.320n.); also 1.313 *ruit imbriferum uer*, 324 *ruit arduus aether*. Cf. also 2.303–14n. on the storm which aids the fire in destroying the trees.

pecudum pestes: cf. 419, of the snake (*pestis acerba boum*) and see n. This is the only reference to the plague as *pestis*.

472 aestiua: sc. *castra*; the military metaphor strengthens the sense of the plague's being an active force and associates it with the heat of summer (479 and n.).

473 The animals are destroyed root and branch, as are the crops by the storm at 1.319–20; cf. the flood which attends civil war at 1.482–3, the fire which destroys the trees at 2.308, and the illness which kills the hive at 4.281–2.

spemque: cf. 73 *spem ... gentis*, and 73–4n.

474–7 The general becomes the particular as V. passes to his *exemplum*, the plague of Noricum, from which, even in his time, the desolation persists. It matters little for the *Georgics* whether or not this plague really occurred (and it seems likely that it did not; cf., recently, Harrison (1979), not refuted by Flintoff (1983)). Cf. 478–566n.

474–6 tum sciat ... si quis | ... uideat 'then would one realize [the apocalyptic nature of plague] if he were to look upon ... '

474–5 Alpis ... Norica ... Iapydis ... Timaui: V. specifies (not very restrictively) the north-east of Italy, from the northernmost point of the Adriatic up to the Austrian Alps. His intention may be in part to show that he is no longer dealing with events and ethnography of distant lands – Libya, Scythia and the like (cf. 339–83, 461–2, where, as in the present instance four proper names define the locations); the plague has come home.

Norica ... tumulis 'the Norican forts on their hillocks'; such pendant prepositional phrases, though rarer than in English, are reasonably common in Latin.

Iapydis: roughly speaking 'Illyrian'; the Iapydes were a northern Dalmatian people.

476   nunc quoque post tanto: chilling testimony to the virulence of the plague.

476–7   desertaque regna | pastorum: see 322–38, 537–45nn. on the annihilation of the pastoral world, and cf. *E.* 1.69–71 (the words of Meliboeus as his own private pastoral existence passes away) *post aliquot, mea regna, uidens mirabor aristas? | impius haec tam culta noualia miles habebit, | barbarus has segetes.*

longe ... lateque: otherwise in V. only at *A.* 6.378 *longe lateque per urbes.*

478–566   The plague

From *causae* and *signa* V. proceeds to the reality of the plague, whose effects and consequences restate on a more profound and final level the theme exemplified by the storm and civil war in Book 1, and by the destructive power of sexual passion in the present book – the failure of *labor*. By the end of the book man's works have been swept away by disease, and, an ominous note immediately before the depiction of the society of the 'bees' in Book 4, man himself is implicated in the contagion (563–6n.). V. pays particular attention to the failure of religious institutions to find a solution to the disaster (486–93), and to the pathetic deaths of the horse (497–514) and the bullock (515–30), the two principal objects of man's *cura* in *Georgics* 3. The rhetorical question at 525 sums up the book, and much of the poem: *quid labor aut benefacta iuuant?* The failure of *labor* is finally attended by a grim 'return to the golden age', an inversion of the cultural progression of 1.118–46, as the disease-ridden wolf no longer threatens the fold, and the snake (along with everything else) disappears from the land (537–45; see n.).

The debt to Lucretius is evident throughout, and has been most systematically examined by Harrison (1979); nowhere else does V.

COMMENTARY: 3.478-480   131

draw so deeply from a single source. Thus Lucretius' account of the
(human) plague of Athens (6.1138–1286) informs and enriches the
Virgilian plague. In addition it furthers the human applications lurking
close beneath the surface in V. – it is not cattle alone that are affected
(563–6n.). Williams (on 470–566) and West (1979) 88 both refer to the
'rhetorical' nature of V.'s lines, and proceed to compare them with those
of Lucretius. Comparative judgements, particularly those of the relative
'rhetorical level', take the focus away from the poetry and make it into
an excerpt. V.'s plague is not a rhetorical response to that of Lucretius,
but a vital component of the *Georgics*. Cf. 2.458–540n. on the distortion
which results from excerpting.

478   Hic quondam morbo ...: V. reveals his model; cf. the first
line in Lucretius' account: 6.1138 *haec ratio quondam morborum* .... V.
retains *quondam* partly to indicate the beginning of a new episode
(152–3n.).

   morbo caeli: cf. *E.* 7.57 *uitio ... aëris*, and 454n.; *A.* 3.138 *corrupto caeli tractu*. Lucretius, in the section immediately preceding the
treatment of the Athenian plague, deals with the airborne nature of
disease (6.1090–1137; cf. 1097 *fit morbidus aër*).

   coorta est: cf. Lucr. 6.1191 *coorta*.

479   tempestas 'season'.

   totoque autumni incanduit aestu: excessive heat and plague are
again linked (*incanduit aestu* 'glowed white-hot'); in classical Latin the
verb is otherwise only used of physical objects, e.g. lead); see 441–4n.
and cf. 459 *incensos aestus* (of the actual fire of plague).

   August and September (*autumni*) are the unhealthiest months of all in
Italy; cf. Hor. *Sat.* 2.6.18–19 *plumbeus Auster | autumnusque grauis, Libitinae
questus acerbae*; at *Epist.* 1.7.1–13 Horace excuses himself to Maecenas for
his absence from Rome in the autumn (*mihi ... aegrotare timenti*) – he will
return in the winter. This is also an important parallel with the disaster
of Book 1: *tempestates autumni*, 311.

480   A conflation of Lucr. 6.1092 *morbida uis hominum generi
pecudumque cateruis* and 1144 *cateruatim morbo mortique dabantur*. In V.'s
plague men (Lucretius' *hominum*) are for the time being spared; but cf.
563–6n. V. establishes a second set of parallels, between plague and
amor; cf. 242–4 – both forces are all-embracing in their effect (*omne
... genus /genus omne*); the point is reiterated at 541 *genus omne natantum*
(see n.).

neci ... dedit: cf. Lucr. 6.1144 (see preceding n.); also 566 (and n.) *cateruatim dat stragem;* 4.90 *dede neci.*

481   corruptitque lacus, infecit pabula tabo: Conington notes that the absence of a copula after *infecit* closely links the two clauses, and that it is a syntactical imitation of Lucr. 6.1140 *uastauitque uias, exhausit civibus urbem.* V. also reproduces the exact word-shapes and rhythms of the Lucretian line, though there is no thematic or dictional repetition – for those cf. Lucr. 6.1125–6 *pestilitasque | aut in aquas cadit aut fruges persidit in ipsas.*

corruptitque: cf. *A.* 3.138 (also of plague) *corrupto caeli tractu.*

482–5   The symptoms are described in general terms; cf. Lucr. 6.1145–98, where the exactness and detail reflect Lucretius' different purpose.

482   nec uia mortis erat simplex 'nor was the road to death uniform'; i.e. excessive heat and thirst were followed by excessive moisture, as V. proceeds to relate. On *simplex* cf. 2.73 (and n.).

482–3   sed ... artus 'but when fiery thirst driven through all the veins had withered their wretched limbs'; an exaggeration of the effect of sexual passion, *subdita flamma medullis,* 271.

484–5   Pervasive heat is followed by pervasive fluid which dissolves all the bones of the body. These symptoms closely resemble those of victims of snake-bites in Nicander's *Theriaca* (414–39n.).

485   minutatim: elsewhere in classical Latin poetry only in Lucretius (seven times, including an instance at 6.1191, where the cold of plague creeps up from the feet 'bit by bit'); cf. 556n. on *cateruatim.*

conlapsa: cf. 557 *dilapsa.*

486–93   In a scene of great horror V. depicts the failure of sacrifice, as the victim falls before the blow can be delivered or, bloodless from disease, frustrates the attempts of the *haruspex.* The futility of religious remedies, already suggested at 456 *meliora deos sedet omina poscens* (455–6n.), is powerfully conveyed, and those who see a connection in the *Georgics* between religious observation and the successful application of *labor* (1.335–50n.) must confront these lines. Williams, for instance, makes no comment on the present vignette, but claims at 1.338 '*in primis uenerare deos*: "above all, worship the gods"; this simply-expressed phrase summarises the basic theme of the *Georgics,* that the farmer can succeed only with the help of the gods of the countryside, which he will have if his attitude is religious and worshipful'. This finds support nowhere in the poem: agrarian failure is never preceded by impiety or religious flaws (cf. 513n.), and the advice *uenerare deos* never brings success in and of itself. The farmer's success comes through knowledge and understanding, which, as here and throughout the poem, are not always enough.

486 in honore deum medio 'in the middle of the gods' ceremony'; the premature death of the victim is all the more disturbing for occurring while the ceremony is under way.

487 'while the woollen headband with its snowy garland is being put round [the victim's head]'. The golden line (1.117n.) recalls the preparations for the sacrifice of Iphigenia at Lucr. 1.87 *cui simul infula uirgineos circumdata comptus* (see also 488n.), from a passage in which religious observance is held up as an evil, *tantum religio potuit suadere malorum*, 1.101.

488 cunctantis: the victims die before the attendants (*ministros*) can complete their preparations. Those attendants are therefore seen as 'lingering'.

moribunda: Lucretius describes Iphigenia as *tremibunda* (1.95) just prior to her death; see 487n.

489 ante: i.e. even if the victim is killed before dropping from plague.

490 neque ... fibris 'neither do the altars blaze up when the entrails are set on them'; this implies not merely that the infected entrails will not burn, but that the offering itself is rejected. Cf. Soph. *Ant.* 1006–7 (a bad omen) ἐκ δὲ θυμάτων | Ἥφαιστος οὐκ ἔλαμπεν, 'fire did not blaze from the offerings'.

491 Haruspicy fails; a progression from 1.483–5 where, after the death of Caesar and as civil war raged, threatening readings were reported.

responsa ... reddere: the technical phrase for the responding of an oracle, etc.; cf. *A.* 5.706–7 [*Pallas*] *haec responsa dabat.*

492 'the knives beneath [the throat] are barely stained with blood' – through the anaemia caused by disease. Ovid, drawing from V., combines this idea with the spontaneous death of the victim (488): *uictima .... | ... subito conlapsa sine ictibus ullis | exiguo tinxit subiectos sanguine cultros, M.* 7.597–9 (537–45n.).

493 'and only the surface of the sand is stained by the thin gore'; the initial placement of *summa* and *ieiuna* emphasizes the victim's anaemia.

494 The calves die in the midst of plenty (*laetis*; also *plena* in 495); a grim reversal of the idealized picture at 2.525–6 *pinguesque in gramine laeto | inter se aduersis luctantur cornibus haedi.*

495 dulcis animas ... reddunt: cf. Lucr. 6.1198 *reddebant ... uitam*; the language, and the Lucretian context, suggest a human death (563–6n.); cf. also the death of the bees at 4.204 *ultroque animam sub fasce dedere.*

plena ad praesepia: cf. 494n.; at 394–5 V. advised keeping the feeding-troughs full.

496 hinc canibus blandis rabies uenit: cf. Lucr. 6.1222–3 *cum primis fida canum uis | strata uiis animam ponebat in omnibus aegre*; on dogs, cf. 404–13n.

blandis 'fawning'; though the adjective is not always pejorative, this contrasts with Lucretius' *fida canum uis.*

496–7 et quatit ... obesis: again V. applies to animals what in Lucretius is a human symptom: *tenuia sputa minuta ... per fauces rauca uix edita tussi*, 6.1188–9; cf. also 6.1147–8 *sudabant etiam fauces intrinsecus atrae | sanguine.*

faucibus ... obesis: cf. 508 *obsessas fauces.*

498–514 These 17 lines on the death of the horse (16 + the parenthesis at 513) together with the 16 which immediately follow on the death of the ox (515–30) effectively respond to and annihilate the *cura boum et equorum* which occupied V. throughout the first half of the book. The numerical structure responds particularly to 49–94 (see n.), where 23 lines on selection of the best cow (49–71) were followed by 23 on selection of the horse (72–94). The detail here frequently refers back to the earlier passages, as V. stresses the change in condition brought by the plague (498–9, 499–500, 500, 507–8nn.). As in those earlier sections, he humanizes the two animals, giving his treatment a moving and tragic dimension, and further suggesting the shared lot of man and beast. Though much of the language is Lucretian (501–2n.), there is nothing quite as personal and tragic as this in Lucretius' plague (478–566n.).

498–9 labitur infelix ... | uictor equus 'the once victorious horse stumbles'; the portrayal opens dramatically with the important verb emphatically placed at the beginning (cf. 515–16n.). The combination *labitur infelix* suggests a human failing, and is used again by V., once, at *A.* 5.329, where Nisus stumbles and falls in the foot-race.

With *uictor* V. refers to an earlier and happier day when the racehorse exulted in victory: *tantus amor laudum, tantae est uictoria curae*, 112; cf. also 102 *quis cuique dolor uicto*.

studiorum atque immemor herbae 'forgetting pursuits and pasture'; *studiorum* goes with *immemor*, not (as some would have it) with *infelix* ('failing in his efforts'), as the rhythm of the line suggests and as is anyway clear from 216, where the cow (and *amor*) have the same effect on the bull, *nec nemorum patitur meminisse nec herbae* – again approximating passion and plague (245, 478–566nn.). This is also how Ovid read V.: *acer equus quondam magnaeque in puluere famae* | *degenerat palmas ueterumque oblitus honorum* [= *studiorum*]..., *M*. 7.542–3. Cf. 520–1n.

499   fontisque auertitur 'turns from' and therefore 'rejects' water. The accusative *fontis* after a passive verb with true middle force may be modelled on the Greek middle ἀμύνομαι + acc. 'to keep something away from oneself'; or perhaps it is an assimilation to the deponent *auersor*, which regularly takes the accusative. The present usage is found here first, then a few times in silver and late Latin.

499–500   pede terram | **crebra ferit:** again a contrast with the horse earlier in the book: *altius ingreditur et mollia crura reponit*, 76. *crebra* is neut. pl., used adverbially ('often'), and as such is unique in V.; it is found once in Lucretius, of a cow bereft of her young: *crebra reuisit* | *ad stabulum*, 2.359–60.

500   demissae aures: in contrast to its previous state: 84 *micat auribus*.

500–1   incertus ... | sudor 'a fitful sweat'; see 443–4n. on *sudor*.

et ille quidem morituris frigidus 'and sweat that is cold as death approaches [lit. 'for those about to die']'; cf. 217n. for *ille quidem*. Cf. the Hippocratic *Aphorisms* 37 'cold sweats, occurring with high fever, indicate death'. At Nic. *Ther*. 254–5 the bite of the viper has a similar effect (414–39n.): 'and a moist sweat, colder than falling snow, envelops the limbs'; cf. 507–8n.

501–2   aret | **... resistit** 'his skin becomes dry, and hard to the touch resists handling [lit. 'the handler']'; cf. Lucr. 6.1194–5 *frigida pellis* | *duraque*. The intensification of Lucretian references in these lines (503, 505, 505–6, 506–7, 507–8, 508, 510–11nn.) has the effect of presenting the horse in very human terms (478–566n.).

The notion of 'touching' (*ad tactum*) is developed in the final four lines of the book (cf. 566 *contactos artus sacer ignis edebat*). Cf. also 416–17 (and n.) *mala tactu* | *uipera* – snake and plague are again closely related.

503   haec ... signa: those that precede: 'these are the signs of death in the first days; but when the disease worsens, then the following symptoms occur'. Page notes the slight lack of logic, in that the disease has been fatal all along, but *sin* (504) must imply a contrast with what goes before.

haec ante exitium ... dant signa: cf. Lucr. 6.1182 *multaque praeterea mortis tum signa dabantur.* V. recalls the world of *signa*, so prominent at the end of Book 1 (1.351n.); there, as here, signs or symptoms of disaster may be learnt, but they cannot avert, and in the *Georgics* regularly precede, those disasters (cf. 440n.).

exitium: cf. 511 *mox erat hoc ipsum exitio.*

504   sin 'but when'.

crudescere 'grow fierce'. The word occurs here for the first time with an impersonal subject (*morbus*); cf. 551–2 (where the plague has become personified in the figure of Tisiphone) *saeuit ... | pallida Tisiphone.*

505   ardentes oculi: so the snake of 433 *flammantia lumina torquens;* cf. Lucr. 6.1190–1 *ardentia morbis | lumina.* The stress on heat continues; cf. 512 *ardebant,* 564 *ardentes papulae.* Cf. 523 (of the ox) *oculos stupor urget inertis.*

505–6   attractus ab alto | spiritus: cf. Lucr. 6.1186 *creber spiritus aut ingens raroque coortus.*

gemitu grauis: cf. 517 (of the dying ox) *extremosque ciet gemitus.*

506–7   imaque ... | ilia: cf. 457 *ima ... ad ossa;* see 457–8n.; also 522–3 *ima | soluuntur latera.*

longo | ... singultu 'with drawn-out sobbing', a very human picture, as at Lucr. 6.1160 *singultusque frequens noctem per saepe diemque.*

507–8   it naribus ater | sanguis: another reversal of its healthy state; cf. 85 *collectumque premens uoluit sub naribus ignem.* The detail is again taken from Lucretius: *multus capitis cum saepe dolore | corruptus sanguis expletis naribus ibat,* 1202–3. This is also a symptom following a bite from one of Nicander's nastier snakes, the Haemorrhois ('Blood-letter') at *Ther.* 301–2 (cf. 414–39, 500–1nn.) αἷμα διὲκ ῥινῶν τε καὶ αὐχένος ἠδὲ δι' ὤτων | πιδύεται, 'blood wells from the nostrils and throat and ears'.

508   obsessas fauces premit aspera lingua: from Lucr. 6.1147–50 *sudabant etiam fauces intrinsecus ... | atque animi interpres manabat lingua cruore | debilitata malis, motu grauis, aspera tactu;* cf. also 497 *faucibus ... obesis.*

509–14 A suggested cure turns out to be only apparently so, bringing the plague back with even greater virulence, and resulting in the disturbingly powerful image of the horse tearing at its own limbs with its teeth.

509 profuit: as is clear from what follows, the sense must be 'some have thought it a help', 'it has seemed helpful'; cf. 459; 4.267nn.

509–10 latices infundere ... | Lenaeos: a return to the *uituperatio uini* of 2.454–7 (see n.); wine will here bring madness and death to the horse, just as it did to the half-horses in Book 2; *ille* [i.e. Bacchus] *furentis | Centauros leto domuit*, 455–6; see n. The detail does not occur in Lucretius; V. clearly intends through self-reference to implicate the 'successful' product of Book 2 (see also 4.102n.).

510–11 ea uisa salus ... | mox erat hoc ipsum exitio: the supposition was not correct. Cf. Lucr. 6.1229 *hoc aliis erat exitio letumque parabat*.

511–512 furiisque refecti | ardebant 'they burned refreshed in their madness', a powerful oxymoron; on *ardebant* cf. 505n. The fiery madness of plague precisely parallels that of sexual passion: *in furias ignemque ruunt*, 244 (see n.).

512–14 ipsique ... artus: V.'s highly original climax (suggested by the plague-victim's self-dismemberment at Lucr. 6.1208–9?), the picture of the horse tearing itself (presumably to death) with its own teeth, creates a pathetic ending to the life of the animal. It also recalls the destruction by *amor* at 267–8, where the inflamed mares of Glaucus tear their master to death (see n.).

512 iam morte sub aegra 'already under the sickness of death'; i.e. in spite of their weakness from plague.

513 'may the gods bring a better fate to the pious, and reserve such madness for the enemy!' *piis* and *hostibus* are general; the imprecation is merely apotropaic, somewhat stronger than that at 435–6 (see n.) *ne mihi tum ... libeat*. For *error* as 'madness' (the Romanus has *ardoremque*), cf. E. 8.41 *ut uidi, ut perii, ut me malus abstulit error*. Given other references to Nicander (414–39, 500–1, 507–8nn.), it is certain that V. is reworking *Ther.* 186 (which explains *hostibus*, and therefore *piis*) ἐχθρῶν πού τέρα κεῖνα καρήασιν ἐμπελάσειε 'be they no friends of mine whose heads these monsters assail' (Gow and Scholfield). Harrison (1979) finds in *errorem* a reference to an error in ritual on the part of the Noric farmer (531–3n.); but the word precedes the purported error by

some 18 lines, and the actions of those lines occur *after* the plague has
had its effects (see n.). The search for a rational cause for the plague is
reasonable, but as with the unseasonable storm of Book 1, so here there
exists none; that is in the nature of the world of *labor improbus*.

514   A golden line ends the account (1.117n.).
   nudis: of the 'bared' teeth, as at Lucr. 5.1064 *duros nudantia dentes*,
rather than of ulceration of the gums.

515–30   The death of the ox follows that of the horse (498–514n.),
with a similar emphasis. V. again paints a very human picture (cf.
518n.), this time implicating the farmer, specifically the ploughman
(*tristis arator*, 517) in the tragedy, and stressing the fact that this death is
undeserved, a cruel return for a life of toil (525n.).

515–16   **ecce autem ... taurus | concidit:** the section, like the
previous one (498–9n.), begins in dramatic and vivid fashion. The verb
concidit mirrors *labitur* (498) in shape, position and sense. V. uses the
opening *ecce autem* only here and nine times in the *Aeneid*, always to
introduce a dramatic episode, for instance as the serpents embark on
their mission against Laocoon: *ecce autem gemini a Tenedo tranquilla per alta
...*, 2.203; or as Polites flees from Pyrrhus: *ecce autem elapsus Pyrrhi de caede
Polites ...*, 2.526.
   duro ... sub uomere: cf. 347 (and n.) *iniusto sub fasce*.
   fumans: cf. 2.542 *fumantia ... colla*.

516   **mixtum spumis uomit ore cruorem:** a heroic image; cf. *A.*
10.349 *crassum uomit ore cruorem*. Lucretius speaks of a calf dying at the
altar: *concidit ... | sanguinis exspirans calidum de pectore flumen*, 2.353–4.

517   **extremosque ciet gemitus:** cf. 506 (of the dying horse)
gemitu grauis; also 226 (of the defeated bull) *multa gemens ignominiam*.
   tristis arator: the ploughman, for the only time in the poem, attains
a degree of pathos, in contrast to his usual characterization (*durus, iratus,*
etc.; cf. 2.207n.)

518   **maerentem ... fraterna morte iuuencum:** the line has a
sepulchral ring, and the human element is all the stronger for V.'s
depicting the death as a *mors fratris*; cf. *A.* 9.735–6 *Pandarus | mortis
fraternae feruidus ira*, and particularly Cat. 68.19–20 *sed totum hoc studium
luctu fraterna mihi mors | abstulit*; Hor. *Epist.* 1.14.6–8 *Lamiae ... | fratrem
maerentis, rapto de fratre dolentis | insolabiliter*.

519   Civilized agriculture stops, soon to be replaced by a grim
reversion to the Saturnian age (537–45n.).

520–2 An elegantly constructed tricolon, with emphatic anaphora of *non* at the beginning of each member.

520–1 non umbrae … animum: the pastoral world (*hic gelidi fontes, hic mollia prata, Lycori,* | *hic nemus, E.* 10.42–3) has lost its appeal, as under the influence of *amor* (216–17). The dying horse is similarly distracted (498–9n.). Cf. Lucr. 2.361–3 (the cow bereaved of its calf, a context relevant to this; and cf. 516n.) *nec tenerae salices atque herbae rore uigentes* | *fluminaque illa queunt summis labentia ripis* | *oblectare animum.*

Orpheus, deprived of Eurydice, is presented in a similar way: *non ulli animum flexere hymenaei,* 4.516.

522 purior electro 'clearer than amber'; imitated from Callim. *H.* 6.28 τὸ δ' ὧστ' ἀλέκτρινον ὕδωρ, 'water as if of amber'. *electrum* has the same meaning as at *E.* 8.54, and does not refer to the metal (as at *A.* 8.624): *purior* implies limpidity, not sheen. The slight ambiguity may be motivated by Callimachus' own ambiguity (amber or electrum?), on which see Hopkinson (1984) ad loc. – he does not mention the Virgilian imitation.

522–4 The references to *latera* and *ceruix* perhaps look back to 52–4, on the appearance of the ideal cow. Cf. 499–500, 500, 507–8nn.

522–3 at ima | soluuntur latera 'his flanks hang loose beneath him'; as at 457–8 and 506–7 (see nn.) *imus* suggests the intensity of the disease.

523 oculos stupor urget inertis: cf. 505 (of the horse) *ardentes oculi.*

524 'and with drooping weight his neck sinks to the ground'.

525–30 Conington cites Scaliger (*Poet.* 5.11): '*malim a me excogitata atque conlecta quam uel Croesum uel Cyrum ipsum dicto habere audientem*'. The lines resonate throughout the poem, and go to its very heart. The words *quid labor aut benefacta iuuant?* imply, as much of the poem has implied, the futility of *labor* when such destruction is visited on its practitioners. The life of simplicity and toil (528–30), carefully contrasted with the life of luxury (526–7) – the reminiscence of the end of Book 2 is strong – has as its reward agony and death. Page, for whom 'a strong sense of the necessity and dignity of labour breathes throughout the poem from beginning to end' (p. xxix) notes on 525–6 only that *iuuat* is to be supplied with *inuertisse*; and Williams sees the two rhetorical questions only as 'conveying the idea of devoted service by the farm animals'. Conington at least sees in the lines 'a gentle accusation of destiny'.

525   quid labor aut benefacta iuuant?: the answer is implicit in the rhetorical question. On *benefacta* cf. 2.515 *meritosque iuuencos*. Orpheus experiences a similar failure as he loses Eurydice: *ibi omnis | effusus labor*, 4.491–2.

525–6   quid uomere terras | inuertisse grauis: from *iuuant*, the singular, *iuuat*, must be supplied; not an anacolouthon since, as Page notes, it is not really impersonal but has as its subject *inuertisse*.

inuertisse: see 1.65n.

526–7   non Massica Bacchi | munera 'no Massic gifts of Bacchus', recalling 2.143 and the characterization of Italy's vines: *Bacchi Massicus umor* – a mark of luxury in both places (2.136–76n.).

527   non illis epulae nocuere repostae: cf. 4.378 *pars epulis onerant mensas et plena reponunt. non illis* implies a contrast, most readily with the luxurious figure at the end of Book 2: *ut gemma bibat*, 2.506.

528   The picture of simplicity and hardiness is similar to that at 231, where the defeated bull trains himself for the return. It is also in contrast to the luxury of 527. As the ethics of *labor* fail, there is perhaps also a suggestion of golden-age self-sufficiency here (cf. 530n.); a new 'golden age' will return at 537–45 (see n.).

529   fontes liquidi: cf. 2.200 *liquidi ... fontes non ... deerunt*; 4.18–19 *liquidi fontes ... | adsint.*

529–30   exercita cursu | flumina 'rivers racing in their course'; for this use of *exercita* ('set in motion') cf. Lucr. 2.97 *exercita motu*.

530   nec somnos abrumpit cura salubris: so the idealized rustic at 2.467 *at secura quies* and 470 *mollesque sub arbore somni*. The absence of *cura* is a mark of the Saturnian age: [*Iuppiter*] *curis acuens mortalia corda* (2.467n.).

531–3   Even the processions to Juno's temple were affected, as wild oxen had to be used in place of domesticated. The reference seems to be to a procession at Argos in which white oxen drew the priestess to the temple of Hera (Herod. 1.31). The relevance is difficult to see; Argos and Juno point to Io, and V. may be recalling a literary context now lost (150–1, 152–3nn.). At Tac. *Germ.* 40.3 a goddess is similarly transported. Harrison (1979) sees the present lines as constituting a ritual shortcoming, resulting in and therefore giving reason to the plague (see also 513n.). But the adverbial phrase *tempore non alio* clearly situates the event of these lines within the *course* of the plague: 'then and only then [as the horse and ox were dying of plague] wild oxen were used ... ' And *ergo* at 534 is to be taken 'therefore [because there were no oxen available] men had to dig with their fingers'.

531 tempore non alio: used to introduce a contemporaneous occurrence, as at 245, and like *nec tempore eodem* ... [*cessauit*] at 1.483 (see nn.).

532 quaesitas: sc. *sed non inuentas*; cf. 549, where remedies are found, but do harm: *quaesitaeque nocent artes*.

uris: see 2.374n. on these odd beasts, somewhat more plausible in the setting of Noricum.

533 imparibus: normally taken to mean that they were of differing size and colour to each other, but given the great size of these things (2.374n.) it could also mean that the two of them were 'not matched' to the *currus*.

donaria: first here as a noun for *templa*.

534 ergo: in the absence of oxen (531–3n.).

aegre ... rimantur: the two words express the futility of agricultural endeavour without the plough: they scratch with difficulty at the earth.

535 infodiunt fruges 'they bury the seed'; for the verb cf. 2.262, 348.

536 A vivid image: throughout the book animals have been presented in human terms; now man takes on the appearance of beast.

537–45 With the failure of the instruments of *labor* a grimly ironic reversion to a diseased golden age takes place, with the sheepfold immune from the wolf, the deer lying down with the dogs and the disappearance of the snake (537–8, 539–40, 544–5nn.). As these phenomena were removed by Jupiter as he brought in the age of *labor* (1.118–46 and n.), so now, when the operations of his age fail, they return, but with a very different implication. The lines stand in stark contrast to the ending of the previous book (2.458–540), where an idealized, and ultimately fictional, golden age was evoked (see n.). The monstrous nature of the details in these lines is also parallel to the ill-omened events attending civil war at 1.464–88.

Ovid, who closely adapts V.'s plague at *M.* 7.523–613, gives as an example of the plague's effect the spontaneous falling off of the sheep's wool (*sponte sua lanaeque cadunt*, 541), a brilliant allusion to the self-dyeing capacity of the golden-age sheep at *E.* 4.45: *sponte sua sandyx pascentis uestiet agnos*.

537–8 non lupus ... obambulat: a clear evocation of the golden age; cf. 1.129–30; *E.* 5.60–1 *nec lupus insidias pecori, nec retia ceruis | ulla dolum meditantur*; also Hor. *Epd.* 16.51 *nec uespertinus circumgemit ursus ouile* (V. transforms Horace's curious bear to the more conventional wolf – a transformation acknowledged by Horace at *Odes* 1.17.7–8 *nec [capri] metuunt ... | Martialis Haediliae lupos*). At *E.* 8.52 the image serves as an *adynaton: nunc et ouis ultro fugiat lupus* (cf. 543n.).

nocturnus: adverbial, in imitation of Horace's adverbial *uespertinus* (see above). Cf. 406–8 (on *cura canum*).

538–9 acrior ... | cura: the pangs of disease are stronger than those of hunger; V. perhaps plays on the senses of *cura*, a key word in the book (123–37, 384–93nn.).

539–40 timidi ... uagantur: much like the golden-age scene of *E.* 4.22 *nec magnos metuent armenta leones*, and a demonstration of the failure of *cura canum*; see 404–13. The immunity of the deer is also a virtual *adynaton* (537–8, 543nn.) at *E.* 8.28 *cum canibus timidi uenient ad pocula dammae*.

541 maris immensi: cf. 1.29 (and n.) *immensi ... maris*.

genus omne natantum: a further parallel between the effects of plague and *amor*; cf. 242–3 *omne ... genus ...* (see n.). Also 480 (and n.) *genus omne*.

V.'s *genus ... natantum* ('the race of swimmers') is a somewhat bold extension of Lucretius 2.342–3 *genus humanum mutaeque natantes | squamigerum pecudes*, parallel to the use of *balantes* ('bleaters') for sheep (457–8n.). Horace's *monstra natantia* occurs in the propempticon to V. (*Odes* 1.3.18), and may refer to this line (1.332n.).

543 proluit 'washes up'; on the emphatic position, cf. 389n.

insolitae fugiunt in flumina phocae: a *monstrum*; the world is not acting normally (*insolitae*; the word otherwise occurs in V. only at 1.475, during the description of portents following the death of Caesar). The words also have the look of an *adynaton* (537–8, 539–40nn.), as they do in what seems to be an adaptation and extension of this line at Hor. *Odes* 1.2.6–8 *noua monstra ... | omne cum Proteus pecus* [sc. *phocarum*] *egit altos | uisere montis*.

544–5 interit ... | uipera: even the snake, the very emblem of plague (414–39n.), dies off – the clearest possible evocation of the golden age (537–45n.): *E.* 4.24 *occidet et serpens* – where | *occidet et* is recalled by | *interit et* in 544. So on Horace's Isles of the Blest (537–8n.) *neque intumescit alta uiperis humus, Epd.* 16.52.

curuis ... latebris: cf. 2.214–16 *curuas ... latebras*, 416–17 *sub immotis praesepibus ... | uipera delituit.*

545 attoniti squamis astantibus hydri: heat and plague have the same effect: cf. *exterritus aestu*, 434. V.'s image, though scientifically incorrect, conveys the horror of the plague.

546–7 In Lucretius' plague birds tended to disappear: *nec tamen omnino temere illis solibus ulla | comparebat auis*, 1219–20; V. recalls Lucr. 6.741–6, describing the lethal effects of Lake Avernus on birds which happen to fly over it (*praecipitesque cadunt*, 6.744; cf. V.'s *praecipites*, 547; also 4.80n.) – a passage closely adapted by V. at *A.* 6.239–42.

546 ipsis: 'i.e. though they [the birds] are its especial denizens and might look for some favour, yet even to them the tainted air shows none' (Page).

non aequus 'unkind', as at 2.225 *uacuis Clanius non aequus Acerris*; a secondary sense may be intended, that the air is not 'balanced' for them, i.e. they cannot support themselves in it.

547 The idea is repeated at *A.* 5.517–18 (of a dove) *decidit exanimis uitamque reliquit in astris | aetheriis.*

548 'moreover it now does not help for their food to be changed'. Cf. 481 *infecit pabula tabo.* There may be a secondary reference to the *pabuli mutatio* which came with the age of Jupiter: 'it does not help that a change of diet occurred'. This would lead well into the clear cultural judgement which immediately follows (549n.). Cf. 1.7–8 (esp. *mutauit*).

549 quaesitaeque nocent artes: medicine not only fails, it is harmful. On a larger scale V. suggests that as the world of *labor* fails, so do its components; cf. 1.133 (of Jupiter's purpose in ending the golden age) *ut uarias usus meditando extunderet artis*, 145 *tum uariae uenere artes*. Lucr. 6.1179 *mussabat tacito medicina timore* has a slightly different and more specific sense.

quaesitaeque: cf. 532 (and n.) *quaesitas.*

cessere magistri 'the experts gave up'; *magister* has been used elsewhere (118, 185, 445) of those who administer *cura* to the animals; it has a somewhat distinct sense here, close to that of 4.283.

550 Phillyrides Chiron Amythaoniusque Melampus: a poetic way of putting it: not the mythical figures themselves, but their contemporary representatives. Chiron, the son of Cronus and Philyra (who figured, the latter unnamed, at 92–4 (see n.)), is famed for his skill in medicine as early as Homer (*Il.* 4.219), and Melampus cured the women of Argos of their madness (Apollod. 1.9.12).

The line has the look of being a transliteration from Greek (Φιλλυρίδης Χείρων Ἀμυθαόνιός τε Μελάμπους), but this is typical of V.'s practice (1.138, 332nn.). The impulse probably comes from Ap. Rhod. *Arg.* 1.554, which begins Χείρων Φιλλυρίδης, 'Chiron, son of Philyra'.

551-2 saeuit ... Tisiphone: like the emergence of the snake, emblem of plague, at 433-4 (553n.). Tisiphone acts like Mars at 1.511; see n. Her function is also similar to that of the gadfly (152-3, and 554-5n.). Cf. *A.* 10.761 *pallida Tisiphone media inter milia saeuit*.

552 Morbos agit ante Metumque: cf. the famous personification of these and other abstractions in the Underworld at *A.* 6.273-81, including 275-6 *pallentesque* (cf. *pallida*, 552) *Morbi ... et Metus ...* The inclusion of *Metus* along with *Morbi* looks to the end of Book 2 (491-2; see n.), where the purpose of knowledge (which here fails) was the banishment of fear to the Underworld – whence it now returns rampant.

553 inque dies 'and as the days proceed'; the phrase belongs mainly to prose.

auidum ... caput altius effert 'raises her head higher', a brilliant figure for the increase in intensity of the plague. Cf. the snake's flight at 422 *timidum caput abdidit alte* (where *alte* has the opposite meaning to *altius* here).

554-5 The anguished sounds resulting from Tisiphone's attack and their echoing through the pastoral world recall precisely the same effects of the gadfly (551-2n.) at 150-1 (see n.).

mugitibus: see 150-1n.

arentesque: again the emphasis on dryness and heat; cf. *sicci*, 151 (and 150-1n.).

556 cateruatim dat stragem: from Lucr. 6.1144 *cateruatim morbo mortique dabatur*; this single instance of *cateruatim* in V. (like *minutatim* at 485; see n.) is to be explained solely through the appearance in Lucretius. Cf. 480.

aggerat 'piles up in heaps'; the first attestation of the colourful verb. The image is developed from Lucr. 6.1262-3 *quo magis aestu | confertos ita aceruatim mors accumulabat*.

556-7 ipsis | in stabulis: in the normal state of affairs, *stabula* are a protection: see 1.354-5 and 1.355n.; here, just as occurred in the parallel context at 1.482-3, they afford no protection: *Eridanus ... cum stabulis armenta tulit*.

557　turpi ... tabo: cf. 441 *turpis ... scabies*.

dilapsa 'decayed'; cf. 485 *ossa ... morbo conlapsa*.

cadauera: the word, an uglier and more clinical variant for *corpus*, occurs in V. only here and of the monstrous corpse of Cacus (*informe cadauer*) at *A.* 8.264; that is, he does not use it of the human body. Cf. Lucr. 6.1155 *rancida quo perolent proiecta cadauera ritu*.

558　humo tegere: of planting at 1.213.

discunt: with grim irony V. suggests that the only cultural development, or *ars*, in the general cultural reversion of the plague (cf. 537–45n.) is the burial of the diseased bodies; cf. 414 *disce*.

559　nam: explains the burial of the corpses.

neque erat coriis usus: *usus*, the object of *labor*, has disappeared; cf. 313 (of goat-hair) *usum in castrorum*.

560　aut undis abolere ... aut uincere flamma: disease has rendered the cleansing powers of water and fire useless; a foreshadowing of the *sudor* and *ignis* which finally infect man himself in the next lines (563–6).

undis abolere 'to destroy [the diseased] flesh with water'.

561–2　morbo inluuieque peresa | uellera 'eaten up by disease and filth'; *peredo* is otherwise used by V. only at *A.* 6.442, of love-stricken suicides in the Underworld: *quos durus amor crudeli tabe* [i.e. *morbo*] *peredit*. Cf. 566 *edebat*.

562　telas: somewhat illogical, since if they could not shear the fleeces there would be no *telae* to touch.

563–6 Though the terminology has been applicable to man, and though V. has drawn heavily from the Lucretian plague, whose effects were almost exclusively felt by man, he postpones the infection of human beings until the final lines of the book. Through contact with infected fleeces and clothing man is suddenly implicated (as, implicitly, he has been all along, through the constant approximation of beast to man). The implication of man provides a transition to Book 4, of which the first half treats the society and eventually the failure through disease of the bees, whose proximity to man is symbolic and fundamental, not merely metaphorical or on the level of suggestion.

564　ardentes papulae atque immundus ... sudor: V. recapitulates, as the plague now affects man, but with the same symptoms as before: cf. 443–4 *inlotus ... | sudor*, 500–1 *incertus ibidem | sudor*, 505 *tum uero ardentes oculi*, 511–12 *furiisque refecti | ardebant*.

564–5   olentia ... | membra sequebatur 'ran along his fetid limbs'.

565–6   nec longo deinde moranti | tempore: *moranti* is dative of interest: 'nor did he have long to wait before . . . '; the construction gives a more personal involvement than the usual *haud/nec mora.*

566   contactos artus sacer ignis edebat: the book ends with the fire which has stood throughout for passion (244 n.) and plague (482–3n.). The term *sacer ignis* has a general sense ('accursed fire of disease'), though in V.'s model (Lucr. 6.660 *existit sacer ignis et urit corpore serpens | quamcumque arripuit partem*) it refers specifically to erysipelas ('St Anthony's fire'): *erysipelas est quem Latini sacrum ignem appellant,* Isid. *Orig.* 4.8.4. In insisting that V. refers specifically to anthrax (which is then slightly confused with erysipelas), Flintoff (1983) 105 (whose aim is to show that V.'s plague was, or could have been, historical) does not attend to the imagery and metaphors which shape this book; V.'s concerns are not here epidemiological.

contactos: cf. 469 *contagia.*

edebat: cf. 561 (and 561–2n.) *peresa.*

Georgics 4

1–7   The proem

The fourth book begins with clear reminiscence of the opening of the second. As that book began with *hactenus,* so V. here starts with *protinus;* the proems in both are brief (eight and seven lines, compared with the more extensive introductions of Books 1 and 3); and in both books, immediately after the proems, the technical material begins with the word *principio* – not otherwise used in the poem (2.9; 4.8); see 2.1, 9nn. V. also recalls the second proem of Book 3 (3.284–94), appropriately, since the first half of Book 4 is similar in theme and movement to the second half of Book 3 (6, 8; 3.563–6nn.). The proem also plays an important part in the programme of the *Georgics,* and to that extent is complementary to those of Books 2 and 3 (cf. 2.41–5, 42–4, 44–5; 3.1–48, 284–94nn.; Introduction, pp. 1–3).

The technical impulse for V.'s treatment comes from Aristotle, *H.A.* 553a17–554b22, and especially Varro, *R.R.* 3.16, but more than with any other subject of the poem, the technical tradition, although constantly visible, retreats in importance. Much has been written on the

bees of *Georgics* 4, and on their relationship to the second half of the book
(315–558n.), and a good survey, together with a perceptive study of the
topic, is to be found in Griffin (1979). One other work should be singled
out, that of Dahlmann (1954), which demonstrates that the structure
and details of the bees' society are based (without strict formal adher-
ence) on those of the ethnographical tradition (see also Thomas (1982a)
70–84) – a tradition otherwise applied exclusively to human societies.
The result is like that produced in Book 3, in which man and animal
were constantly conflated: the bee society is intended to evoke a human
society. And this equivalence was a part of V.'s inherited technical
tradition: Varro, *R.R.* 3.16.6 *haec ut hominum ciuitates, quod hic est rex et
imperium et societas.* The question which the fourth book then poses (and it
is perhaps the most difficult question of the poem) concerns the *nature* of
that human society (see particularly 149–96n.).

1   Protinus: cf. 2.1 (and n.) *hactenus*; also 1–7n.

aërii mellis caelestia dona 'the heavenly gifts of honey from the
sky'; a reference to the notion, firmly held by Aristotle, that, while the
bees made wax from flowers, honey itself fell from the sky: μέλι δὲ τὸ
πῖπτον ἐκ τοῦ ἀέρος, 'honey is what falls from the air', *H.A.* 553b29. V.
knew of the realities (169, 181–3), and the purpose of this statement is
partly to link the bees to some sort of divinity (*caelestia*; cf. 219–27 and
n.) and, perhaps, through the word *dona* to anticipate Jupiter's special
participation in the nature of the bees (cf. 149–50n.).

2   exsequar: cf. 3.340 *prosequar.*

hanc etiam, Maecenas, aspice partem: creates a strong link with
the second half of Book 3, in the proem to which V. states *superat pars
altera curae*, 286 (*pars* = 'section' is confined to these two places in the
poem); cf. 1–7, 10–11, 13nn.

Maecenas: in the second line, as in Book 1 (1.2n.). The imperative
aspice parallels those imperatives or virtual imperatives addressed to
the poet's patron at 2.39–44 (*ades*, etc.), and its sense is resumed by
spectacula, 3.

3   admiranda ... spectacula: with the nouns in 4–5 the object of
dicam (5), though at first sight the words have the look of a subject (with
sunt understood). *admiranda* suggests that the society of the bees is a θαῦμα
('marvel') – as it is to become (309n.).

leuium ... rerum 'of a tiny world'. Throughout the early part of the
description V. applies to the bees the words *tenuis, leuis* and *angustus* (6,
19, 38, 55, 83), while he also suggests the magnitude of the world from

their point of view, or the greatness of their endeavour within it (20 *ingens*, 26 *grandia*, 68 *magno*, 76 *magnisque*, 79 *magnum*). The antithesis reaches a peak at 83 *ingentis animos angusto in pectore uersant* (a line which also has a programmatic dimension; see n., and 4-5, 6nn.), and especially in the comparison to the Cyclopes at 170-5; cf. 176 *si parua licet componere magnis* (see nn. and 295-7n.).

The juxtaposition of large and small and the very choice of the bees as subject clearly create a danger of producing an amused response, what is normally regarded as 'mock-heroic'. But V.'s world is one whose constituent elements, be they plants, birds, beasts or bees, are all capable of sentient powers equivalent to those of man. He certainly intends that the reader notice the disparity between size and tone (for instance at 86-7; see n.), but that need not imply humorous intent; it is one of the marks of the Virgilian genius that this poem constantly risks, but *when viewed as a whole* avoids, producing an effect of humour or the absurd.

4-5 The enumeration of topics suggests an ethnographical orientation, a suggestion strengthened by the use of *ordine* ('in due order'), and by the prosaic style which connects six nouns by five conjunctions. The word *mores* in particular suggests the focus of the ethnographer (νόμοι); cf. Dahlmann (1954); Thomas (1982a) 70-84.

magnanimosque: the word has obvious epic dimensions; cf. 83 *ingentis animos*.

duces ... et proelia dicam: in the *Eclogues* the Callimachean V. was forbidden such pursuits (6.3-4), in the *Aeneid* he confidently undertook them (7.41-2); here in the *Georgics*, as befits a transitional attitude, he sings of such themes, but their lofty nature is to be mitigated by the attenuated status of the bees (cf. 6n.); see Introduction, pp. 1-3. Horace may be specifically recalling V.'s antithesis in his own *recusatio* at *Odes* 1.6.5-9 *nos, Agrippa, neque haec dicere ... | conamur, tenues grandia*; also 3.3.70-2 *desine ... | magna modis tenuare paruis*; cf. 3n.

6 in tenui labor; at tenuis non gloria: the antithesis is familiar from the second proem of Book 3: *angustis hunc addere rebus honorem*, 290; on the Callimachean language, and the programmatic sense of the line, see Introduction, pp. 1-3.

This line also suggests that the stylistic approach will be correctly Callimachean (*tenuis* = λεπτός), while the theme and the glory accruing from it will be of a larger, non-Callimachean nature; or, in other words, *ars* and *ingenium* will both be accommodated. V. surely noticed Varro's characterization of the bees at *R.R.* 3.16.3 *uolucres, quibus plurimum natura ingeni atque artis tribuit.*

in tenui labor: i.e. *in tenui re laboratur.*

6–7   si ... Apollo 'if the adverse powers permit one, and Apollo listens to prayer'; *quem* is indefinite.

auditque uocatus Apollo: cf. *A.* 3.395 *aderitque uocatus Apollo.* Apollo Nomius, guardian of shepherds, appeared at 3.2 (3.1–2n.), but here he is the god of poetry, a function inherited from Alexandria by the Augustan poets.

The wording is formal, *uoco* defining the act of prayer, *audire* the god's (favourable) response; cf. Hor. *Odes* 2.18.40 *uocatus atque non uocatus audit*; 3.22.3 *ter uocata audis.* On *uoco* in such contexts, see 1.42; 3.392–3nn.

8–50   de situ apium

The first category in the ethnographical tradition concerns the *situs* of the people in question, both the geography of their land, and their own position within that geography (Thomas (1982a) 1–3, 71). Varro's description of the bees' society already shows a debt to the tradition, and may well have suggested to V. the potential for an ethnographical approximation: *R.R.* 3.16.12 *primum secundum uillam potissimum, ubi non resonant imagines (hic enim sonus harum fugae existimatur esse protelum), esse oportet aere temperato, neque aestate feruido neque hieme non aprico, ut spectet potissimum ad hibernos ortus, qui prope se loca habeat ea, ubi pabulum sit frequens et aqua pura, si pabulum naturale non est, ea oportet dominum serere, quae maxima secuntur apes.* Varro includes weather conditions and food-supply, the second and third categories of the tradition, which are also treated in V.'s lines.

8   Principio: cf. 2.9 (and n.); also 3.295 *incipiens*, which immediately follows the second proem of Book 3 (1–7n.), and like *principio* in the present line introduces *stabula* (here *sedes statioque*); see following n.

sedes ... statioque petenda: cf. 14, where the beehives are called *stabula.* This is the first of many parallels drawn between the worlds of smaller animals and bees, the greatest of which is the culmination in disease and death (251–80, 281–2nn.). The words also strengthen the human dimension; V. completely avoids the word *aluus* (= 'beehive') in his description (*aluaria* occurs once, at 34; see 33–4n. and 2.452–3n.).

On *sedes* see also 65n.

apibus: indirect object, 'for the bees', not dative of agent with *petenda*.

9–12 quo ... atterat: the subjunctives are consecutive: '[such] a place where there may be no approach for the winds, etc.' (after the first clause *ubi* is understood from *quo* = 'whither'); cf. 2.266–7 *ubi prima paretur | arboribus seges et quo mox digesta feratur*. To take them as final subjunctives (*ut eo*: so Page) produces less of an emphasis on the selection of the ideal place.

9 neque sit uentis aditus: cf. 3.302 (of sheep and goats; cf. 8n.) *et stabula a uentis hiberno opponere soli*.

10–11 neque oues haedique petulci | floribus insultent: a reversal of 3.295–321; there V. treated the steading and protection of sheep and goats, while in the present lines it is precisely those animals which threaten the bees and create the need for a safe hive. Cf. also 2.371–5, on the protection of young vines from animals. Cf. Lucr. 2.367–8 *haedi | ... agnique petulci*.

11 errans: as often, with the implication *pascens*; cf. *E.* 2.21 *mille meae Siculis errant in montibus agnae*; see Thomas (1979).

12 decutiat rorem: another connection with Book 3; cf. 3.324–6, where the animals enjoy the dewy grass.

13 absint: otherwise in V. only at 3.385 (8n.). The word is balanced by *adsint* at 19 – prohibitions followed by prescriptions.

picti squalentia terga lacerti 'lizards with their colourful scaly backs'; *terga* is an accusative of respect. Cf. 91 (of the king-bee itself) *maculis ... squalentibus*.

14 stabulis: cf. 8n.

meropesque: *Merops apiaster*, 'bee-eater'.

aliaeque uolucres: 'and other birds (such as the swallow)': *et* in 15 is epexegetic; cf. *A.* 11.272 for the usage.

15 Procne was changed into a swallow while being pursued by her husband Tereus; with the help of her sister Philomela (who was turned into a nightingale) she had murdered and served up her son in revenge for Tereus' infidelity. The stain of her crime persists on the bird's plumage – a detail which constitutes the aetiological link between mythical character and bird. Ovid's account concludes with similar detail (he treats both sisters): *neque adhuc de pectore caedis | excessere notae, signataque sanguine pluma est*, *Met.* 6.669–70. At *E.* 6.78–81 V. refers to the tale, but mentions only Philomela, as here he mentions only Procne. At some point in the tradition the two became interchangeable.

16   omnia ... uastant 'their devastation [of the bees] is complete', not 'they destroy everything [and carry off the bees as well]'.

uolantis 'on the wing'.

17   ferunt dulcem ... escam: cf. 2.216 *dulcem ferre cibum* (where the subject, however, is *agros*).

dulcem nidis immitibus escam 'as a sweet morsel for their cruel young'; the metonymy *nidis* for *pullis* seems to occur here for the first time. Cf. 56; *A.* 12.474–5 *hirundo,* | *pabula parua legens nidisque loquacibus escas.*

18–32   Another parallel between the bees and the flocks of Book 3, where (300–1, and n.) fresh running water is also to be provided (see also 18, 24, 29nn.). V.'s description has the ring of a *locus amoenus.*

18   liquidi fontes: cf. 3.529 *fontes liquidi.*

stagna uirentia musco: cf. 3.144 (of the ideal setting for cattle) *flumina, muscus ubi et uiridissima gramine ripa*; also *E.* 7.45 *muscosi fontes.*

19   tenuis 'tiny', 'trickling'; cf. 3n.

20   uestibulum: doubtless intended to suggest a human habitation (8, 22, 26–7nn.), though there is a precedent in Varro, who uses the word of the platform in front of a pigeon-house (*R.R.* 3.7.4).

ingens: from the bee's perspective (3n.); perhaps with the sense 'natural' – the *oleaster* is not a cultivated tree; cf. Mackail (1912).

21   After *ut, cum* the order is that of a golden line (1.117n.).

reges: with a very few exceptions, ancient writers considered the queen-bee to be a male; e.g. Varro, *R.R.* 3.16.8 *regem suum secuntur*; even if V. knew the truth, it would have been in his interests to suppress it (cf. 88–102n.).

22   uere suo: 'in the spring which is dear to them' (cf. 190 *sopor suus*); or perhaps 'in the spring, which is the appropriate time for them'.

ludetque: cf. 103 *examina ludunt,* 105 *ludo prohibebis inani.*

iuuentus: the first occurrence of the word referring to other than human youths (cf. 3.105–6n.); the next (and there are very few others), is in imitation of V.: *noui duces procedunt cum sua iuuentute,* Colum. 9.9.2.

23   decedere ... calori 'to give way to the heat'; i.e. 'to go into the shade'. Cf. 3.467 (and n.); *E.* 8.88 *decedere nocti* 'to retire before the night'.

24   The word order (A–n–V–a–N) is artistically equivalent to that of the golden line; cf. 2.531n.

obuiaque 'in their path'.

hospitiis ... frondentibus: a poetic inversion: 'with its welcoming foliage'; so Hor. *Odes* 3.2.10 *umbram hospitalem.* Cf. 3.300–1 (on care of goats) *frondentia capris | arbuta sufficere.*

25 Picks up 18: *stabit ... umor | stagna; profluet umor | liquidi fontes.*

26–7 grandia ... consistere: a poetic reshaping of Varro, *R.R.* 3.16.27 *in qua aqua iaceant testae aut lapilli, ita ut exstent paulum, ubi adsidere et bibere possint.* V.'s *pontibus* makes the setting more human (8, 20nn.), while *grandia* creates empathy by once more presenting the detail from the bee's perspective – *testae* and *lapilli*, which become *saxa* in V.'s lines, are 'huge' only to the bee.

V. omits Varro's detail, *ut ... bibere possint*, which is in fact erroneous; the bees take up water to use in ventilating the hive.

27–8 alas | pandere ad aestiuum solem: cf. 1.398–9 (a sign of fair weather) *non tepidum ad solem pennas in litore pandunt | ... alcyones*; also see *A.* 3.520 (of setting sail) *uelorum pandimus alas.*

28 morantis: i.e. those slow in returning to the hive when rain comes on ('loiterers'); at 70 it means 'laggards'.

29 sparserit 'has sprinkled'.

praeceps Neptuno immerserit Eurus: the magnification and elevation of language increase the sense of danger; the high epic metonymy, *Neptuno*, avoided in the *Aeneid* (a cliché?), depicts the pool (two or three fingers deep at Varro, *R.R.* 3.16.27) from the bee's point of view.

Cf. 3.303–4, referring to the threat posed by the elements to the *stabula* of sheep and goats.

30–2 casiae ... | serpylla ... thymbrae | ... uiolaria: *casia* (some sort of aromatic laurel, distinct from *casia*, 'cinnamon', at 2.466) and rosemary are associated with bee-keeping at 2.212–13 *glarea ... | uix humilis apibus casias roremque ministrat, casia* and thyme at 304 *thymum casiasque recentis, casia* and various other plants at 181–3. Thyme (*serpylla = Thymus serpyllum*; the species otherwise appears in V. only at *E.* 2.11) is the plant most commonly associated with bees and the production of honey (169, 181, 241, 270; *E.* 5.77; *A.* 1.436). Winter savory (*thymbra = Satureia montana*; Sargeaunt thinks it may be summer savory, *Satureia hortensis*) does not otherwise figure in V., but Columella (9.4.6) considers it second only to thyme for flavour imparted. *uiola* can be used of several flowers, but V. probably intends the sweet violet (*Viola odorata*); at 275 the curative plant *amellus* seems to be related, at least in colour: *uiolae sublucet purpura nigrae.*

Taken together the lines almost constitute a description of a garland, common in pastoral, and familiar from *E.* 2.45–55 (where *uiolae* and *casia* are included); cf. 30–1n. There is a similar list at 181–3.

30–1 olentia late | serpylla: cf. *E.* 2.48 *bene olentis anethi.* The words match *grauiter spirantis ... thymbrae* in 31.

31 grauiter spirantis ... thymbrae 'strong-smelling savory'. Cf. *A.* 7.753 (where *grauiter* is more ominous) *grauiter spirantibus hydris*; also see 270 *graue olentia Centaurea*, and 49 *odor caeni grauis*.

32 inriguumque bibant uiolaria fontem: cf. 2.218 [*terra*] *bibit umorem*; *E.* 3.111 *sat prata biberunt.* Adapted by Tibullus at 2.1.44 *tum bibit inriguas fertilis hortus aquas.*

33–4 ipsa ... aluaria 'now as to the *hives* ...'; *ipsa* acts as a connective and assists the transition to the next topic.

seu ... texta 'whether you have one sewn from hollow bark or woven with pliant osier'. Varro lists five types of hive: *alii faciunt ex uiminibus rotundas, alii e ligno ac corticibus, alii ex arbore caua, alii fictiles, alii ex ferulis quadratas*, *R.R.* 3.16.15. V., not concerned with instruction, has merely taken the first two; at 2.452–3 he mentioned a third type (see n.).

corticibus ... cauatis: cf. 2.453 *corticibusque cauis*; also 44 *pumicibusque cauis.* The adjectives belong more naturally with a different type of hive; cf. Varro's *ex arbore caua* (see n. above). Cf. also 2.387 (of masks) *corticibus ... cauatis.*

aluaria: the only instance of *aluus/aluarium* in the book; see 8; 2.452–3nn.

35 angustos habeant aditus: cf. Varro, *R.R.* 3.16.16 *media aluo, qua introeant apes, faciunt foramina parua dextra ac sinistra*; also 3.16.18 *ut eas coangustent.* V. uses *angustus* of the bees' world at 83 (see n.), 206, 228 (see n.) and 296.

35–6 The familiar threats, excessive heat and cold, so destructive of the animal world (3.441–4n.), are here introduced into the bees' society. These elements eventually attend the failure of the hive (259, 261–3nn.). Aristotle prescribed narrow entrances as a means of excluding intruders (*H.A.* 623b30), and Columella, though specifying excessive temperature as a threat, considers cold to be the only real danger: *nec tamen ita nocet huic generi calor aestatis ut hiemale frigus*, 9.7.4 (see 37n.).

37 utraque uis apibus pariter metuenda: though Varro, *R.R.* 3.16.12 supports this (*esse oportet aere temperato*), Columella (35–6n.)

suggests that heat is not such a problem. V.'s wording takes the reader back to the world of the plague (*pallida Tisiphone Morbos agit ante Metumque*, 3.552, and n.), and to the world of *labor* in general, where the uncontrollable forces of nature are a constant source of fear: *et iam maturis metuendus Iuppiter uuis*, 2.419 (and n.). Here he merely establishes the terminology, but the fear will shortly be realized (251–80, 280–1nn.). Cf. also 2.491–2n.

utraque ... pariter: suggests there are views to the contrary; see 35–6n.

37–8   neque ... | nequiquam: litotes: 'and not without success'.

38–9   certatim ... linunt 'they compete in smearing the tiny crevices with wax'.

tenuia: cf. 3n.

39–40   fucoque ... | explent 'and they fill the edges with paste from flowers'. Though the ancients were uncertain of the use to which flowers and pollen were put by bees, it is best to take *fucoque et floribus* as a hendiadys, referring to *propolis* or 'bee-glue', a resinous substance collected chiefly from the buds of trees and used to seal the hive. Some have seen it as a reference to pollen, but as Page notes *fuco* implies something that can be 'smeared or daubed'. He also notes that this interpretation finds support from 160 *narcissi lacrimam et lentum de cortice gluten*, where the bees seal their hives with the exudation of flowers and trees; and at 250 *floribus* means 'with the gum from flowers'. The subject is treated by Varro at *R.R.* 3.16.23–5.

oras 'edges', of what it is not quite clear; perhaps of the crevices. Some see a reference to the entrances. Cf. 188 *oras et limina circum*.

40–1   collectumque ... Idae 'and for this very purpose they gather and store up glue, more binding than lime or the pitch of Phrygian Ida' (cf. 39–40n.). Cf. 3.450 (ingredients in the ointment smeared on sheep) *Idaeasque pices et pinguis unguine ceras*; the words further connect the end of Book 3 with the bees.

42–3   saepe ... larem: though bees will inhabit rocky crevices or existing holes, they certainly will not excavate the ground themselves, and this is not one of the methods mentioned by Varro (33–4n.). V. is perhaps drawing a parallel with the Scythians: *ipsi in defossis specubus secura sub alta | otia agunt terra*, 3.376–7; see 44n.

si uera est fama: an indication that the detail is a θαῦμα ('marvel'), a common element of ethnography (Thomas (1982a) 80).

fouere larem 'they make a snug home'; *fouere* is a gnomic perfect. Cf. 45–6 *fouens*, 56 *progeniem nidosque fouent*.

larem: cf. 155 *penates*; V.'s language is constantly that of man, though this need not imply a specifically *Roman* society (3.344n.).

43 penitusque: an exaggeration (42–3n.), or possibly another instance of the bees' perspective (26–7n.).

44 pumicibusque cauis: cf. 33–4n.

exesaeque arboris antro 'in the hollow of a decayed tree'; cf. the *specus* of the Scythians (42–3n.). The detail is perhaps developed from Varro, *R.R.* 3.16.15 *alii ex arbore caua* (cf. *pumicibusque cauis*).

exesaeque: cf. 2.214–15 (the home of snakes) *exesa . . . | creta.*

45 tu tamen: even though they fare well by themselves, help them by insulating with clay and foliage from the outside; the tone is strongly didactic.

rimosa cubilia 'the chinks of their chambers' (lit. 'their fissured chambers'). *cubile* is used of the mole at 1.183, rooks at 1.411, the bull at 3.230, and bees again at 243, and quite commonly of animals elsewhere.

46 fouens 'keep them snug', as they do themselves (*fouere larem*, 43, and 42–3n.); also 56 and n.

raras 'a few'.

superinice: apparently the first instance of the verb; compound verbs formed from two prepositions are rare in Latin, perhaps imitated from Greek (cf. *prosubigit*, 3.256 and n.), and this seems to be the first attestation of one beginning with *super-* (most other instances are rare and post-classical).

47–50 Ribbeck placed the lines after 17, but no modern editors follow this measure, which forces a dogmatic ordering on the poem.

neu . . . neue . . . neu: cf. 2.298–302n.

47 neu propius tectis taxum sine: yews are highly toxic; cf. 2.257 *taxique nocentes*. At *E.* 9.30 they pose a particular threat to bees: *sic tua Cyrneas fugiant examina taxos.*

47–8 neue rubentis | ure foco cancros: the detail, which is oddly specific, may be intended as representative; cf. Colum. 9.5.6 *grauis et taetri odoris non solum uirentia sed et quaelibet res prohibeantur, sicuti cancri nidor, cum est ignibus adustus . . .* Pliny (*N.H.* 11.62) claims that the smell is fatal to them. For the view that 'burnt crabs were used as a specific manure for certain trees' (Kennedy, cit. Page) there seems to be no ancient evidence.

49   aut ubi odor caeni grauis: cf. 31 (and n.) *grauiter spirantis.*
Varro says of the bees (*R.R.* 3.16.6) *secuntur omnia pura. itaque nulla harum
adsidit in loco inquinato aut eo qui male oleat, neque etiam in eo qui bona olet
unguenta.*

49-50   aut ubi ... imago: a poetic reworking of Varro, *R.R.*
3.16.12 (on the best place for the hive) *ubi non resonant imagines.* Cf. also
Lucr. 4.570–1 (on the dispersal of sound) *pars* [sc. *uocum*] *solidis allisa locis
reiecta sonorem | reddit.* Conington notes the slight impropriety of *imago*
with *offensa*; strictly it is the *uox* which 'strikes' the rock.

saxa sonant: the sound reflects the sense of *resultat*; cf. 2.328;
3.338nn.

51–66   The bees at work when winter ends

These lines are characterized by the same sense of joy and rebirth which
marked the growth of the new plants at 1.43–70, and the springtime
emergence of the animals at 3.322–38 (see nn.). This second parallel is
somewhat ominous, as it foreshadows the similar deaths, through disease or plague, of both flocks and bees (1–7, 251–80, 281–2nn.).

51   Quod superest: cf. 2.346n.

51-2   ubi ... terras: cf. 1.43–4 *uere nouo, gelidus canis cum montibus
umor | liquitur*; see 51–66n.

52   caelumque aestiua luce reclusit: cf. 3.296 *dum mox frondosa
reducitur aestas.*

53   saltus siluasque peragrant: just like the flocks of 3.322–3 *in
saltus ... atque in pascua*; cf. *A.* 4.72–3 *illa fuga siluas saltusque peragrat |
Dictaeos.*

54   purpureosque metunt flores et flumina libant: for both
sound and sense cf. Lucr. 3.11 *floriferis ut apes in saltibus omnia libant.*

55   summa leues: the enjambment separates and stresses the two
adjectives: 'lightly, on the very surface'.

55-8   hinc ... hinc ... | hinc: the words express a causal, not just a
temporal, link: 'hence', 'therefore'; the warm weather is the catalyst for
their various activities.

55   nescio qua dulcedine laeti 'glad with some joy'; like the crows
when fair weather comes: *nescio qua praeter solitum dulcedine laeti*, 1.412 (see
56n.).

56 progeniem nidosque fouent: cf. 42–3, 46nn.; *nidosque* is perhaps a metonymy for *pullosque*, as at 17 (see n.). As in 55 cf. the crows of Book 1: *iuuat . . . | progeniem paruam dulcisque reuisere nidos*, 413–14.

arte: the first real suggestion in the book, implicit at the outset of the poem (1.4 *apibus quanta experientia*), that the bees belong in the cultural setting of the age of Jupiter: 1.145 *tum uariae uenere artes* (cf. 149–96n., and cf. esp. 156–7 *laborem | experiuntur*). See also 57n.

57 excudunt 'mould'; lit. 'forge'. The verb otherwise occurs in the poem only at 1.135 (of the actions of man after the age of Saturn; see 56n.) *ut silicis uenis abstrusum excuderet ignem*.

mella tenacia fingunt: cf. 179 *daedala fingere tecta*.

58 emissum caueis ad sidera caeli: cf. 3.551 *in lucem Stygiis emissa tenebris*.

sidera caeli: a favoured formula: cf. 2.1; *A.* 1.259; also 2.342; *A.* 4.578 *sidera caelo*.

59 nare: cf. *A.* 6.16 (of Daedalus' flight) *enauit*.

per aestatem liquidam 'through the clear summer air'; cf. 1.404 *liquido . . . in aëre*. *liquidam* contributes to the image of *nare*.

60 obscuramque trahi . . . nubem: cf. 557 (also of a cloud of bees) *immensasque trahi nubes*; *A.* 7.705 (of birds) *uolucrum . . . nubem*.

mirabere: cf. 42–3, 309, 554–5nn.

61 contemplator: cf. 1.187n.

61–2 aquas . . . petunt: the prescribed features of their *situs* at 18–24.

62 tu: a didactic touch.

iussos 'prescribed'; referring either to 63, or to the tradition in general – Varro, at *R.R.* 3.16.10, recommends the planting of thyme, *cytisus* and *apiastrum, quod alii meliphyllon, alii melissophyllon, quidam melittaenam appellant* (63n.). Cf. 3.300 *iubeo*.

63 melisphylla: the contraction (*metri causa*) for *melissophylla* (62n.) occurs only here and in Columella (9.9.8) and Palladius (1.37.2) – doubtless following V.

cerinthae 'bee-bread'; called *erithace* by Varro (*R.R.* 3.16.23) and others, the only other appearance of *cerintha* before V. being in Aristotle (*H.A.* 623b23 κήρινθος). Cf. Plin. *N.H.* 11.17 *erithace quam aliqui sandaracam, alii cerinthum uocant*.

ignobile: because it grows commonly.

64   Varro (*R.R.* 3.16.30) claims that the sound frightens them; the wording suggests that V. is contradicting him: *circumtinniendo aere perterritae* (cf. *tinnitusque ... circum*). Aristotle (*H.A.* 627a18) was unsure whether the bees congregated at loud sounds through pleasure or fear. The line looks to 150–2 (see n.)

Matris ... cymbala: cymbals were used in the worship of Cybele, 'the great mother'; cf. Cat. 63.19–21 *simul ite, sequimini | Phrygiam ad domum Cybebes, Phrygia ad nemora deae, | ubi cymbalum sonat uox, ubi tympana reboant*; also *A.* 9.619–20 *tympana uos buxusque uocat Berecyntia Matris | Idaeae*.

65   **ipsae ... ipsae:** the anaphora emphasizes the co-operation of the bees if the prescribed actions are carried out.

consident ... sedibus: the gloss provides a reference to the subject which has thus far concerned the poet: *sedes apibus statioque petenda*, 8.

medicatis: here = 'scented'; perhaps with a reference to the failure of *medicina* at the end of Book 3 (3.455–6, 549nn.), a failure which will recur in the bees' world (281–2n.).

66   **more suo** 'after their fashion'; i.e. with certainty. The reference to their *mos* also has an ethnographical dimension (4–5n.).

sese ... condent: sets up a transition to the next topic and a contrast with the very next line: *sin ... exierint.*

67–87   *Swarming*

V. knew well what he was describing, for Varro had given a clear account of the swarm at *R.R.* 3.16.29–31: *cum examen exiturum est, quod fieri solet cum adnatae prospere sunt multae ac progeniem ut coloniam emittere uolunt ...* Here, however, the phenomenon is presented as a battle, and V.'s purpose is clear, to create a closer approximation to a human situation, and to provide a basis for the section which follows, the discussion of selection of the best king, and suppression of the inferior one (88–102) – a theme which follows naturally on the topic of civil discord. The image may have been suggested by Varro, *R.R.* 3.16.30 *consonant uehementer, proinde ut milites faciunt, cum castra mouent*, but it is typical of V.'s practice that the simile has become a reality.

The diction is epic throughout, looking back to the programme of 3–5 (see esp. 4–5n.), and as in the proem V. indicates that the large-scale treatment is balanced by the attenuated subject-matter (83, 86–7).

Many see all this as an instance of mock-heroic, but that term implies a humorous intent, for which there is no place here.

67 Sin ... exierint: V. begins in didactic vein, setting up an apodosis containing advice to the bee-keeper – an apodosis which never comes, however, as V. gives the impression of being swept up into the narrative of the battle. Cf. 251–2n.

ad pugnam: see 67–87n.

exierint: cf. the beginning of Varro's section: *R.R.* 3.16.29 *cum examen exiturum est.*

nam: partly explanatory of *ad pugnam exierint*, but also indicating the beginning of an episode (= Gr. καὶ γάρ).

68 regibus: cf. 21n.

incessit magno discordia motu: developed from Varro, *R.R.* 3.16.18 (not the section on swarming) *praeterea ut animaduertat ne reguli plures existant; inutiles enim fiunt propter seditiones.* The words recall 2.496 *infidos agitans discordia fratres* (also 2.459 *discordibus armis*), and suggest that the bees belong to a culturally 'advanced' society (149–96n.).

69 uulgi: as with *discordia* (68), the terminology is human and political.

69–70 trepidantia ... | corda: cf. 73 *trepidae*; also 3.105–6 (of the horses just before the race – a parallel situation) *exsultantiaque ... | corda.*

70 licet longe praesciscere: *praesciscere* occurs only here in V.; the words are developed from Varro, *R.R.* 3.16.29 ... *huius quod duo solent praeire signa scitur.*

morantis: cf. 28n.

71 Martius ille aeris rauci canor 'that warlike ring of harsh-sounding brass'; a bold way of referring to the agitated sound of the bees, softened and explained by *imitata* in the next line.

71–2 uox | auditur fractos sonitus imitata tubarum: developed from Varro, *R.R.* 3.16.9 *iique duces conficiunt quaedam ad uocem ut imitatione tubae.* This is the only place where V. refers to the bees' actions as *similar* to those of man (the constant stance of Varro); elsewhere they *are* those of man.

fractos sonitus: i.e. intermittent, broken sounds, as at *A.* 3.556 *fractasque ... uoces*; and cf. Tac. *Germ.* 3.1 *adfectatur praecipue asperitas soni et fractum murmur.*

73 trepidae: cf. 69 *trepidantia.* With one exception (1.296), all other instances of *trepidus, trepido* occur in the *Aeneid.*

coeunt: otherwise in V. only at *A.* 7.582, where the Latins mass before battle, *undique collecti coeunt Martemque fatigant* (75–6n.).

pennisque coruscant 'and their wings flash'; cf. 98 *fulgore coruscant.*

74   spiculaque exacuunt rostris: 'sharpen their stings with their beaks' rather than 'sharpen the stings on their beaks'. Neither sense respects the facts, but the former may at least be explained by a misconception gained from observing the bee's cleaning its abdomen with its mandibles (*rostris*), and with *exacuunt* an instrumental ablative seems more natural.

75–6   circa … | miscentur: cf. *A.* 7.585 (as the Latins prepare for war) *certatim regis circumstant tecta Latini. praetorium,* the technical term for a general's headquarters (tent or building), occurs only here in V.

76   The sound of the line reflects the noise and activity which it portrays.

77   ergo ubi uer nactae sudum: sc. *sunt* with *nactae*, 'therefore when they have obtained a clear spring day'. The verb strengthens the sense of an army waiting for the right conditions for battle; e.g. Caes. *B.G.* 4.23.6 *et uentum et aestum uno tempore nactus secundum.*

78   The asyndetic style suits the context of a battle narrative: 'out they burst, they clash together, a din goes up, they mass together, they fall headlong'. The alternation of personal with impersonal verbs makes the sequence more vivid.

erumpunt portis: cf. *A.* 10.604 *tandem erumpunt et castra relinquunt.*

concurritur: collective action is frequently expressed by the passive of intransitive verbs; cf. 189 *siletur.*

aethere in alto: bees do not actually fight in the air.

79   fit sonitus: so at 188, when the bees first return to the hive in the evening.

magnum mixtae glomerantur in orbem 'they mingle together and are massed into a great ball'. Cf. Varro on the bees just prior to their swarming: *conglobatae* (*R.R.* 3.16.29). *glomero* is used of the violence of the storm at 1.323, and of the fire-storm at 2.311 (see n.).

80   praecipitesque cadunt: cf. Lucr. 6.744 (of birds) *praecipitesque cadunt* (3.546–7n.).

non densior aëre grando: conjuring up an appropriately epic atmosphere; cf. *A.* 9.667–70 *pugna aspera surgit | … quam multa grandine nimbi | in uada praecipitant*; also *A.* 5.458–9.

81   'nor do the acorns rain so thick from the shaken oak'; with *tantum
... glandis* V. treats the acorns as a collective. As in 80, the image is also
epic; see e.g. Hom. *Il.* 6.146–9.

82   ipsi: i.e. the kings themselves, distinct from the general popu-
lace, the subject so far.

insignibus alis: Columella says of the wings of the king (9.10.1)
minus amplis pinnis pulchri coloris et nitidi. V.'s reference foreshadows the
striking prescription of 106–7 *tu regibus alas | eripe* (see n.).

83   ingentis animos angusto in pectore uersant: a brilliant
characterization of the diminutively epic status of these creatures. The
antithesis between great (*ingentis*) and small (*angusto*) is operative
throughout (3n.). Here V.'s words have an almost programmatic ring,
supporting his earlier suggestion (4–5, 6nn.) that the treatment of the
bees represents a blending of attenuated Callimacheanism with the
larger issues which were coming to concern him (Introduction, pp.
1–3). Propertius seems to have reworked the line into an intensely
Callimachean context at 2.1.39–40 *neque ... | intonet angusto pectore Cal-
limachus,* 45 *nos contra angusto uersantes proelia lecto.* See 86–7n.

angusto: cf. 35n.

84–5   'struggle on, refusing to yield until the pressure of the victor
has forced one side or the other to turn its back and flee'.

usque adeo: expresses the intensity of their struggle; cf. *E.* 1.11–12
undique totis | usque adeo turbatur agris.

aut hos | aut hos: the anaphora from line-end to line-beginning,
together with the use of two monosyllables, creates an unusual rhythm;
cf. *A.* 10.9–10 *quis metus aut hos | aut hos arma sequi ferrumque lacessere suasit?*

86–7   Most commentators have detected humour, seeing the couplet
as providing relief for what would otherwise become pure exaggeration.
But V., here as in Books 2 and 3, in spite of the obvious dangers,
consistently ascribes human qualities not only to animals but even to
plants – and the bees continue to be depicted in human terms throughout the rest of the account. Three points need stressing: (*a*) the detail is
traditional; V., at the end of this section, as at the beginning (67n.),
draws from Varro, who observes that swarming can be prevented: *a
mellario cum id fecisse sunt animaduersae, iaciundo in eas puluere et circumtinniendo aere perterritae,* R.R. 3.16.30 (see also 71–2n.); (*b*) the couplet
contributes to the theme of a blending of large and small (3n.), and the

response to this carefully sustained theme need not be humorous; (*c*) the lines also suggest the frailty of the bees (and ultimately the frailty of man is only different in degree), a theme which occupies V. through much of the book (251–80, 281–2nn.), as frailty in general concerns him through much of the poem.

86   motus animorum: cf. 3.521 *mouere animum.*

86–7   tanta | ... exigui: cf. 3, 83nn.

88–102   *The importance of selection*

Both Aristotle (*H.A.* 624b21–7) and Varro (*R.R.* 3.16.18–19) had treated the markings of the superior bee, both king and worker, and V. seems to know of both accounts (92n.). His chief purpose here is to draw yet another parallel between the bees and the animals of Book 3; for in subject-matter and diction there are close similarities to the passages on selection (3.49–71, of cows; 72–94, of horses; 384–93, of rams). See 89, 89–90, 91nn.

The lines on the good and bad king have been seen as pure allegory, representing Octavian and Antony, but V.'s treatment of the bees, while symbolic, does not suit such a strict equation (1–7n.). How would the bee-keeper, prominent in this section (88 *reuocaueris*, 90 *dede neci*, 101 *premes*) fit into such a fabric, and what of the advice at 106–7 (which would be directed against Octavian) *tu regibus alas | eripe*?

88   Verum ubi: used at 1.417; 4.405, 443.

89   deterior: cf. 90, 92 *melior*; also 3.51 (of cows) *optima*, 82 (of horses) *deterrimus* (88–102n.). There is only one other instance of this comparative or superlative in V. (*A.* 8.326 *deterior ... aetas*).

uisus: sc. *erit.*

89–90   eum, ne prodigus obsit, | dede neci 'lest he be a waste and a burden, kill him'. The tone is very close to that of 3.387–90 (on rejection of the tainted ram) *illum autem ... | reice, ne maculis infuscet uellera pullis | nascentum* (88–102; 3.389nn.); also to that of 3.96 (of the old horse) *abde domo.* Cf. also 3.480 (of the plague – which will shortly also come to the bees) *et genus omne neci pecudum dedit, omne ferarum.*

90   sine regnet: almost all the instances in Latin of *sino* with a jussive noun clause occur with the imperative (*sine/sinite = peto, oro,* etc.); cf. *E.* 9.43 *insani feriant sine litora fluctus*; *A.* 2.669–70 *sinite instaurata reuisam | proelia.*

aula: cf. 8n.

91   alter: the *melior*, as is revealed in 92.

maculis auro squalentibus ardens 'bright with specks which are rough with gold'; *maculis* is to *ardens* as *auro* is to *squalentibus*. The superior *plebs* have a similar appearance (98–9). The line establishes a firm connection with the selection of cows at 3.56 (see n.) *nec mihi displiceat maculis insignis et albo.* Cf. also *A.* 10.314 *tunicam squalentem auro.* On *auro*, cf. 92n.

92   nam duo sunt genera: the words appear innocent enough, but are in fact intended polemically. Aristotle knew two species of kings, the one red and the other black (*H.A.* 624b22), perhaps the common and Ligurian (*Apis mellifica* and *A. ligustica*), but Varro, who seems to be referring to that passage, is somewhat confused, first specifying three, then in mid-sentence appearing to change his mind: *et quidam dicunt, tria genera cum sint ducum in apibus, niger ruber uarius, ut Menecrates scribit, duo, niger et uarius, qui ita melior ut expediat mellario, cum duo sunt in eadem aluo, interficere nigrum, R.R.* 3.16.18. V.'s words look specifically to Varro's *tria genera cum sint* and to the confusion which follows (cf. 3.54–5n. for a similar 'correction'). V. departs from the tradition in his manner of treating colour: his superior king is appropriately of regal gold, while the inferior type (and its *plebs* with it) is merely squalid and ugly (96–8n.).

melior: the final syllable is treated as long at the point of ictus.

92–3   hic ... squamis 'the better one is of conspicuous appearance and bright with gleaming scales'; the first *et* is postponed. V. seems to draw on these lines in describing the appearance of Turnus at *A.* 11.487–8 *iamque adeo rutilum thoraca indutus aënis | horrebat squamis* (he otherwise uses *rutilus* only at *G.* 1.454).

93–4   ille ... aluum 'the other one [*deterior* is understood from 89 and from *melior* in 92] is squalid from sloth and unseemly as he drags around his broad paunch'. V., to create an ethical contrast not in Aristotle or Varro, deliberately confuses the inferior king with the drone; cf. Varro, *R.R.* 3.16.19 *fur qui uocabitur, ab aliis fucus, est ater et lato uentre.* Aristotle (*H.A.* 624b27) calls the drone 'lazy' (νωθρός; cf. V.'s *desidia*).

horridus: brilliantly transferred from Varro's description of the sick bee (*R.R.* 3.16.20) to V.'s inferior one; cf. 96 *horrent*, and see 96–8n. The word implies neglect. It is also used of the sick bees at 254–5 *horrida uultum | deformat macies.*

inglorius: like *desidia* and *horridus* creating a moral dimension absent from the technical tradition.

95 ut binae regum facies, ita corpora plebis: V., concerned as ever with a precise human approximation, has two varieties of bee under each of the two kings, neatly related in appearance to their leaders (96, 99nn.). In fact Aristotle and Varro, after discussing the two (or three) types of bees, proceed to talk of other types (workers, drones, wasps, etc.), in no way related to the two kings; only one type is desirable, the worker, who is not distinct by species: *de reliquis apibus optima est parua uaria rotunda*, Varro, *R.R.* 3.16.19.

96 namque aliae turpes horrent: the *apes deteriores* take after their leader (93 *horridus*; see 93–4n.). The feminine *aliae* assumes *apes*, which does not in fact occur in the vicinity.

96–8 ceu ... | aridus: a vivid simile, developed from two words in Varro, *ut puluerulentae* (*R.R.* 3.16.20), which apply to the sick bees, with whom V. has already equated the inferior type of king (93–4n.).

The image of the thirsty traveller may owe something to Cat. 68.58–61 *riuus ... , dulce uiatori lasso in sudore leuamen*, that of spitting to Callim. *H.* 6.6 μηδ' δκ' ἀφ' αὐαλέων στομάτων πτύωμες ἄπαστοι, 'nor when fasting spit from parched mouths'.

98 aliae: the better bees, matching the better king of 91–3 (96, 99nn.).

fulgore coruscant: cf. 73 *pennisque coruscant*.

99 'their bodies ablaze and covered with equal specks of gold'; lit. 'blazing as to bodies covered with gold and equal specks'. *corpora* is accusative of respect, while *auro et ... guttis* is best taken as a hendiadys; cf. 1.346n. and 2.192 *pateris ... et auro*.

100–1 haec potior suboles, hinc ... | dulcia mella premes: again bee and animal are depicted in close terms; cf. 3.308 *densior hinc suboles, hinc largi copia lactis*. In both cases V. states the superiority of offspring and product.

dulcia mella premes: cf. 140–1 *spumantia cogere pressis | mella fauis*.

101–2 nec tantum dulcia quantum | et liquida et ...: it is sweet, but its sweetness is surpassed both by its clarity and its capacity for mellowing the flavour of wine.

102 durum Bacchi domitura saporem: reminiscent of the hostility to wine at 2.454 7 (see n., and 3.509–10n.). With *domitura* V. perhaps intends a reminiscence of 2.455–6 *ille* [sc. *Bacchus*] *furentis* |

Centauros leto domuit. The future participle has potential force: 'capable of overcoming'.

103–15   Keeping the bees near the hive

Two general methods are prescribed: immobilizing the king (106–7), and supplying the appropriate plants in the vicinity of the hive. The chief function of the passage is, through this second topic, to create a transition to the theme of gardening, and the 'excursus' on the old man of Tarentum (116–48).

103 Their aimless behaviour is in contrast to the purposeful expedition of 53–4.

ludunt: cf. 105 *ludo.*

104   frigida: predicative: 'leave their hives which become cold'.

105   instabilis animos: Conington compares Soph. *Ant.* 343 κουφονόων τε φῦλον ὀρνίθων, 'the tribe of light-hearted birds', and, perhaps more appropriate to the present context, Aristoph. *Aues* 169–70 ἄνθρωπος ὄρνις, ἀστάθμητος [= *instabilis*], πετόμενος, | ἀτέκμαρτος, 'the man's a bird, unstable, flighty, inconsistent'.

ludo: cf. 103 *ludunt.*

prohibebis: for the imperative, cf. 3.155n.

106   nec magnus prohibere labor: cf. 6 *in tenui labor.* Given the symbolic level of the advice which immediately follows (106–7n.), the words have a certain cool irony.

106–7   tu regibus alas | eripe: an emphatic didacticism: 'do you tear the kings' wings off'. This is 'no great task' in terms of didactic reality (removing the wings from queen-bees), but in terms of the human status which the bees enjoy throughout the advice comes abruptly and in contrast with the words *nec magnus prohibere labor*; and the detail is not found in Aristotle or Varro. Those who see the two kings of 88–94 as strictly representative of Octavian and Antony (88–102n.) must confront the present words.

eripe: cf. 3.389n. for the emphatic position.

107–8   non illis quisquam cunctantibus altum | ire iter … **audebit:** cf. 1.456–7 *non illa quisquam me nocte per altum | ire … moneat.*

cunctantibus: since they are without wings; something of a euphemism. Cf. 28, 70 *morantis.*

iter: a cognate accusative (with *ire*).

castris ... uellere signa: a continuation of the military language of 67–87.

109–11   The transition to the subject of gardens begins. The jussives *inuitent* and *seruet* stand for didactic imperatives, as V. includes the bee-keeper only obliquely in these lines – he is merely *ipse* (twice) at 114.

109   inuitent 'they should be attracted by'; like the setting of 23 *uicina inuitet decedere ripa*.

croceis halantes floribus 'with the fragrance of saffron flowers'.

110–11   custos furum atque auium ... | Hellespontiaci ... tutela Priapi 'he who watches against thieves and birds ... the guardian Priapus of the Hellespont'; the expression is somewhat odd, as the subject changes from *custos* to the abstract *tutela* (lit. 'the guardianship of Priapus'). Ithyphallic wooden statues of Priapus watched over gardens. *tutela Priapi* is an epicizing periphrasis for *Priapus tutelarius*. Cf. Hor. *Sat.* 1.8.3–4 (spoken by a statue of the god) *deus inde ego, furum auiumque | maxima formido.*

111   One of the six lines in the poem consisting of only four words; see 1.470n. As at 1.502 the phenomenon results from the use of a Greek proper name extending from the beginning of the line to the third-foot caesura.

Hellespontiaci: Priapus was originally worshipped in Lampsacus on the Hellespont.

112–13   ipse ... ferens ...: the bee-keeper (*ipse*) is like the herds-man of 3.395 *ipse ... ferat*; in both cases the intensifying pronoun (here repeated twice in 114) indicates personal effort. The syntax is reversed between the two passages, the relative clause preceding the main clause in Book 3, following it in the present couplet.

pinosque: *tinosque* has better MS support, and is *lectio difficilior*, but it is problematic. The gum from trees (*propolis*) is used in constructing the hive (40 *collectumque haec ipsa ad munera gluten*, 160 *lentum de cortice gluten*), and at *E.* 7.68 the pine is mentioned as a garden tree (*pinus in hortis*). *tinus*, on the other hand, seems to be the shrub laurustinus (*Viburnum tinus*), which is one of the least hardy of the viburnums and does not therefore suit the words *de montibus altis* (it even does well in salty, coastal areas). Moreover, it flowers early in the year, so is of little use to bees anyway. See also 141n.

113   tecta: cf. 8n.

114–15   A tricolon, with anaphora of *ipse* in 114 resuming the instance in 112, ends the section.

114   ipse labore manum duro terat: man shares in the bees' toil, a feature of their existence which will shortly come to the fore (149–96n.). The words recall the important statement at 1.145–6 *labor omnia uicit | improbus et duris urgens in rebus egestas*; cf. also 2.412 *durus uterque labor*. Something is owed to Lucr. 5.1358–60 *uellent | . . . durum sufferre laborem | atque opere in duro durarent membra manusque.*
At 203–4 the bees themselves are presented in similar terms: *duris errando in cotibus alas | attriuere.*

114–15   feracis | . . . plantas: cf. 2.79–80 *feraces | plantae*, where, however, the reference is specifically to an engrafted scion. The force of *feracis* ('fruitful') is strongly felt; the shrubs or trees must produce abundant blossom to be of use.

115   amicos inriget imbris: i.e. he should water the new shoots. Cf. *A.* 1.123 (of the waters of a storm) [*naues*] *accipiunt inimicum imbrem.*

116–48   Gardens; the old man of Tarentum

One of the most famous passages of the poem, but also one of the most difficult. It is cast in the form of a *praeteritio*, the device which purports to minimize, but in fact creates emphasis (cf. 116–19, 147–8nn.). The lines constitute the skeleton of a fifth book of *Georgics*, treating the important topic of gardens (119, 147–8nn.), but this topic is merely used as a transitional device to the description, which Virgil conveys in an intensely personal mode (125–7n.), of the existence of the old man of Tarentum. The status of this existence within the fabric of the poem is clearly of great importance. The old man lives in a private world, the product of the poet's imagination, as has been shown by Perkell (1981), and it has been argued (Thomas (1982a) 56–60) that the success he enjoys and the tranquillity he attains are deliberately situated outside the bounds of the agricultural areas which form the premise for the rest of the poem (128–9n.). More recently Kenney (1984) xxxvi–xxxix, liv–lv and Ross (1987) 201–6 have argued that the passage is either impossibly idealized or pointedly fictitious in the claims it makes for the old man's environment. It needs to be said, however, that the old man's success, unlike that of the idealized rustic at the end of Book 2, occurs within the operations of a *real* (albeit personal) world, free from associations with the golden age that has passed, and to that extent it is a success plausible within the cultural setting of the age of Jupiter, on which the realities of the *Georgics* are predicated. See 125–48n.

Little need be said of the attempts (as old as Servius and surely older, but rightly no longer in fashion) to find a specific individual with whom to identify the old man; V.'s portrait is no doubt finely characterized, but it need not imply the existence of an actual personality outside his own poetic imagination; see 127n.

116–19 The *praeteritio* (116–48n.) is presented through a contrary-to-fact conditional, to which 147–8 provides a closing frame (see n.). The present subjunctives in the protasis give a more vivid effect: 'but for the fact that I am almost at the end of my task, I should go on to sing of . . .'

116   equidem: the word recurs, forming a frame (116–19n.) at 147. In V. it occurs (37 times) only with the first person, showing that he, like many, believed it was formed from *ego* + *quidem*, which seems not to be the case.

extremo . . . sub fine laborum: cf. 2.39 *ades inceptumque una decurre laborem.*

116–17   ni . . . | uela traham et terris festinem aduertere proram: the end of the metaphor employed at 2.39–45 *tuque ades . . . | Maecenas, pelagoque uolans da uela patenti. | . . . ades et primi lege litoris oram; | in manibus terrae.*

118–20 'perhaps I should be singing of the cultivation which decks out rich gardens, and singing of the rose-gardens of twice-blooming Paestum, and of how endive rejoices . . .'; so with *rosaria* taken as the object of *canerem*, but it may also be taken as the object of *ornaret*, in which case it is linked to *hortos*: 'cultivation which decks out gardens and rose-beds'.

119   canerem: cf. 1.5n. for V.'s use of the word at the outset of Books 1–3; it is appropriate here at the beginning of what 'might have been a fifth Georgic' (Conington).

biferique rosaria Paesti: at 2.150 (see n.) V. made the patently false claim *bis grauidae pecudes, bis pomis utilis arbos*; the present claim looks similarly fantastic. Propertius (*uidi ego odorati uictura rosaria Paesti*, 4.5.61), Ovid (*tepidique rosaria Paesti*, *M.* 15.708) and Columella (*Paestique rosaria*, 10.37; see 147–8n.) refer to the rose-gardens of Paestum, and to V.'s line, but both suppress the epithet *bifer*; Martial reproduces it at 12.31.3 *bifero cessura rosaria Paesto*. If V.'s words have a basis in fact he is referring to the Autumn Damask Rose (*Rosa × bifera*), which blooms in the spring and autumn and which, though not otherwise known in Italy before the seventeenth century, may be represented in Pompeian frescoes; cf. Thomas (1961) 67–8. Alternatively he intends a θαῦμα ('marvel'), and if so perhaps has in mind Hom. *Od.* 7.117–21, the fabulous description of the continuously blooming and fruiting trees in the garden of Alcinous.

120   potis ... riuis 'the streams which it [the endive] drinks'.

gauderent: cf. 2.179–81 *difficiles ... terrae ... | Palladia gaudent silua uiuacis oliuae*; *E.* 9.48 *astrum quo segetes gauderent frugibus.* See 121n.

intiba: the word appears in V. only here, and in the same line of Book 1 (125–48n.).

121   et uirides apio ripae: an elegant inversion of 120: while the *intibum* rejoices in the stream which nurtures it, the banks rejoice in the *apium* which they nurture.

apio: wild celery, smallage (*Apium graueolens*), not parsley, as is clear from *E.* 6.68 *apio ... amaro.*

121–2   tortusque ... cucumis '[and how] the cucumber snakes through the ground and swells into a paunch'. V. well captures the two very noticeable growing features, first of the stem, then of the fruit, of the cucumber. Cf. Prop. 4.2.43 *caeruleus cucumis tumidoque cucurbita uentre.*

122   sera comantem 'late-blooming'; for the neuter of the adjective, used adverbially with the participle, cf. 270 *graue olentia*; 3.149 *acerba sonans.*

Cf. 137 *comam ... hyacinthi.*

123   narcissum: used by the bees at 160.

flexi ... acanthi: cf. *E.* 3.45 *molli ... acantho.*

tacuissem: the change of tense from *canerem* is merely more graphic: 'nor should I have kept silent'.

124   pallentisque hederas: cf. *E.* 3.39 *hedera ... pallente*, 7.38 *hedera ... alba.*

amantis litora myrtos: cf. 2.112 (and n.) *litora myrtetis laetissima.* On *amare* in such contexts, see 2.113n.

125–48   The actual account of the old Corycian begins (116–48n.). The lines are significantly placed in the same relative position as those occupied by the account of the transition from the age of Saturn to that of Jupiter (1.125–49), and may be seen as a portrayal of the successful workings of private man within the terms of the age of *labor*; see 116–48, 128–9; 2.458–540nn.

They are also intended to produce a favourable contrast with both the *laudes Italiae* (2.136–76) and the description of life in Scythia (3.349–83), all three passages showing a clear debt to the tradition of ethnographical writing (126, 128–9nn.; Thomas (1982a) 35–60).

125   namque: indicates, like καὶ γάρ in Greek, that what follows will be an independent episode; so at *E.* 6.31 the song of Silenus begins *namque canebat uti* . . . ; or the ecphrasis on Dido's temple at *A.* 1.466 *namque uidebat uti* . . . Cf. 287 *nam.*

sub Oebaliae . . . turribus arcis: the periphrasis for Tarentum is in the Alexandrian manner. Oebalus was a king of Sparta, father of Tyndareus, and his name is here somewhat boldly used to create an epithet for Tarentum, which was founded by the Spartans (the word is used before V. of Laconia); see 126n. Horace, who draws from the present lines (126, 145–6nn.; and cf. 2.197n.), also suppresses the name Tarentum, but uses the name of a different king, Phalanthus, who is supposed to have founded the city: *regnata . . . Laconi | rura Phalantho, Odes* 2.6.11–12.

125–7   memini me . . . uidisse: creates a strong sense of the poet's personal experience – which need not, however, imply an existence for the *senex* outside V.'s imagination; cf. 1.193 (and n.), 197, 318 (and 316–18n.) *uidi.*

126   qua niger umectat flauentia culta Galaesus: as often in ethnographical contexts, the *situs* is defined by the specifying of a river; cf. 3.350 (and n.) *turbidus et torquens flauentis Hister harenas.*

Galaesus: the river occurs in Polybius (8.33.8), where it is given the variant name Eurotas (after the river of Sparta). When considered with *Oebaliae* (125 and n.), it looks as if V. is drawing from a specific geographical source, doubtless Hellenistic. Callimachus may have mentioned the Galaesus in his treatise on the rivers of the known world (*frag. gram.* 457–9 Pf.). After V. the Galaesus is mentioned by Horace (*Odes* 2.6.10; see 125n.) and Propertius (2.34.67), with specific reference to V. (Thomas (1982a) 59).

127   Corycium ... senem: commentators since Servius have sought a specific identification for the old man. The most popular has been a Cilician pirate settled in the area by Pompey, but few now read the passage as a mere recounting of personal experience, and the designation doubtless has a literary justification. Ethnographical studies regularly specify the *origo* of the inhabitants under study, and the

answer may be simply that V. is tying his account to that tradition
(Thomas (1982a) 56–7). However, as Ross (1987) 204–5 has argued,
V. may intend a connection with a different Corycian locale, not in
Cilicia, but on Mt Parnassus, specifically with the Corycian cave
(placed by a confused Servius in Cilicia), whose nymphs are mentioned
by Callimachus at *Aet.* 3, fr. 75.56 Pf. They also appear at Ov. *Her.*
20.221–2, in association with the island of Cea.

127–8   cui pauca relicti | iugera ruris erant 'who had a few
acres of waste land'. As in what follows (128–9n.), the old man's world is
set apart from that of civilized society; this is land which is unappro-
priated by those who pursue conventional agriculture or other, more
sinister, activities. Horace speaks critically of the encroachment of
civilized man on the land at *Odes* 2.15.1–2 *iam pauca aratro iugera regiae |
moles relinquent*; and cf. Tibullus of large land-holdings: 1.1.1–2 *alius ...
teneat culti iugera multa soli.*

128–9   nec fertilis ... Baccho: some have suspected *pecori*, since
the lines must constitute a rejection of all three areas of agriculture (the
subjects of Books 1–3; see 2.143–4n.). But so they do already: 'but
neither was that land rich enough for ploughing-oxen [i.e. to produce
crops], nor suitable for a flock, nor favourable for the vine'.

In the *laudes Italiae* all three categories of agriculture flourished
(2.143–4 and n.), while in the description of Scythia the three were
mentioned (3.352–3 and n.), but the climate prevented their success.
Here all three are again mentioned, only to be rejected – the land is not
suitable for their production. In their place there exists the minimum for
personal, rather than public, self-sufficiency: a vegetable garden, some
herbs, flowers for the bees, and a few fruit-trees. When the reader recalls
the fate of the crops in Book 1 (destruction at the hands of the storm), of
livestock in Book 3 (annihilation by plague), and of the vine in Book 2
(success along with vituperation of the product and of the vine itself; see
2.454–7n.), these lines seem to offer an alternative, not necessarily
idealized (134–43n.), to the problems and disasters besetting agricultural existence.

130   hic ... tamen: cf. 3.354 *sed ...*, immediately following the
parallel negation of agricultural activity (128–9n.). *hic* is the adverb: 'he
had a few acres of waste land, no good for normal agriculture; nevertheless on this land [*hic*] he ...'; this is better than taking it as the pronoun
(so Forbiger, Conington).

rarum ... olus: not 'the odd vegetable' (which would make less credible the self-sufficiency of the old man), but 'spaced-out vegetables'; i.e. in rows. The garden could have included lettuce, onions, turnips, cabbage, and more. This is V.'s only general reference to vegetables.

131 lilia uerbenasque: not merely ornamental, for the lily was used to make ointment and oil (Plin. *N.H.* 21.23), and vervain was prized for medicinal (and magical) purposes.

premens 'planting', as at 2.346.

uescumque 'small' (of the seed), or 'slender' (of the stem); cf. 3.175 and n.

132 regum aequabat opes animis 'he matched in contentment the wealth of kings'. Similarly Horace as he dines on the *holuscula* (cf. 130) from his own garden: *o noctes cenaeque deum!*, *Sat.* 2.6.65. Some see an irony or impossible idealization in these words; while the glorification of simplicity may have such connotations (e.g. Ovid's complex account of the simple fare of Baucis and Philemon at *M.* 8.629–78), a serious or 'straight' intent is quite possible, and indeed necessary if subsequent parody is to be effective.

132-3 seraque reuertens | nocte: cf. 185–7 (of the bees) *easdem | Vesper ubi e pastu tandem decedere campis | admonuit*; also 3.467 *serae solam decedere nocti*; *A.* 7.492 *ipse domum sera quamuis se nocte ferebat.*

133 dapibus mensas onerabat inemptis: cf. Hor. *Epd.* 2.48 [*pudica mulier*] *dapes inemptas apparet*; presumably one imitated the other. Though in the final lines of the Second Epode the irony of the situation (as the reader is told that the speaker is the money-lender Alfius) to some extent infects the whole poem, the statement in itself is not parodistic either for Horace or V. (132n.).

dapibus mensas onerabat: cf. 378 *epulis onerant mensas.*

134-43 The Corycian works within the realities of the seasons, all mentioned in these lines; cf. 2.319–22n. In this his environment is distinct both from the fictitious situation of the *laudes Italiae* (2.149 *hic uer adsiduum*) and from the restrictive hardship of Scythia (3.356 *semper hiems*). The details of these lines also separate the old man from the Saturnian rustic at the end of Book 2, for his success is within the confines of the real, seasonal world.

134 An elegant line with *uere* looking to *autumno*, *rosam* to *poma*, and *carpere*, a prolative infinitive with *primus* rather than a historical infinitive, controlling both clauses.

primus: repeated at 140; cf. 2.408–10n.

135–6   cum … hiems … frigore saxa | rumperet: something of a rhetorical exaggeration, given the climate of Tarentum; V. desires to have the old man successfully working at an early stage of the growing season.

136   glacie cursus frenaret aquarum: Lucretius speaks of the power of ice (*uis magna geli*) as *magnum duramen aquarum*, 6.530.

137   ille comam mollis iam tondebat hyacinthi: a difficult line, taken by commentators to mean 'would already be cutting the flower of the *hyacinthus*'. But in spite of *comantem* at 122 the combination *comam tondere* here surely has its natural sense 'cut back the foliage'; cf. 2.368 *tum stringe comas, tum bracchia tonde*; Ov. *M.* 11.46–7 *arbor | tonsa comas*. It is fairly common practice with some bulbous plants to leave the old foliage intact until just before the growing season, since nutrients are thereby returned to the bulb. While it is natural enough to have the old man cutting back the dead foliage of his plants in the winter (135–6) in preparation for the new growth of spring, it makes no sense to have him culling flowers at such a time: (*a*) it is clearly impossible (and not just an idealization); (*b*) what need to curse the slowness of summer's coming (138 *aestatem increpitans seram*) if he could have blossoms in winter? (*c*) the actions of 137–8 lead to the result of 139–41 (*ergo*), that is, to an abundant supply of honey. Such a result is hardly to be produced by picking one's flowers at all, and certainly not by doing so before the bees emerge from the hive in the spring.

tondebat: cf. 1.138n. for the 'lengthening' of the final syllable.

hyacinthi: the bees also feed on them at 181–3 *pascuntur … ferrugineos hyacinthos*. The identity of the flower is disputed; it is clearly a member of the Liliaceae, either an asphodel, or some sort of lily.

138   aestatem increpitans seram: cf. 137n.

139   ergo: as a result of his tending the flowers in the winter; cf. 137n.

apibus fetis 'with bees which had produced young'; inconsistent with 199 (*nec*) *fetus nixibus edunt*. These bees are just 'bees', unlike those outside 125–48, which are depicted with particular cultural and ethical concerns; see 198–9n.

140   primus: cf. 134n.

abundare et … cogere: prolative infinitives dependent on *primus*, like *carpere* at 134.

141 tiliae: cf. 183 *pinguem tiliam.*

uberrima 'in abundance' or 'luxuriant'; with *tiliae* and *pinus.*

pinus: most modern editors prefer *tinus* (112–13n.), which is indeed *lectio difficilior.* The claim of Serv. Auct. that V. wrote both words reflects the difficulty of the choice (cf. 1.25n.). However, Columella, who gives a large list of desirable trees and shrubs at 9.4, includes *pinus* (used predominantly for *propolis*, but also for pollen) and *tilia*, but not *tinus.*

142–3 'and as many fruits [i.e. 'flowers', 'incipient fruits'] as the productive tree had dressed itself with in its early bloom, so many did it retain when it came to maturity in autumn'. The old man's fruit-trees behave normally, if with great bounty, unlike the fantastic ones of the *laudes Italiae: bis pomis utilis arbos,* 2.150.

144–7 seras … umbras: when transplanted the old man's elms are advanced in growth, his pear-tree is already hard, his thorn-bushes are producing plums and his plane giving shade. There is an element of exaggeration in the details (Ross (1987) 201–6), aimed at demonstrating the old man's successful arboriculture, but terms such as *seram* and *eduram* are relative; they need not imply that these trees are fully grown. Cf. Hor. *Epd.* 2.9–10 *adulta uitium propagine | altas maritat populos.*

145 eduramque 'which have been hardened out'; a back-formation from *edurare*, occurring here and at 2.65 (see n.), subsequently only in Tertullian.

145–6 spinos … umbras: the plum (*prunus*) has been grafted on to the *spinus* (blackthorn?), and therefore produces plums. Horace similarly claims of his farm at *Epist.* 1.16.8–10 *quid si rubicunda benigni | corna uepres et pruna ferant? si quercus et ilex | multa fruge pecus multa dominum iuuet umbra?* He is specifically recalling, and creating an association with, the old man's plot, as is clear from what follows: 11 *dicas adductum propius frondere Tarentum* (147–8n.).

ministrantem platanum potantibus: cf. Hor. *Odes* 2.11.13–17 *cur non sub alta uel platano uel hac | pinu iacentes … | potamus?*

147–8 The closing frame for the *praeteritio* signalled at 116–19 (see n.). Subsequent authors took literally the words *aliis post me memoranda relinquo* – merely a part of the fiction of *praeteritio*; Horace clearly identified V.'s setting with his own farm (145–6n. and Thomas (1982a) 13–15), and Columella, in the preface to his treatment of gardens (10, *praef.* 3), which is written in poetry and in dactylic hexameters in honour of V., states: *postulatio tua … ut poeticis numeris explerem Georgici carminis* *omissas partes, quas tamen et ipse Vergilius significauerat posteris se memorandas relinquere.*

147 equidem: cf. 116 (and n.).

spatiis exclusus iniquis: cf. Cic. *Verr.* 2.1.148 *angustiis temporis excluduntur*; also *A.* 5.203 (in a different sense) *spatio . . . iniquo*.

148 praetereo atque . . . relinquo: a formulaic part of the *praeteritio*; cf. Cic. *Verr.* 2.3.106 *audistis haec, iudices; quae nunc ego omnia praetereo et relinquo.*

149–96 de apium natura et laboribus

Having treated *situs*, climate, and to some extent produce, V. proceeds to the major ethnographical category, which is also the core of his account, the description and cultural assessment of the inhabitants. He deals in the same cultural terms as have pertained throughout; the bees belong to the age of Jupiter (149–50, 154, 177, 178–9, 193nn.) and are practitioners of *labor* (156–7, 184nn.). Along with this essential characterization V. depicts them as an intensely communal society (again a feature of the ethnographical tradition), lacking in individual motives and existing only for the good of the hive. Many of the details of the description are traditional, taken chiefly from Aristotle (*H.A.* 623b26–627b22) or Varro (*R.R.* 3.16.4–9), but V. develops this material with two major concerns: the bees' society is the equivalent of a human one (the bee-keeper and the didactic addressee are absent) and in its *nature* their society is motivated by toil.

149–50 Nunc age . . . | expediam: the tone is elevated, as in the two other instances of this combination in V. (*A.* 6.756–9 – the beginning of Anchises' prophecy; *A.* 7.37–40 – the invocation of Erato and beginning of the second half of the *Aeneid*). The device is Lucretian in flavour (2.62–6; 6.738–9).

naturas apibus quas Iuppiter ipse | addidit: the words characterize the nature of the bees as post-Saturnian. This connection is ensured by *addidit*, which V. otherwise uses in the poem (also with Jupiter as subject) only in the account of the transition from the age of Saturn at 1.129 *ille malum uirus serpentibus addidit atris.*

150–2 'in payment for which they fed the king of heaven in the shelter of a cave on Mt Dicte, as they followed the melodious sounds and clashing bronze of the Curetes'. V. refers to the concealment of Jupiter

from Saturn on Crete, and to his rewarding the bees who nurtured him
by imparting to them their *natura*. This particular detail, although the
basic story is as old as Hesiod (*Theog.* 453–80), may be V.'s own
contribution. Callimachus (*H.* 1.49–50) has the 'works of the bees' first
appear on Mt Ida in Crete while Zeus was being hidden there, while
Nicander seems to have had bees born on Crete in the time of Saturn (*ap.*
Colum. 9.2.4). Aratus has the god nursed by bears (*Phaen.* 30–5). V. has
adapted the whole story to the cultural system of the *Georgics*: Jupiter's
reward for the bees is a *natura* which is characterized by *labor*, the key
element of his age; before this time honey was produced spontaneously
as a component of the age of Saturn, a feature which Jupiter ended
(1.131 *mellaque decussit foliis*).

V. has conflated the role of the bees with that of the Curetes, the
inhabitants of Crete who were said to have covered the cries of the infant
god by dancing around him and clashing their shields; in this he is
adapting Callim. *H.* 1.51–2 οὖλα δὲ Κούρητές σε περὶ πρύλιν ὠρχήσαντο |
τεύχεα πεπλήγοντες, 'and around you the Curetes danced a war-dance in
quick tempo, beating their armour'. V. suggests that the bees were
attracted by the sound (*secutae*), as they are by the cymbals of 64
tinnitusque cie et Matris quate cymbala circum.

150–1: the sound supports the sense: c̱anoros̱ | C̱uretum s̱onitus̱
c̱repitantiaque aera s̱ecutae.

152 Dictaeo ... sub antro: reminiscence of Callimachus
(150–2n.) is replaced by the influence of Apollonius: *Arg.* 1.509 Δικταῖον
ναίεσκεν ὑπὸ σπέος, 'he [the child Zeus] dwelt in a Dictaean cave'.

153–5 Some (including Servius) see the emphasis on the communal life of the bees as showing a debt to Plato, *Rep.* 457c10–d10, but
the claim for such a shared existence is a part of the ethnographical
tradition (Thomas (1982a) 89 n. 22), and V. probably has no specific
source in mind.

153, 155 solae: in contrast to 1.186 *inopi metuens formica senectae*, but
V. is concerned with the uniqueness of the bees' society (156–7n.).

communis ... consortia: emphatically placed and dominating the
line: 'in common they have their children, jointly they hold the dwellings of their city'.

154 magnisque agitant sub legibus aeuum: appropriate to the
age of Jupiter (cf. 149–96n.), for laws are necessary only after the
passing of the golden age; cf. *A.* 7.202–4 *'neue ignorate Latinos | Saturni*

gentem haud uinclo nec legibus aequam, | *sponte sua ueterisque dei se more tenentem'*; Ov. *M.* 1.89–90 *aurea prima sata est aetas, quae … sine lege fidem rectumque colebat.*

For the wording cf. *A.* 10.235 (where the sense is more concrete) *aeuumque agitare sub undis.*

155   patriam solae … nouere: *patria* is also used of trees (2.116), and horses (3.121); see 153n.

penatis: cf. 43 (and 42–3n.) *larem.* V. does not otherwise use *penates* of non-human beings (1–7n.), and it seems to be used elsewhere in this way only at Stat. *Silu.* 3.5.58–9 *uernos non sic Philomela penatis* | *circumit.*

156–7   uenturaeque … reponunt: cf. 1.186 (of the ant; 1.185–6n.) *inopi metuens formica senectae*; also *A.* 4.402–3 (of the Trojans) *ac uelut ingentem formicae farris aceruum* | *cum populant hiemis memores tectoque reponunt.* Cf. 3.403 (of man) *hiemique reponunt.*

laborem | **experiuntur:** identifies the age of Jupiter, controlled by the ethics of toil (149–96; 1.145–6nn.). Cf. also 1.4 *apibus quanta experientia parcis*, 118–19 *labores … experti.*

in medium quaesita reponunt: cf. 1.127 (of man in the Saturnian age) *in medium quaerebant*; but here forethought and thrift, absent from and unnecessary in the golden age (see n.), are in evidence.

158–69   V. describes the division of labour among the bees, employing *uariatio* in the nouns and pronouns he chooses: *aliae … pars … aliae … aliae …* | *sunt quibus.* This division continues in the simile of 170–5 *alii … alii.*

158   uictu inuigilant 'watch over the collecting of food'; *uictu* is dat., like *concubitu* for *concubitui* at 198.

159   agris 'in the fields', locative. The absence of *in* is here perhaps due to the fact that *exerceo* tends to be used for 'train somebody in [a skill, etc.]'; cf. Cic. *N.D.* 2.161 *exerceri in uenando.*

saepta domorum 'their enclosed dwellings'; for the construction (lit. 'the enclosures of their dwellings') cf. 1.478 *obscurum noctis*; *A.* 2.332 *angusta uiarum*, 725 *opaca locorum*; and esp. 11.882 *tuta domorum.*

160   narcissi lacrimam: though the exudation of flowers is elsewhere referred to as 'tears' (cf. δάκρυον in Greek), Servius may well be right in supposing that V. intends a secondary reference to Narcissus' weeping over his own reflection; cf. from Ovid's version of the story at *M.* 3.475 *lacrimis turbauit aquas.*

lentum de cortice gluten: i.e. *propolis*; cf. 40 (and 40–1 n.) *collectum-que haec ipsa ad munera gluten.*

161   prima … fundamina 'as the first foundations', in apposition to *lacrimam* and *gluten.*

161–2   tenacis | suspendunt ceras: cf. 247 (of the hive's enemy) *laxos in foribus suspendit aranea cassis.*

162–9   Reproduced (without 165–6) almost verbatim at *A.* 1.431–6, in a simile for *human* activity, the building activities of the Carthaginians (*qualis apes … | exercet … labor*). Cf. the inversion between 170–5 (bees compared to Cyclopes) and *A.* 8.449–53, where the lines are reproduced, but now applied to the *reality* of the Cyclopes' work. In two consecutive passages, then, reality is used to create a simile, and simile to create reality.

162   spem gentis: in apposition to *adultos | … fetus.* Cf. 3.73 *spem … gentis*, 473 (and n.) *spemque gregemque simul cunctamque ab origine gentem.* The second of these refers to the utter destruction of the livestock, and the present words come somewhat ominously, to be recalled when the hive too fails; see 281–2 and n.

162–3   adultos … fetus: they are full-grown because not produced by sexual generation; cf. 198–9.

educunt: they are led out to be taught their tasks, not, as some think, as a swarm. There is perhaps a play on *educatio* 'upbringing'.

164   liquido … nectare: a periphrasis for honey, repeating the idea of the previous clause. At *E.* 5.71 *nectar = uinum.*

165   sorti: predicative dative: 'there are those to whom guard-duty at the gates has fallen as a lot'. Some see it as an archaic ablative, the phrase *cecidit sorti* ('it falls to them by lot') being paralleled by *sorti euenit*, found in Livy (4.37.6; 28.45.11; 31.6.1). But V. elsewhere uses *sorte* for the ablative, as he could have done here – the one exception, at *A.* 9.271, is not at line-end.

166   speculantur aquas et nubila caeli: the verb is used of prognostication at 1.257 *nec frustra signorum obitus speculamur et ortus.* It is a mark of the bees' cultural status (149–96n.) that they observe *signa.*

167   agmine facto: only used by V. of bees (here and *A.* 1.434) and the winds (*A.* 1.82).

168   ignauum fucos pecus 'the drones, an idle bunch'; for the enclosing word-order see 2.146–7n. *pecus* has a strongly derogatory tone, as at Hor. *Sat.* 1.3.100 *mutum et turpe pecus* and *Epist.* 1.19.19 *o imitatores, seruum pecus.*

praesepibus: otherwise used in V. (and, it seems, in Latin) of the stalls of cattle, horses, and the like; cf. 3.416–17 (where the *praesepia* are also threatened, by the snake). V. again suggests the shared nature of his worlds.

169   Encapsulates the results of the preceding activity.

feruet opus: cf. *A.* 4.407 (of ants, in a simile) *opere omnis semita feruet*, 409–10 (of the Trojans, outside the simile) *cum litora feruere late | prospiceres.* Page sees the verb ('is aglow') as an anticipation of the image of the Cyclopes at their smithy.

170–5   The simile is reproduced, no longer in a simile (162–9n.), at *A.* 8.449–53, describing the making of Aeneas' armour. V. doubtless took the account from Callim. *H.* 3.46–61 (cf. 173, 174–5nn.; for a secondary source, cf. 172–3n.). See 171–2, 173, 175nn. for significant differences in language between the two passages – the change from *magna* (174) to *multa* (*A.* 8.452) is insignificant.

V. again plays on the element of size (3n.), equating the tiny bees with the giant Cyclopes, and subsequently commenting on the disparity: 176 *si parua licet componere magnis.* Those who see V.'s bees as bees and nothing more generally feel that the comparison is excessive, and label the lines mock-heroic (86–7n.).

170–1   **ac ... properant** 'and just as the Cyclopes when they are busied in forging bolts from malleable ore ...' The introduction to the simile is (naturally) not a part of the description in *A.* 8.

ac ueluti: see 176n.

171–2   **alii ... alii:** responds to *aliae ... pars ... aliae*, etc. at 158–69 (see n.).

taurinis follibus 'with ox-hide bellows'; cf. Plaut. *Bacch.* 10 *folles taurini.* Elsewhere the epithet seems to be used (until Statius) to mean 'of or from a bull' (e.g. Cat. 66.34 *taurino sanguine*), and at *A.* 8.449 V. replaces it with *uentosis* (less audacious?).

auras | accipiunt redduntque 'make the blasts come and go'; i.e. work the bellows.

172–3   **stridentia tingunt | aera lacu:** significantly developed from Hom. *Od.* 9.391–2 (a simile describing the blinding of the Cyclops by Odysseus and his men) 'as when a blacksmith dips a great axe-blade or adze, greatly screaming [cf. *stridentia*], into cold water, and so tempers it'.

lacu: not merely an epicism for *aqua* (so Page), but also reflecting the scale of the Cyclopes; though the root sense is 'basin', V. doubtless intends 'lake'.

173 gemit impositis incudibus Aetna: cf. 2.540 *impositos duris crepitare incudibus ensis*, where swords are placed on the anvil, while in the present line it is the anvil which is placed in Aetna. The personification of Aetna groaning with the weight of the anvils may owe something to the aetiological account (well known from Pindar's first Pythian ode) which connects the volcano's activity with the groaning of Typhoeus, buried by Zeus beneath the mountain. Callimachus is also an influence: cf. *H.* 3.56 αὖε γὰρ Αἴτνη, 'for Aetna cried out' (as the Cyclopes worked their forges); see 170–5, 174–5nn.

Aetna: changed to *antrum* at *A.* 8.451, perhaps to avoid repetition, since the workers at 8.440 had already been referred to as *Aetnaei Cyclopes*.

The Cyclopes are traditionally associated with Mt Aetna (e.g. at Eur. *Cycl.* 20), and figured in this connection at 1.471–3 (see n.).

174–5 illi inter sese magna ui bracchia tollunt | in numerum: adapted from Callim. *H.* 3.59–61 εὖθ' οἵ γε ῥαιστῆρας ἀειράμενοι ὑπὲρ ὤμων | ... χαλκὸν ... | ἀμβολαδὶς τετυπόντες, 'when they lifted their hammers above their shoulders and struck the bronze with rhythmic swing'. V. conveys the rhythm of the work with five spondees in 174. There is debate about Callimachus' ἀμβολαδίς, but V. (whose view is not considered by the commentators on Callimachus) clearly took it to mean 'rhythmically' (*in numerum*).

Line 174 recalls 3.220 (the battle of the rival bulls) *illi alternantes multa ui proelia miscent*, and at *A.* 12.720 (also such a battle, in a simile) V. seems to conflate that line with this: *illi inter sese multa ui uulnera miscent*.

175 ferrum: changed to *massam* at *A.* 8.453, a word already used at 170; see 173n. V. perhaps suggests that the raw material, the ore, has now become iron.

176 non aliter: with *ac ueluti* (170) providing the entrance to and exit from the simile, as at *A.* 12.715–23 *ac uelut ... non aliter.*

si parua licet componere magnis: see 170–5n., and cf. *E.* 1.23 *sic paruis componere magna solebam.*

177 Cecropias: the honey from the bees of Athens, specifically of Mt Hymettus, was proverbial.

innatus ... amor ... habendi: the words have a distinct cultural connotation: at *A.* 8.326–7, when the age of Saturn finally ends in Latium, it is replaced by the war and acquisitiveness of an inferior age: *deterior ... ac decolor aetas | et belli rabies et amor successit habendi*; and cf. Ovid's bronze age: *amor sceleratus habendi, M.* 1.131. In those two passages the critical stance is explicit, whereas here the implications are more subtle, but they undoubtedly set the bees' society in the age of Jupiter, and present it as subject to the ethics of that age (149–96n.).

178 munere quamque suo 'each in his own sphere of activity'.

178–9 'the aged have charge over the towns, both the building of hives and the fashioning of intricately worked houses'. The two infinitives in 179 are in apposition to the idea contained in *oppida curae*, which should therefore be followed (as it is not in most editions) by a comma.

grandaeuis: a lofty word (cf. *grandaeuus Nereus*, 392), used outside the human sphere only here, at Prop. 2.25.6 (with obvious mock elevation) *grandaeuique negant ducere aratra boues*, and in Cassiodorus.

oppida ... munire: the mention of towns and the building of walls (*munire* is from *moenia*) again suggests the age of Jupiter; cf. *E.* 4.31–3 *pauca tamen suberunt priscae uestigia fraudis | ... quae cingere muris | oppida ... iubeant*; see also 193; 2.155–7nn.

daedala fingere tecta: the bees have *ars*, which sets them in the age of *labor*; cf. 56–7 (and 56, 57nn.) *arte ... mella tenacia fingunt.*

180 fessae multa referunt se nocte: cf. 3.467 (of the sick sheep) *serae solam decedere nocti*; also 4.132–3 *seraque reuertens | nocte domum.* The words *multa ... nocte* ('far into the night') fly in the face of fact and are designed to stress the toil of the bees.

minores: in contrast with *grandaeuis,* 178.

181 crura thymo plenae 'their legs loaded with thyme'; *crura* is accusative of respect.

181–3 Cf. 30–2n. for a similar list – there the bee-keeper is to plant them in the vicinity of the hive. Of the six mentioned here three occur elsewhere in connection with bees: *casia* (30, 304; 2.213), linden (141) and *hyacinthus* (137).

181 pascuntur: also in the initial position at 3.314 (of goats) *pascuntur uero siluas et summa Lycaei*; see n.

182   glaucas salices: cf. 2.13 *glauca canentia fronde salicta.*

183   pinguem tiliam: cf. 141, where *uberrima* is ἀπὸ κοινοῦ with *tiliae* and *pinus*; it is called 'rich' for the *propolis* it supplies.

ferrugineos: probably 'purple', 'dark blue', which seems to be the sense of *obscura . . . ferrugine* at 1.467 (see n.), but certainty is hindered by doubts about the exact meaning of *hyacinthus* (137n.).

184   An artful line, with anaphora of *omnibus* and *una/unus* helping to convey the communal nature of the bees' entire existence.

labor omnibus unus: cf. 3.244 *amor omnibus idem,* and see 1.145–6n. on the ways in which V., particularly between the *Eclogues* and *Georgics,* suggests a connection between *amor* and *labor,* two of the key themes of the two poems. Cf. too 212 *mens omnibus una est.*

185   mane ruunt portis, nusquam mora: the asyndeton conveys a sense of bustle and activity. Cf. 3.110 *nec mora nec requies; at . . .* ; 4.548 *haud mora, continuo matris praecepta facessit.*

ruunt portis: cf. 78 *erumpunt portis.* In both cases military activity is implied; cf. Livy 27.41.8 *eques pedesque certatim portis ruere.*

186–7   Vesper ubi e pastu tandem decedere campis | admonuit: the words have a strong pastoral flavour; cf. 434 *Vesper ubi e pastu uitulos ad tecta reducit*; also 3.467 *serae solam decedere nocti.* See too 1.381 *e pastu decedens.*

decedere: cf. 1.456–7n.

187   tecta: the dwellings are described in human terms; cf. 189 (and n.) *thalamis,* 191 *stabulis,* 193 *sub moenibus urbis.*

tum corpora curant: an expression belonging to the human domain, normally referring to eating, washing, etc.; cf. *A.* 3.511 *corpora curamus.*

188   fit sonitus: as at 79, just prior to the battle.

mussantque oras et limina circum: 'this beautiful phrase descriptive equally of the bees and of an evening gossip on the doorstep' (Page); cf. *A.* 11.454 (of the muttering of Latin elders) *mussantque patres*; also 12.718 *mussantque iuuencae. oras,* distinct in sense from *oras* at 39 (39–40n.), seems to be synonymous with *limina.*

189   post, ubi . . . : on adverbial *post,* followed by a temporal clause introduced by *ubi,* see 3.235n.

thalamis: the only non-human (or non-divine) application of the word – though the epigrammatist Nicias (third century B.C.) has κηρο-παγὴς θάλαμος, 'waxen chamber', *A.P.* 9.564.4.

189–90 siletur | in noctem 'silence reigns on into the night'; cf. *A.* 7.8 *aspirant aurae in noctem.*

190 sopor … occupat artus: cf. *A.* 7.446; 11.424 *tremor occupat artus.*

suus: 'which is dear to them', or 'which they have deserved'; cf. 22 *uere suo.*

191–6 An expansion of Arat. *Phaen.* 1028–30 'and when a great storm approaches the tawny bees do not go a great distance to gather their wax, but they circle right by their honey and their hive [lit. 'works']'. V. had omitted this detail in his adaptation of Aratus' storm-signs at 1.351–92 – doubtless saving it for the present context (cf. 191n.).

191 nec uero a stabulis … recedunt: so when the storm threatens at 1.354–5 *quid saepe uidentes | agricolae propius stabulis armenta tenerent.*

pluuia impendente: cf. 1.365 *uento impendente*; 191–6n.

192 credunt caelo 'trust the sky'; cf. *A.* 5.870 *o nimium caelo et pelago confise sereno.* This is easier than understanding *se*: 'entrust themselves to the sky [i.e. to flight]'.

aduentantibus Euris: cf. 1.356 *uentis surgentibus.*

193 tutae sub moenibus urbis aquantur: creates not only a human image, but an image of man in a culturally advanced setting (cf. 149–96, 178–9nn.). The line also has military implications: *aquor* is used almost exclusively of armies, etc. replenishing their water-supplies.

194–6 et saepe | … librant: V. has taken this erroneous idea from Aristotle: 'whenever a great wind comes up they take on a pebble as a defence against its blasts', *H.A.* 626b24. The detail conveys the fragility of the bees' existence and leads into the appealing simile of 195.

195 'as unsteady skiffs take on ballast when the sea is tossing'.

196 inania 'insubstantial'; cf. *A.* 10.82 *uentos … inanis.*

197–209 Reproductive habits and life-expectancy

How bees are generated seems to have been a ζήτημα ('matter of debate'). Aristotle (*H.A.* 553a16–25) gives various theories: they are produced either by the flower of *callyntron* (an unidentified shrub), reed or olive, or by the king. He also reports a view that is half correct, that the male drone mates with the female worker. V., although earlier implying copulation (139 *ergo apibus fetis*; see n.), here chooses to deny any sexual means of reproduction, having a female worker-bee pick young bees from the leaves. This denial allows him to stress their real *amor*, which is of toil and the production of honey (205n.), a love for which they even give up their lives.

197   morem (νόμον) suggests another ethnographical category (marriage and child-bearing are of great interest in this tradition, from Herodotus on), while *mirabere* suggests that the practice of the bees is an ethnographical θαῦμα ('marvel').

198   concubitu: cf. 3.130n. on V.'s restricted use of the word.

198-9   nec corpora segnes | in Venerem soluunt: these bees are distinguished from the rest of the world's creatures; cf. 3.242-4 *omne adeo genus in terris . . . | in furias ignemque ruunt; amor omnibus idem.* Orpheus, after losing Eurydice, is depicted in a similar way: *nulla Venus, non ulli animum flexere hymenaei*, 516.

nec ... fetus nixibus edunt: an apparent contradiction of 139 (see n.) *apibus fetis*; also 197-209n.

200-1   ipsae ... ipsae: i.e. without the help of males, also with the suggestion of spontaneous generation, 'of their own accord'; cf. 1.127-8 *ipsaque tellus | omnia . . . ferebat*; see n.

201   legunt: V. has them 'gathering' the young from the leaves, Aristotle (cf. 197-209n.) has them 'fetching' them (φέρειν).

regem paruosque Quirites: i.e. the entire population. Although the application of *Quirites* to the bees is audacious and apparently unparalleled, it need not imply that the bees stand allegorically for specifically Roman citizens. V.'s only other use of the word is also outside the context of Rome, an allusion to the false etymology (for which cf. Varro, *L.L.* 6.68) connecting *Quirites* with *Curenses: A.* 7.710 *priscique Quirites*.

202   aulasque et ... regna: the human approximation continues; with *regem* in the previous line *regna* looks forward to the next section (210-18, on the bees' loyalty to their king).

cerea regna: cf. *A.* 12.589 *cerea castra*.

203-5   In pursuit of their work they make the supreme sacrifice. The change of topic comes rather abruptly, and some have argued for transposition of the lines to follow 196. There is however a logic in the thought: the bees' individual devotion to the collective good results (206 *ergo*) in the continuance of the hive (206-9).

204   ultroque animam … dedere: as they do for their king at 218 *pulchramque petunt per uulnera mortem*; cf. also 238 *animasque in uulnere ponunt*. See also 3.495 (of the dying cattle) *animas … reddunt*; 3.547 (of the dying birds) *uitam … relinquunt*.

sub fasce: like the Roman soldier of 3.347 *iniusto sub fasce*.

205   tantus amor florum: cf. 2.301 (of the young vine-shoot) *tantus amor terrae*; 3.112 (of the stallion) *tantus amor laudum*. See too 2.272n.

206–7   ergo … | excipiat: *angusti* is emphatically placed: 'and so, though it is a short life whose limit awaits the individual bees [*ipsas*] …'

angusti: cf. 35n.

207   (neque enim plus septima ducitur aestas) 'for it does not extend beyond the seventh summer'; *quam* is omitted.

208   at genus immortale manet: the first suggestion of the hive's immortality (219–27n.); it is abandoned when disease strikes (281–2). In any case, in the very next words *immortale* is modified: *multosque per annos*.

208–9   multosque per annos | stat fortuna domus: the language suits a human situation; cf. *A.* 2.56 *Troiaque nunc staret, Priamique arx alta maneres.*

209   aui numerantur auorum: V.'s striving to depict the bees in human terms creates a logical inconsistency with his claims about regeneration at 197–202.

210–18   Devotion to the king

The bee's devotion to its leader is a traditional detail; cf. Varro, *R.R.* 3.16.8 *regem suum secuntur quocumque it, et fessum subleuant, et si nequit uolare succollant, quod eum seruare uolunt*. But V.'s mode of presenting this information, within the constant equation of bee and man, is hardly encouraging: the bee gives even greater reverence to its king than do the peoples of the east to their monarchs. Foremost of the eastern *exempla* is Egypt, and the words *regem non sic Aegyptus … obseruant* may refer to the *Aegyptia coniunx* (*A.* 8.688) of Antony, defeated by Octavian two years before the publication of the poem.

210   Praeterea: also used to begin a new section at 1.204; 2.83.

210–11   V. varies his manner of reference: *Aegyptus* (210–18n.) and *Lydia* are virtual metonymies (for Egyptians and Lydians), *populi Parth-*

orum is a straightforward reference to the Parthian peoples, while the
Medes are referred to by the river Hydaspes (in fact a tributary of the
Indus, but V.'s main concern here is merely to provide a strong eastern
flavour).

212   obseruant 'pay homage to'; in this sense (*OLD* s.v. 8) used
exclusively in political contexts, generally with opprobrium.

mens omnibus una est: cf. 184 (and n.) *omnibus una quies operum,
labor omnibus unus*. V. is unlikely to have considered such an outlook as
purely laudable.

213-14   Again the language is political: revolution follows the loss of
the king.

rupere ... | diripuere ... soluere: the perfects are either gnomic
('have been known to') or (so Page) express the rapidity of these actions
following the death of the king (like *ruperunt* at 1.49).

constructaque ... fauorum 'tear down the honey they have built
up and break up their trellised combs [lit. the trellises of their combs]'.

215   admirantur: cf. 3 *admiranda ... leuium spectacula rerum*; V.
otherwise uses the verb only twice, in the *Aeneid*. With a personal object
it implies respect or reverence, like *obseruant* at 212.

216   circumstant fremitu denso stipantque frequentes: V.
reproduces the shape of the line, with the same framing words, at *A.*
6.486 *circumstant animae dextra laeuaque frequentes*.

stipantque frequentes: so Dido's subjects throng about her: *stipante
caterua, A.* 1.497; 4.136.

218   pulchramque petunt per uulnera mortem: repeated in
a battle scene at *A.* 11.647, and cf. 9.401 (of Nisus) *pulchram properet
per uulnera mortem?*; also 204 (and n.) *ultroque animam sub fasce dedere*,
where *ultro* implies the same willingness for self-sacrifice as *pulchram*
here.

219-27   On the immortality of the bees

Some have inferred from the bees' behaviour that they have a share of
the divine and that their souls are immortal. Richter has a good treatment of the philosophical basis to this theory, which goes back at least
to Aristotle. Some use the passage as evidence that the bees are distinct
from all other creatures subject to *labor*, and that the rebirth they will
find through *bugonia* (cf. 281–314n.) ensures them an immortality which
constitutes the redeeming element, the success, of the poem. Such a view

needs to be weighed against the fact that the passage, in its pantheism, makes the same claims for bees as for other, larger, creatures (223 and n.), and to that extent the bees are merely being elevated to the level of man and the beasts – on which they have already existed throughout. It also must be pointed out that the present lines are completely in indirect speech (219–21n.), forming the equivalent of a footnote, a citation of the views of some people (219 *quidam*). See also 225n.

219–21 V. nowhere commits himself to the theory – there is no indicative other than *dixere*. Nowhere else in the poem does he dissociate himself in this way (219–27n.).

220–1 esse ... dixere 'have said that the bees have a share of divine intelligence and drink of heavenly ether'; their partial divinity is presented metaphorically, as they are imagined as 'drinking in' the ethereal elements. Cf. Petron. *Sat.* 56 *apes enim ego diuinas bestias puto*; by this time the idea is clearly a topos. For V.'s wording cf. Hor. *Sat.* 2.2.79 *diuinae particulam aurae.*

221–2 Pure pantheism, held by commentators to be typical of the Virgilian attitude throughout the poem (but cf. 219–21n.). The view is in essence a combination of Stoic and Pythagorean theory, but V. may also have in mind the famous opening of Aratus' *Phaenomena*: μέσται δὲ Διὸς πᾶσαι μὲν ἀγυιαί, | πᾶσαι δ' ἀνθρώπων ἀγοραί, μεστὴ δὲ θάλασσα | καὶ λιμένες, 'full of Zeus are all the streets and all the market-places of men, full of him is the sea and the harbours', 2–4.

222 Repeated from *E.* 4.51. Cf. *A.* 1.58; 3.193; 6.724 for variations on the tricolon referring to earth, sea and heavens; also see 3.242–3n. Cf. 1.152–3n. on the quantity of the first *-que.*

223 hinc: i.e. *ex deo*; cf. 225 *huc.*

pecudes, armenta, uiros, genus omne ferarum: bees are equated with man and the larger creatures of the world (219–27n.). Cf. 3.242–3 *omne adeo genus in terris* ... ; in those lines they are all affected by a different power: *in furias ignemque ruunt; amor omnibus idem*, 244. Cf. too *A.* 6.728 (a similar context, the cosmology of Anchises) *inde hominum pecudumque genus uitaeque uolantum.*

224 '[from god] each one of these, as it comes to life, draws its thin-spun life to itself'.

225 scilicet: here used to qualify the assumption to which it is attached, and thus to contribute to the distancing effect of the indirect speech (219–27n.): 'and they evidently say that everything is restored to him ...'

huc: i.e. *ad deum*; cf. 223 *hinc*.

reddi . . . ac resoluta referri: the repeated prefixes stress the idea of the soul's returning to the deity from which it derived, though *resoluta* ('broken down') is somewhat different from the other two verbs.

226   uiua uolare: cf. Enn. *Epigr.* 18 V. *uolito uiuus* (and see 3.8–9n.).

227   sideris in numerum 'into the place of a star'; i.e. 'so as to rank as a star'. The singular *sideris* rules out the sense 'into the number of the stars', which as Conington notes is not really paralleled by Lucr. 1.436 (*corporis augebit numerum*), where *corpus* is used in a collective sense.

228–50   *Methods and seasons for gathering honey; pests*

The didactic stance, in abeyance since 115, returns, and with it an ominous progression develops. After telling how and when to collect the honey V. advises fumigating the hive with thyme, for this keeps away the various pests which are prone to attack it. In the very next section (251–80) disease will be the topic, and by 281–2 the hive has been wiped out. This is, in microcosm, the very pattern which developed at the end of book 3: the advice to fumigate (3.414–15) was justified by the tendency of those more dire *pestes*, snakes, to get into the stable (416–39 *saepe* . . . ; cf. 4.242 *nam saepe* . . .), and treatment of them was immediately followed by the disease and plague which destroyed the livestock and tainted the countryside (440–566). See 251–80, 281–2nn.

Varro treats the gathering of honey at *R.R.* 3.16.32–8.

228   Si quando: used at 1.259; 2.128; 3.98, only here as the first words of a paragraph.

angustam: this reading, found in the Romanus and a number of ninth-century MSS, is rejected by modern editors in favour of *augustam*, which the lofty word *thesauris* is considered to support. However, though *thesauris* is apt for storehouses of honey, there seems no good reason for a lofty adjective to modify *sedem* (particularly given the purely didactic nature of the advice which follows at 229–30). On the other hand, *angustus* is used throughout (35, 83, 206, 296) to define the bees' world, and Varro (*R.R.* 3.16.15–16) stresses the need for narrow hives (*coangustent . . . angustissimas*). Given the political resonances in V.'s treatment of the bees, and particularly the recent depiction of their monarchy (210–18), *augustam* will easily have ousted *angustam*. It is worth noting that the adjective *augustus* is very rare in V., and is reserved for a single special application: it occurs only at *A.* 7.153 and 170 of the city or palace of Latinus.

229   relines 'unseal', 'uncork', a very rare word, otherwise found, in a more literal sense than here, perhaps only at Ter. *Heaut.* 460 *releui dolia omnia.*

229–30   prius haustu sparsus aquarum | ora foue 'first with a draught of water sprinkle and freshen your mouth'. At 2.135 *ora fouent* is used of freshening the breath. V. has already noted the bees' sensitivity to foul smells at 49 (*odor caeni grauis*), and Columella (9.14.3) recommends general cleanliness when approaching the hive, including cleanliness of breath: *abstineatque omnibus redolentibus esculentis.* The variant *ore faue* ('keep silence') is clearly less to the point.

231   Cf. 2.150 *bis grauidae pecudes, bis pomis utilis arbos.* The subject of *cogunt* is unspecified, a feature familiar from Book 3 (3.123–4n.). *fetus* refers to the honey.

V. follows Aristotle (*H.A.* 626b29) in recommending two gatherings, one in May and one in November (Aristotle merely specifies spring and autumn), while Varro has a third gathering at the beginning of September (*R.R.* 3.16.34).

232–3   V. produces a literary intensification in this periphrasis for the rising of the Pleiades (in Varro merely *Vergiliarum exortu*, *R.R.* 3.16.34); the same phenomenon was treated with similar care at 1.221–2 (see n. and 1.222n.). With the appositional *Taygete ... Pleas*, he has one of the seven standing for the whole group (the Pleiades were the daughters of Atlas and Pleione); this detail probably comes from Arat. *Phaen.* 263, where all seven are named (Callimachus seems to have had his own list, different from that of Aratus except that it includes Maia; see fr. 693 Pf.). At the same time, in the wording of 233 V. alludes to Aratus' characterization of the constellations of the Bears at *Phaen.* 48 (which he had already closely adapted at 1.244–6; see n.) κυανέου πεφυλαγμέναι ὠκεανοῖο, 'which shun the blue ocean'. But a secondary reference seems to be active in the words *spretos pede*, for which V. is indebted to the famous ending of Callim. *H.* 2 (ποδί τ' ἤλασεν, 'spurned with his foot', 107), describing Apollo's actions against Envy, immediately preceding his rejection of the 'great flood of the Assyrian river', which, as Williams (1978) 85–9 has shown, is itself a reference to the Homeric 'flood of Ocean', from which all rivers flow (so V.'s *Oceani ... amnis*).

232 os terris ostendit honestum: like Bacchus at 2.392 *quocumque deus circum caput egit honestum.*

234–5 For a similar but more allusive periphrasis for the setting of the Pleiades cf. 1.221 and n.

234 Piscis aquosi: i.e. in the rainy season of November (though the sun does not enter Pisces until late winter). At *A.* 4.52 V. signifies winter in a similar way: *dum pelago desaeuit hiems et aquosus Orion.*

235 For a similarly vivid depiction of the setting of a constellation cf. *A.* 7.719.

236 illis ira modum supra est: this looks like an ethical judgement; cf. Hor. *Epist.* 1.2.59 *qui non moderabitur irae | infectum uolet esse dolor quod suaserit et mens.*

236–7 laesaeque ... inspirant 'and when hurt they breathe poison into their bites'; the counterfeit Ascanius was to have a similar effect on Dido at *A.* 1.688 *occultum inspires ignem fallasque ueneno.*

237 spicula caeca 'unseen darts'; cf. 74 *spiculaque exacuunt.* As in 236–7 there seems to be a hint of the darts of love; cf. *A.* 4.1–2.

238 adfixae uenis 'having fastened on the veins'; *adfixae* has middle force.

animasque in uulnere ponunt: cf. 204 (and n.) *animam sub fasce dedere*; the awareness that the bee, in stinging, often loses part of its intestines is at least as old as Aristotle.

239 sin duram metues hiemem: as the bees themselves do at 156 (156–7n.) *uenturaeque hiemis memores.* Cf. 2.333n. on the connection between *metus/metuo* and the forces of nature.

240 The style is lofty; cf. *A.* 2.13 *fracti bello fatisque repulsi,* 170 *fractae uires*; 3.53 *opes fractae Teucrum.*

241 at: also introduces the apodosis, and follows the protasis, at *A.* 1.542–3 *si genus humanum et mortalia temnitis arma, | at sperate ...*

241–2 at suffire thymo ... | quis dubitet?: fumigation is recommended, as at 3.414 *disce et odoratam stabulis accendere cedrum*; see 228–50, 242–50nn.

cerasque recidere inanis: the advice is traditional; cf. Varro, *R.R.* 3.16.34 *faui qui eximuntur, siqua pars nihil habet aut habet incunatum, cultello praesicatur.*

242–50 Fumigation and cleaning are necessitated by the threat of various *pestes,* just as the threshing-floor (1.181–6) and the stable (3.414–39) were threatened, in the first case by a similar variety of creatures, in the second by the snake (*pestis acerba boum,* 3.419); see

228–50n. Varro merely states the need to clear out vermin (*uermiculos eicere*, *R.R.* 3.16.17), but V. has incorporated the topic into his larger scheme.

242 nam saepe ... adedit | stelio: with *saepe* and the gnomic perfect V. looks back to 3.416–17 *saepe* ... | *uipera delituit*, which also immediately follows the need to fumigate (242–50n.), and itself leads into the account of disease (228–50n.); cf. also 1.181–2 (the attack on the threshing-floor) *saepe exiguus mus ... posuitque ... atque ... fecit.*

243 stelio 'newt'; the *i* is consonantal.

et ... blattis 'and swarms of light-shunning beetles'; *adederunt* must then be supplied from *adedit*. This is rather an odd way of putting it (cf. in English 'whole roomfuls of beetles'), but seems preferable to the syntactical disjunction which comes from supplying *sunt* with *congesta*: 'their chambers have been crowded with beetles' (the construction with *adedit* then has to be resumed at 244).

lucifugis: the first neutral instance of the adjective, used by Lucilius and Cicero of men, as a term of abuse.

cubilia: cf. 45n.

244 'and the drone who sits without sharing the toil at a meal which belongs to others'; the drone seems to have stirred V. to moral outrage; cf. 168 (and n.) *ignauum fucos pecus* – though he is not unique in this attitude: *fur qui uocabitur, ab aliis fucus ...*, Varro, *R.R.* 3.16.19. In fact he is adapting two passages from Hesiod, who compares the man who does not work (ἀεργός = *immunis*) to a drone which 'eats without working' (ἀεργοὶ | ἔσθοντες, *W.D.* 305–6) and which elsewhere 'reaps the toil of others into its own belly' (ἀλλότριον [= *aliena*] κάματον σφετέρην ἐς γαστέρ' ἀμῶνται, *Theog.* 599). Some see a reference to the description of Penelope's suitors as men who 'with impunity eat up the substance of another' (ἀλλότριον βίοτον νήποινον ἔδουσιν, Hom. *Od.* 1.160), but the Hesiodic passages seem to provide the necessary literary details. The connection between idleness and sponging is natural; cf. Ter. *Eun.* 265 (of the parasite Gnatho) *uiden otium et cibu' quid facit alienu'?*

245 imparibus se immiscuit armis 'closes with their [the bees'] ill-matched arms'; *armis* is dative, rather than ablative ('with its [the hornet's] superior arms'): cf. *A.* 10.796 and 11.815, where *se immiscuit* is found with unambiguous instances of the dative *armis.*

246 dirum tiniae genus: cf. 2.146–7n. for the enclosing word-order, and see esp. 168 *ignauum fucos pecus.* Cf. Hor. *Sat.* 2.3.118–19 *stragula uestis,* | *blattarum et tinearum epulae.*

246–7 inuisa Mineruae | ... aranea: an oblique reference, in the Alexandrian mode (1.14–15n.), to Arachne (ἀράχνη, 'spider'), the Lydian weaver who challenged Minerva to a weaving contest and was turned into a spider for her arrogance. Servius charges V. with confusion in his use of the feminine *aranea* (normally 'spider-web') instead of *araneus*; but for his allusion to the myth V. needed the feminine, and he had the precedent of Cat. 68.49 *tenuem texens sublimis aranea telam.*

248–9 quo magis exhaustae fuerint, hoc acrius ...: cf. 3.309–10 *quam magis exhausto spumauerit ubere mulctra, | laeta magis ...*

249 generis lapsi sarcire ruinas 'to repair the ruin of their fallen race', foreshadowing the end of the hive through disease: 281–2 (see n.).

250 foros 'rows [of cells]', derived from the sense 'rows of seats' (in the theatre), rather than 'paths', 'passages' (*OLD*).

251–80 Disease

Like the animals of Book 3 the bees succumb to disease (cf. 251–2, 252, 253, 254, 259, 261–3, 264, 267, 269, 270, 271–8onn.), and to a disease which is as final as the plague of that book (281–2n.). On the plausibility of *bugonia* as a remedy see 281–314n.

251–2 The protasis lacks an apodosis, as at 67 (see n.). It might have been expected to contain didactic remedies ('if the bees become ill, they can be cured in the following way'); its absence implies the absence of a cure.

quoniam casus apibus quoque nostros | uita tulit: bees are no more exempt from disease than the rest of the world which, including man (cf. 3.563–6n.), was subject to affliction and destruction.

251 The rhythm is unusual, with coincidence of accent and ictus only in the sixth foot.

252 tristi languebunt corpora morbo: a clear reminiscence of the Lucretian plague (and through it of the end of *Georgics* 3): 6.1156–7 *omne | languebat corpus leti iam limine in ipso,* 1221 *languebant pleraque morbo; langueo* occurs only here in the *Georgics.*

253 Knowledge of *signa*, symptoms, does not bring remedy. So at 3.440 (the opening line of the account of disease and plague) *morborum quoque te causas et signa docebo.* And in Book 1 civil war came in spite of the *prognostica* which preceded it: 1.351 (see n.), 394.

254 continuo est aegris alius color 'when they become ill their colour changes immediately'; cf. 91–9 on the markings of the healthy bee. See 3.498–9, 499–500, 507–8nn. for a similar progression from the description of healthy to diseased livestock.

254–5 horrida uultum | deformat macies: the sick bee somewhat resembles the inferior king (*ille horridus alter*, 93), as well as his people (*aliae turpes horrent*, 96). V. is drawing from Varro, *R.R.* 3.16.20 *minus ualentium signa, si sunt pilosae et horridae.*

255–6 tum ... ducunt: the language is that of human burial: *exporto* (like *effero*; Gr. ἐκφέρω) is virtually a technical verb, as is the combination *funera ducere*. Columella (9.13.7), who uses the verb *effero*, likens the bees' actions to a public mourning: *ut in publico luctu.*

luce carentum: used of the shades at 472 *simulacraque luce carentum* = Lucr. 4.35 (of visions).

257 illae: draws attention to the subject (3.217–18n.).

pedibus: with *conexae*, rather than *pendent* (though in a sense it goes with both): 'with feet linked they hang at the entrance-ways'; cf. the hanging bees at *A.* 7.66–7.

259 ignauaeque fame: hunger causes them to resemble the drones: 168 *ignauum fucos pecus.*

contracto: it is hard to decide whether V. intends the adjective as a strict modifier of *frigore* ('with the cold they have caught') or as transferred from the bees ('torpid with pinched cold').

frigore: cold also attended the disease of Book 3: 441–3; and see 261–3n.

260 tum sonus auditur grauior: cf. 71–2 (as the bees are about to swarm) *et uox | auditur.*

tractimque susurrant 'there is a drawn-out rustling'.

261–3 The three similes abbreviate and modify Hom. *Il.* 14.394–9, where the clash between Greeks and Trojans is compared first to the roaring of the sea under the force of the North wind, then to the sound of a forest-fire, and finally to the sound of the wind among the oaks. V. compresses to a single line the two lines Homer gave to each vignette, and rearranges the order and the details so that the cold South wind (*frigidus ... Auster*) and the heat of the fire (*aestuat ... ignis*) frame the series (cf. 441–2n.). The illness of the bees is thus presented in terms of excess and imbalance of temperature, as was the disease of Book 3 (3.441–4n.).

261   ut quondam 'as at times'; cf. the simile at 3.99 *ut quondam in stipulis magnus sine uiribus ignis.*

262   mare sollicitum: cf. 2.503 (and n.) *sollicitant alii remis freta caeca.*

stridit: where it is possible to tell, V. prefers *strido* to *strideo* (556; *A.* 2.418; 4.689; 8.420; 12.691). Cf. 1.455–6n. on *ferueo/feruo.*

263   clausis ... fornacibus: cf. 1.472 (of Aetna) *ruptis fornacibus.*

264–80   Neither here nor at 3.445–69 do the suggested remedies avert the onset of disease (281–2n.). Columella paraphrases V.'s lines at 9.13.7.

264   galbaneos suadebo incendere odores: a clear reminiscence of 3.414–15 (the prelude to plague; see 3.414–39n.) *disce et odoratam stabulis accendere cedrum | galbaneoque agitare grauis nidore chelydros.* No other sure instance of *galbaneus* is found in Latin.

264–5   incendere ... inferre: for the infinitive following *suadeo, persuadeo,* etc. cf. 2.315–16n.

266   hortantem ... uocantem: agreeing with *te,* to be understood as the subject of *incendere* in 264: 'as you freely encourage them and call them in their weariness to their familiar food'.

fessas 'weary from disease'. The adjective creates a human pathos; it is used of the bees three times (cf. 180, 190), once of Proteus (403).

267   proderit: another ominous note; the verb (*profuit*) was used of remedies for the plague at 3.459, 509, remedies which turned out in the latter instance merely to revitalize the disease: *mox erat hoc ipsum exitio,* 3.511; see 3.509–14, 509nn.

tunsum gallae ... saporem: *tunsum* is a transferred epithet: 'the flavour of pounded oak-galls'; galls are an excrescence from trees, chiefly the oak.

268   igni pinguia multo: i.e. the must is concentrated by being boiled down.

269   psithia passos de uite racemos: actual wine, not just dried grapes; so at 2.93 *passo psithia utilior.* The suggestion recalls 3.509–14, where wine was given to the plague-ridden horse, only to bring on an even more violent death (cf. 267n.); cf. too 279n.

270   A *spondeiazon.*

Cecropiumque thymum: Mt Hymettus in Attica was famous for its thyme, as for its bees (177 *Cecropias ... apes*).

grave olentia: cf. 31 *grauiter spirantis,* 49 *odor ... grauis.*

centaurea 'centaury'; so called because it was the 'medicinal root of Chiron' (Χείρωνος ἐπαλθέα ῥίζαν, Nic. *Ther.* 500), whose art failed to cure plague at 3.549–50, as the plant fails to prevent the death of the hive (281–2n.).

271–80 The style is very much like that of the similar account of the gadfly at 3.146–56. This helps further to tie the illness of the bees to the troubles of the livestock in Book 3, for which the gadfly was a clear paradigm; 3.150–1, 152–3nn. The plant is probably a starwort (*Aster amellus*); it otherwise figures only in Columella (who is indebted to V.; see 264–80n.) and Sidonius, and V.'s motivation is surely entirely etymological (271–2, 277–8nn.).

271–2 est ... agricolae: the style is ecphrastic, with the emphatic *est* placed first and followed by the noun (*flos*) which will be the focus of the aetiology: cf. 3.146–7 *est lucos Silari circa ... uolitans, cui nomen asilo | Romanum est* (see n.). As the *asilus* came from Silarus (*a-Silaro*), so the *amellus* comes from the river Mella (*a-Mella*, 278). V. perhaps intends a secondary etymology: the plant cures sick bees, which presumably produce 'no honey' (*a-mell-*; i.e. α-privative).

nomen ... | fecere agricolae: a standard part of such *aetia*; cf. 3.280–1 *hippomanes uero quod nomine dicunt | pastores*, and see 3.280–3n.

272 facilis quaerentibus herba: unlike aconite, which can be collected by mistake – though not in the *Saturnia tellus* of Italy; cf. 2.152 and n.

273–4 namque ... ipse 'for itself golden [i.e. its centre], it raises a great bush from a single clump'; somewhat exaggerated.

274–5 sed ... nigrae 'but on its petals there is a crimson sheen beneath the dark violet'. Columella refers to this same combination of gold and purple at 9.4.4 (*amelli ... cuius est frutex luteus purpureus flos*), though he seems to have taken *ipse* as the foliage (264–80n.).

276 Being used often to decorate altars, it is also easily identified.

277 asper in ore sapor: like the citron of 2.126–7 (also aetiologically treated) *Media fert tristis sucos tardumque saporem | felicis mali*.

tonsis: by the animals grazing there (cf. 1.15 *tondent dumeta iuuenci*); some take it as a temporal indicator: 'when the hay has been cut'.

277–8 illum | pastores ... legunt: cf. 3.280–2 (and see 271–2n.) *hippomanes ... quod saepe malae legere nouercae.*

278 curua ... prope flumina Mellae: cf. Cat. 67.33 [*speculae*] *flauus quam molli praecurrit flumine Mella*, which specifies it as the river flowing by Brixia, north of the Po, of which it is a sub-tributary. It is otherwise obscure, and is doubtless chosen by V. purely for its etymological potential (271–2n.).

279   odorato radices incoque Baccho: wine is again used as a 'cure' (269n.).

280   Adapted from Varro, *R.R.* 3.16.28 *alii uuam passam et ficum cum pisierunt, affundunt sapam atque ex eo factas offas apponunt ibi quo foras hieme in pabulum procedere tamen possint.*

281–314   The death of the hive and bugonia

Like the livestock of Book 3 and in spite of prescribed remedies, the hive does fail suddenly (281 *subito*), completely (281 *proles . . . omnis*) and without hope of renewal (282). The plausible, technical material of the *Georgics* ends at 282, with the death of the hive, for what follows, the spontaneous birth of the bees through *bugonia*, has no place in the real world of the Italian farmer. Though the practice is mentioned by technical writers (not, however by Aristotle), since it is a fiction and an impossibility, it is not described in any detail by, for instance, Varro (*R.R.* 2.5.5; 3.16.4), who regards it as a piece of traditional lore (at 2.5.5 it is included with Jupiter's metamorphosis into a bull to abduct Europa). V. himself knew it was an impossibility, and he says as much by presenting it as an eastern θαῦμα ('marvel'); 287–94, 309nn. And who in the Mediterranean world would kill an ox in order to gain a hive? In *real* terms, then, the *bugonia* cannot stand as the solution to the problems of man and beast in the world of *labor*, the issue which has concerned V. throughout the poem. The sequence serves partly as a means of transition to the stories of Aristaeus and Orpheus, which occupy V. for the remainder of the book, and which set the poem on a different plane (Introduction, pp. 22–4). The *bugonia* reappears, and provides a frame for the second half of the book, at 537–58.

281–2   Belies the statement of 208 *at genus immortale manet* and recalls the fate of the livestock at 3.473, where the destruction is also total, *spemque gregemque simul cunctamque ab origine gentem*; cf. also 162n.

282   'and does not know from where to recall his race in a new line'. The expression is forced: *genus . . . nouae stirpis* is pleonastic and *nouae* is logically incompatible with *reuocetur*.

283   tempus: sc. *est*.

Arcadii ... magistri: an Alexandrian reference to Aristaeus – the only type of reference to him so far; cf. 1.14–15 (and n.). He is not named until 317 (315–32n.).

284 quoque modo: so at 120 – one of the few ways in which *quomodo* can appear in the hexameter; cf. 2.226n.

saepe: V. counters the fact that the process is miraculous and impossible by asserting its frequent occurrence, as at 3.274–5 (of the wind's impregnation of mares) *et saepe sine ullis | coniugiis uento grauidae (mirabile dictu)*.

285 insincerus 'rotting'; cf. Varro, *R.R.* 2.5.5 [*boue*] *putrefacto*.

altius: normally understood 'more deeply', the sense being elaborated by 286; and this is the sense of *altius expediam* at Tac. *Hist.* 4.12.1. But as *altius* belongs more to *expediam* than *repetens*, it should perhaps be taken 'in a higher mode', an entirely legitimate characterization of the style of the rest of the book (to which V. clearly refers with *omnem ... famam*); cf. Cic. *Fat.* 35 *licuit uel altius* [*dicere*]. Cf. *E.* 4.1 *paulo maiora canamus*.

286 expediam: the verb is somewhat elevated (285n.), as at 149–50, where it occurs with *nunc age* (see n.). Cyrene uses it of the explanation Proteus is to give to Aristaeus: *ut omnem | expediat morbi causam*, 396–7.

prima repetens ab origine: indicates that what follows is aetiological (as does *nam* in 287). So Aeneas, in response to questions about his identity from the disguised Venus: *o dea, si prima repetens ab origine pergam ..., A.* 1.372; and Dido instigates the narrative of *Aeneid* 2 and 3 with the command: *immo age et a prima dic, hospes, origine nobis | insidias ... Danaum ..., A.* 1.753–5.

287–94 V. takes eight lines to say '*bugonia* is practised in Egypt'. Some have seen this excess as a residual element of the *laudes Galli*, somewhat out of place once those lines had been removed following Gallus' disgrace and death. This is most unlikely (Introduction, pp. 13–16), and the lines must be understood in the context of the poem as V. published it (they could with some adjustment have been removed along with the hypothetical *laudes*). This colourful ethnographical notice serves to situate a miraculous phenomenon (*bugonia*) in the east, the provenance of ethnographical θαύματα ('marvels') in general. V. has entered the world of the sowing of dragons' teeth and harvests of warriors (2.140–2), and he characterizes *bugonia* as being of this nature by defining it as a θαῦμα at 309 (*modis ... miris*) and later at 554 (*dictu mirabile monstrum*); 281–314, 287, 289nn.

According to the requirements of the ethnographical tradition, V. defines the *situs* of Egypt by reference to its boundaries – Canopus in the west, Persia to the east and India to the south (somewhat imprecise).

287 nam: cf. 286n.; also 125 (and n.) *namque*.

Pellaei: i.e. Macedonian; a reference to Egypt through the Ptolemies, first used in such a way here.

fortunata: generally taken to refer to the richness of the soil, but more importantly it is appropriate to the mythical ethnographical nature of the passage. The adjective is regularly used of the Utopian Isles of the Blessed, traditionally described in the format of ethnography and home of θαύματα, like Egypt here (287–94n.); cf. Plaut. *Trin.* 549–51 *sicut fortunatorum memorant insulas, | quo cuncti qui aetatem egerint caste suam | conueniant*; also *A.* 6.638–9 (of Elysium, which is in the same Utopian tradition) *locos laetos et amoena uirecta | fortunatorum nemorum sedesque beatas*. See Thomas (1982a) 21–5.

289 'and sail about their countryside in painted skiffs' (instead of going in wagons, on foot, etc.). Another traditional, Herodotean θαῦμα, leading up to the central θαῦμα, the *bugonia*. The detail is identical in ethnographical status to that at 3.361–2 *undaque iam tergo ferratos sustinet orbis ...* The descriptive epithet (*pictis*) is typical in such contexts.

circum pictis uehitur sua rura phaselis: cf. Hor. *Sat.* 1.6.58–9 (with the same tmesis) *circum | me Satureiano uectari rura caballo*.

290 pharetratae 'quiver-bearing'; again an ethnographical epithet (cf. 289 *pictis*, 293 *coloratis*), very much like that at 2.168 (see n.) *Volscosque uerutos*. On the association between easterners and archery cf. 2.125 (and n.).

292 diuersa ruens septem ... in ora: the standard way of referring to the Nile; cf. *A.* 6.800 *septemgemini ... ostia Nili*. In Greek it is called 'seven-pathed' (ἑπτάπορος, Mosch. 2.51), 'seven-channelled' (ἑπτάρους, Aristoph. fr. 300), etc.

292–3 discurrit ... deuexus: the two compounds are carefully descriptive: the Nile branches *out* into its seven mouths after travelling *down* from India; *de-* is equivalent to Greek κατα-, used of progress towards the coast from either direction.

293 Ever so casually, V. states that the source of the Nile is in India; he was doubtless aware that the issue was perhaps the greatest geographical ζήτημα ('matter of debate') in antiquity. Callimachus has the river say ὃν οὐδ' ὅθεν οἶδεν ὁδεύω | θνητὸς ἀνήρ, 'I whose source no mortal man knows', *Ep. et Eleg. Min.* fr. 384. 31–2 Pf.; and cf. Hor. *Odes* 4.14.45 *fontium qui celat origines*. The debate was as old as Herodotus (2.28–34), and older.

coloratis: cf. 289 *pictis*, 290 *pharetratae*, and nn.

291 In the three major MSS 291 is found in three separate places – following 290 in the Palatinus, 292 in the Mediceus, and 293 in the Romanus. It clearly belongs after 293, whence it was perhaps displaced (to follow 290) because the scribe's eye went from *urget* in 290 to *et* of *et uiridem*, rather than *et* of *et diuersa*. Some earlier editors have seen the line as an interpolation, but this seems unnecessary; it is not crucial, but it contributes to the ethnographical colouring and finds parallels in 2.139, 3.350 and 4.126, likewise ethnographical in nature.

nigra: black soil is the best for crops; cf. 2.203–5 *nigra … terra* | … | *optima frumentis.*

294 'the entire region places its sure preservation in this art'; the wording conveys a slight *diffidentia*, or scepticism – they set great store by the practice, but is their trust justified? See following n.

iacit: a unique use of the verb (= *ponit, habet*); cf. *ThLL* VII. 1.42.32. It perhaps denotes a certain recklessness, but may merely suggest building (Servius compares it to *fundamenta iacio*), the topic which immediately follows.

295–314 The actual *bugonia* is not cast in didactic form, directed to a second-person addressee, but is rather presented as a description. This has the effect of separating it from the real technical advice of the poem (281–314n.). This is the first extant account of the curious process, though Florentinus (*Geop.* 15.2) has a similar description, for which he acknowledges Democritus and Varro (it is only mentioned in passing in *R.R.*; cf. 281–314n.).

295–7 V. stresses the smallness of the enclosure: *exiguus, contractus, angustique, artis.* In Florentinus (295–314n.) it is larger, but cf. 3n.

295 **ipsos contractus in usus** 'confined for this very purpose'.

297 **parietibusque:** the first *i* is consonantal, as at *A.* 2.442; 5.589.

297–8 'they add four windows with slanted light, set away from the four winds'. Some take *a uentis* to mean 'facing the four winds' (on the face of it possible), but V. seems to be thinking of shelter, presumably from both wind and light. Cf. Lucr. 6.1110–11 (of the four climates) *quae cum quattuor inter se diuersa uidemus | quattuor a uentis et caeli partibus esse.*

quattuor ... | quattuor: used twice at the end of the book (538, 541), though in a different context, perhaps to provide a frame (cf. 308–9, 309, 310nn.).

299   bima curuans iam cornua fronte 'whose horns are just now arching on his two year-old forehead'; Florentinus (295–314n.) refers to a 'thirty-month-old ox' (τριακοντάμηνον βοῦν).

300–2   The object of this brutal-sounding exercise is to keep the blood from escaping – so the skin is not damaged (*integram*, 302). This is at odds with the repeated details at 542 *sacrum iugulis demitte cruorem* – a further indication that V. has no technical interest in *bugonia*.

301   multa reluctanti: concessive: 'in spite of its great struggles'. For adverbial *multa* with the present participle, cf. 320 *multa querens*; 3.226 *multa gemens*; V. may have in mind the Homeric expression πόλλ’ ἀεκαζόμενος, 'much against one's will'.

301–2   'and when he has been beaten to death his carcass is pounded through the intact hide until it disintegrates'; cf. the effect of the plague at 3.484–5. See too 308–9.

302   A golden line (1.117n.).

303   sic positum in clauso 'they leave him in this condition in the enclosure'; at 543 the dead animals are left in the open: *corporaque ipsa boum frondoso desere luco* (300–2n.).

304–5   ramea ... fragmenta: i.e. sticks, twigs; the adjective seems to occur only here, and is perhaps a coinage of V.'s.

305   thymum casiasque recentis: presumably as being attractive to bees; cf. 30 (and 30–2n.), 270; 2.213.

305–7   The *bugonia* takes place in early spring (305 *primum*), the time of generation (cf. 2.323–45). The details are traditional; cf. Hor. *Epist.* 1.7.12–13 *te, dulcis amice, reuiset | cum Zephyris ... et hirundine prima.*

306   ante nouis rubeant quam prata coloribus: cf. 2.319 *uere rubenti*. For the image of the field's changing colour cf. *E.* 4.28 *molli paulatim flauescet campus arista.*

307   garrula ... tignis nidum suspendat hirundo: strictly speaking, this should refer to the house-martin rather than the swallow (which does not hang its nest from the rafters), but *garrula* and the association with spring point to the swallow, and V. may not have bothered about the distinction. Cf. 247 *laxos in foribus suspendit aranea cassis.*

308-9   interea teneris tepefactus in ossibus umor | aestuat:
cf. 555 *liquefacta boum per uiscera*. As at 301–2 (see n.) V. seems to recall
the details of the plague; cf. too the effects of *amor*, also aided by the
warmth of spring, at 3.272.

309   uisenda modis animalia miris 'wondrous creatures, a sight
to behold'; *modis . . . miris* (also at 1.477) goes with *animalia*, and defines
the event as a θαῦμα ('marvel'), as does the framing reference at 554
mirabile monstrum.

310-13   A vivid picture of the emergence of the bee: *primo . . . mox . . .
magis magis . . . donec . . . erupere.*

310   trunca pedum 'footless'; *pedum* is best seen as a genitive of
separation, a Greek construction. Cf. Sil. 10.310 *truncus capitis*. The
ablative would be more regular; cf. Luc. 8.436–7 *trunci | . . . ceruice duces*.

stridentia pennis: cf. 555–6 *toto | stridere apes utero*; also *A.* 1.397 (of
swans) *stridentibus alis*.

311   miscentur 'they swarm together'.

magis magis: cf. Cat. 64.274 *magis magis increbescunt*.

aëra carpunt 'tentatively take to the air'.

312   ut aestiuis effusus nubibus imber: like the bees after their
battle at 80 *non densior aëre grando*; also *A.* 5.317 *effusi nimbo similes*.

313   ut neruo pulsante sagittae 'like arrows from the twanging
string'; cf. *A.* 5.502–3 *neruo stridente sagitta | . . . diuerberat auras*; also 12.856
where the image also leads immediately to thoughts of the Parthians.

314   Almost a golden line (depending on the disruption felt by *si
quando*), appropriately at the end of the section (332; 1.117nn.).
On the Parthians cf. 2.125; 3.31nn.

315-558   Aristaeus, Proteus and Orpheus

Though it will return at the end (537–58), the *bugonia* has served its
purpose, as a means of transition to the true second half of the book, the
accounts of Aristaeus' loss of his bees, of his mission, aided by his mother
Cyrene, to the seer Proteus, and of the response of Proteus, in effect a
song on Orpheus' loss of Eurydice. The whole sequence unfolds as a
progressive series (Aristaeus, 315–32; Aristaeus and Cyrene, 333–414;
Aristaeus and Proteus, 415–52; Orpheus, 453–527; see nn. for the
importance of each), which then briefly retraces itself (Proteus, 528–9;
Aristaeus and Cyrene, 530–47; Aristaeus, 548–58), with this last section
treating *bugonia* and providing (with 281–314) a frame and outer ring to

the whole of the second half, of which Orpheus occupies the thematic centre.

As is often noted, the lines are in the style of an epyllion, in movement (with frame and picture constituting the whole as, for instance, with Cat. 64) and in language, which is elevated throughout, influenced first chiefly by various disparate Homeric contexts, then by the style of Hellenistic and neoteric poetry (see nn. passim); here, more than anywhere else in Roman literature the loss of the poetry of the previous generation (of Calvus and Cinna, to name the two most important) is most keenly felt. On connections with Cat. 64 cf. Crabbe (1977).

The question of the meaning of these lines, and of their relationship to the first half of the book and the *Georgics* as a whole, is perhaps the most difficult exegetical problem in Roman poetry, and it is certainly the most written-about (see Griffin (1979) 61 for a bibliography of 17 interpretations over a period of 12 years); it is doubtless this difficulty which led to the fictitious Servian claim that the whole of the second half was originally occupied by the praises of Gallus; on this, and on the second half in general, cf. Introduction, pp. 13–16, 21–4.

Ovid covers the whole story in 18 lines (*Fasti* 1.363–80), as a demonstration of the evils of sacrifice.

315–32   *The lament of Aristaeus*

Aristaeus, the *cultor nemorum* of 1.14, now a *pastor* who has come to represent all areas of agriculture (that is, all four books of the poem – see 329–31 and n.), comes lamenting to his mother, the nymph Cyrene, after losing his bees to illness and starvation (318n.). The passage finds its literary impulse in a general way in the two laments of Achilles to his nymph-mother Thetis at *Il.* 1.348–56 and 18.79–93, though other, more specific, Homeric reminiscence is superimposed (323n.), and there may well be a debt to the laments in epyllion, such as those of Ariadne at Cat. 64.132–201 and Dido at *A.* 4.305–30 and 365–87 (320, 322–5, 504–5nn.).

In spite of the intense literary reference, which continues throughout the rest of the poem, the role of Aristaeus, along with his connections with *bugonia* and with Proteus, is clearly original to V.; a new poetry is created from a patchwork of old.

315   The sudden elevation, with the theme presented through a question addressed to the Muse, initiates a Homeric tone, recalling in part the first line of the *Odyssey*, in part the style of *Od*. 9.14 (as Odysseus begins his own song) τί πρῶτόν τοι ἔπειτα, τί δ᾽ ὑστάτιον καταλέξω; 'What then shall I recite first, what later on?' Cf. *A*. 9.77–8 *quis deus, o Musae, tam saeua incendia Teucris | auertit?*

hanc ... extudit artem: cf. 328 *extuderat*. Aristaeus belongs culturally to the age of Jupiter (316, 327–8nn.); cf. 1.133–4 (of Jupiter's motives in ending the Saturnian age) *ut uarias usus meditando extunderet artis | paulatim* – the verb otherwise occurs in V. only once in the *Aeneid* (8.665), of Vulcan's metal-working. The *bugonia* is referred to as an *ars* at 294.

316 'from what source did this strange new practice of man take its beginnings'; as often, *nouus* means more than just 'new' (see 2.82 and n.).

experientia: otherwise in V. only at 1.4 (see n.), of the 'skill gained by practice' of the bees themselves; and cf. 156–7 *laborem | experiuntur*. As in 315, the age of Jupiter is suggested, as Servius noted in his explanation of the noun: *nullo docente ars per usum reperta* (cf. 1.133) – to which Page objects that a god, not man, discovered the *ars*.

317 pastor Aristaeus: cf. 1.14–15n. The reference is to Pind. *P*. 9.39–65 or Ap. Rhod. *Arg*. 2.500–27, which tell of the birth of Aristaeus to Apollo and Cyrene, of his epithets 'Hunter' and 'Shepherd', and of his subsequent status as healer and prophet (this last detail is not in Pindar). V. clearly no longer depicts him as a healer (318n.), his chief function in Apollonius, and in Callimachus (*Aet*. 3, fr. 75.32–5 Pf.); he rather takes on new associations, pertinent to the more immediate context of the *Georgics* (cf. 315, 327–8, 329–31nn.).

Peneia Tempe: the Thessalian locale is the home of Cyrene, who lives in the waters of the Peneus (355). In Pindar and Apollonius she is transported to Libya, which may play a part in V.'s placing of the *bugonia* in Egypt.

Pēnēiă: four syllables; a Greek formation, though not found in Greek (cf. 461n.).

318 amissis ... apibus morboque fameque: a glance back to the real world of the bees (252 *morbo*, 259 *fame*), destroyed like those of Aristaeus (281–2). The rest of the georgic world will be implicated in this destruction at 329–31 (see n.).

ut fama: a virtual footnote, suggesting a prior version; for the device see Norden on *A*. 6.14. In fact the story is almost certainly V.'s own invention, but the phrase by implying a tradition creates credibility.

319 As at 355 (see n.), Aristaeus takes on the look of the elegist–lover (cf. *E.* 6.64 *errantem Permessi ad flumina Gallum*), a figure embodied in Orpheus himself at 508–9. Lamentation beside water, though perhaps indebted to Hom. *Il.* 1.348–50, becomes a special feature in the neoteric epyllion (Cat. 64.124–31) and in elegy (Prop. 1.15.9–10 *Calypso | desertis olim fleuerat aequoribus*). The influence of Gallus may already be at work (351, 354–6n.; Introduction, pp. 15–16).

tristis: so he is at 335, and cf. 531 *tristis ... curas*; it is also used of Gallus at *E.* 10.31.

caput: i.e. *fontem*; *caput* can refer to either end of a river, but Cyrene and her nymphs will more naturally be at the source; at 363–73 their setting is identified with the source of several rivers (cf. 368 *caput*).

320 multa querens: cf. 3.226 (and n.) *multa gemens*; also 515 and n. The words suggest the harangue of epyllion: Cat. 64.130 *extremis ... querellis*; *A.* 4.360 *tuis ... querelis*.

321–2 mater, Cyrene mater, quae gurgitis huius | ima tenes: the anaphora, with the intervening word modifying and restricting the range of the repeated word, creates a mannered effect; cf. *E.* 6.55–6 *Nymphae, | Dictaeae Nymphae*; *A.* 8.71 *Nymphae, Laurentes Nymphae*. The second of these instances is perhaps conflated with 321–2 at *Anth. Lat.* 5.215.1–2 Burm. (not found in other editions) *Nymphae, fonticolae Nymphae, quae gurgitis huius | aeternum roseo tunditis ima pede*. On Cyrene cf. 317n.; the first syllable is here long, as at Ap. Rhod. *Arg.* 2.500 (317n.), whereas in Callimachus it is short in three out of four instances.

gurgitis huius | ima: for *gurgite hoc imo*; cf. 3.459–60 *inter | ima ... pedis*. The construction appears occasionally even in prose; cf. Livy 33.17.8 *ima urbis plana sunt*; also 385 *ad summum tecti*.

gurgitis: used four times in the second half of this book (cf. 387, 395, 524), otherwise only at 3.446; it is a somewhat elevated word, used in prose almost exclusively in its primary sense, 'eddy', 'whirlpool', and is one of the favoured words for sea in Cat. 64, where it appears four times (14, 18, 178, 183).

322–5 A series of despairing questions, filled with emotion, is one of the features of the lament in epyllion; cf. Cat. 64.177–83 *nam quo me referam? quali spe perdita nitor?*, etc.; also *A.* 4.368–71 *nam quid dissimulo ...?*, 305–14. See 504–5n.

323 The reproach, which here involves a questioning of the mother's morality as well as her word, is Homeric in origin: 'Poseidon

... if truly I am your son, and you avow that you are my father', *Od.*
9.528-9. Ovid makes this the basis for Phaethon's visit to Apollo: *M.*
1.760-1 *at tu* [sc. *Clymene*], *si modo sum caelesti stirpe creatus, | ede notam tanti
generis meque adsere caelo!* – he had been taunted by his companion
Epaphus *'matri'que ait 'omnia demens | credis et es tumidus genitoris imagine
falsi'*, 753-4. The taunt can also be directed against the son; cf. *A.* 2.540
at non ille, satum quo te mentiris, Achilles ...

Thymbraeus: the epithet is odd in connection with Aristaeus.
Thymbra is an otherwise obscure place in the Troad mentioned at *Il.*
10.430 and famous for a shrine to Apollo. According to Apollodorus
(*Epit.* 3.32) it was at the altar of Apollo in this shrine that Achilles killed
Troilus, who, like Aristaeus, was reputedly the son of Apollo, his mother
being Hecuba. The words *si pater est Thymbraeus Apollo* belong as a taunt
in the mouth of Achilles as he is about to kill Troilus (suggesting that the
latter get help from his 'father'), and it is quite possible that V. has
adapted them (whether Greek or Latin cannot be known) to a new
situation. Callim. fr. 491 Pf. is an unplaced line treating Troilus' early
death. Cf. 355n.

324   inuisum fatis: cf. *A.* 2.647 (Anchises, of himself) *inuisus diuis.*

324-5   aut quo tibi nostri | pulsus amor?: cf. *A.* 2.595 (where
the situation is reversed as the divine Venus addresses her mortal son)
aut quonam nostri tibi cura recessit?

325   quid me caelum sperare iubebas?: cf. the words of Ariadne
at *Cat.* 64.140 *non haec miserae sperare iubebas.*

325-6   caelum ... mortalis: not only are his hopes for heaven
destroyed, but also his mortal glory.

326   hunc ipsum uitae mortalis honorem: so Achilles com-
plains that not only is he to be short-lived, but Zeus has also taken away
his honour (τιμή), *Il.* 1.352-6.

327-8   quem ... extuderat '[the glory] which skilful tending of
crops and herds had with difficulty hammered out for me as I en-
deavoured all'; i.e. which I had achieved through absolute devotion to
labor. Aristaeus looks very much like the *agricola* of Books 1-3 (315,
329-31nn.).

328   te matre, relinquo: the ablative absolute is concessive: 'even
though you are my mother [and a deity at that], I lose these'.

329-31 Aristaeus invites Cyrene, if she has so little regard for him,
to destroy his works, his trees, stables, crops and vines; in other words he

invites precisely what has happened in the real world of the *Georgics* (the destruction of crops by the storm in Book 1, of trees by the fire-storm in Book 2, of the herds by plague in Book 3). His bees have already been lost (318 *amissis . . . apibus*), as they were in the real world, to plague, at 281–2 (315, 327–8nn.).

Cf. 2.133–4n. for reference throughout the poem to the subjects of Books 1–3.

329   quin age 'come on, then'; indicates a challenge, as in the only other instances in V.: *E.* 3.52 *quin age, si quid habes*; *A.* 5.635 *quin agite et mecum infaustas exurite puppis.*

ipsa manu: cf. 3.395 *ipse manu* (also with a command).

felicis erue siluas: as the winds did to the crops at 1.319–20 *grauidam late segetem . . . eruerent*; cf. too 2.210 (of the farmer's own actions) *antiquasque domos auium cum stirpibus imis | eruit.*

330   fer stabulis inimicum ignem: as happened in the second half of Book 3, where the plague, depicted as a fire (566 *sacer ignis*; see n. and 3.244n.), destroyed the herds and piled up their corpses *ipsis | in stabulis*, 556–7.

interfice messis: the verb appears in V. only here, but cf. 1.152 (the result of a relaxation of *labor*) *intereunt segetes*; 3.368 *intereunt pecudes*, 544–5 (during the plague) *interit . . . | uipera.* V. does not otherwise use *intereo*; clearly neither verb is felt to be appropriate to epic.

331   ure sata: cf. 2.196 (of the goat's bite) *urentis culta capellas.*

332   A line which is almost golden (1.117n.) ends the section, as at 314 (see n.).

laudis: the praise associated with farming is mentioned at 3.288 *hic labor, hinc laudem fortes sperate coloni.*

333–86   Cyrene and the catalogue of nymphs; reception of Aristaeus; catalogue of rivers

Cyrene and the nymphs hear the lament of Aristaeus, and he is brought down to their realm to be entertained prior to Cyrene's instructions (387–414). The passage gives the impression of intense Homeric influence; a catalogue of nymphs in the vicinity of a lament by a mortal son to his nymph-mother can only recall Achilles, Thetis and the catalogue of Nereids at *Il.* 18.34–147 (where Achilles' lament occurs in the presence of Thetis, and after the catalogue). But V.'s 12 nymphs, for

the most part obscure figures, do not coincide in a single instance
(though see 345–7n.) with the 33 Homeric nymphs, nor, for that matter,
with the 50 Hesiodic nymphs (*Theog.* 240–64); his nymphs, set in an
archaic context, are pointedly non-archaic. They seem to be either
sylvan figures or have associations with singing, and many of them look
to be Hellenistic (see nn.). For the view that they come from the
Callimachean treatment of nymphs, the Περὶ Νυμφῶν (of which only one
name is preserved, that of Nonacrina, who is as obscure and non-archaic
as the Virgilian instances; *frag. gram.* 413 Pf.), cf. Thomas (1986b)
190–3. Such an explanation would help to account for V.'s inclusion of
land nymphs. Cf. 339, 341–2, 343nn.

The catalogue of nymphs is balanced by the catalogue of eight rivers
at 367–73, and this is almost certainly in some way a reference to the
parallel Callimachean treatise on the rivers of the known world (*frag.
gram.* 457–9 Pf.), a work which seems to have been used by other Roman
poets.

333–4   At mater sonitum thalamo sub fluminis alti | sensit: a
clear reminiscence of the opening of the Homeric sequence (333–86n.):
'and his lady mother heard him as she sat in the depths of the sea', *Il.*
18.35–6; cf. 349–50.

thalamo: so called at 374; perhaps a secondary reference to Soph.
O.T. 194–5 (of the Atlantic) μέγαν | θάλαμον Ἀμφιτρίτας, 'the great
chamber of Amphitrite' – a Nereid at Hes. *Theog.* 243.

334   eam circum: cf. Hom. *Il.* 18.37 μιν ἀμφαγέροντο, 'they gathered
around her'.

334–5   Milesia uellera ... | carpebant: cf. 1.390 *carpentes pensa
puellae*; also 3.306–7 (and n.) *Milesia ... | uellera.* It is not clear why these
nymphs are engaged in wool-working; cf. 348–9n.

335   hyali saturo fucata colore 'dyed with the rich hue of glass';
hyalus, a transliteration of Greek ὕαλος, occurs only here in classical
Latin. Cf. 2.465 (and n.) *Assyrio fucata lana ueneno.* Cf. 350n.

336   Drymoque Xanthoque Ligeaque Phyllodoceque: the line
sounds and looks Greek, that is Homeric, and is an exact rhythmical
imitation of *Il.* 18.45 Λωτώ τε Πρωτώ τε Φέρουσά τε Δυναμένη τε, but it is
doubtless of V.'s own construction (333–86n.). See 1.470n. on lines of
four words.

Drymo ('Oak', from δρυμός) and Phyllodoce ('Leaf-Receiver', from
φυλλοδοκέω) are names not found in Greek; Xantho ('blonde', from

ξανθός) appears as a woman in Philodemus, and is a good singer (*A.P.* , 9.570), while Ligea ('clear-voiced', λίγεια) is a siren in Lycophron (*Alex.* 726). Such provenances would well suit a source in Callimachus (333–86n.).

337 'their shining locks flowing over their fair necks'; for the accusative *caesariem* retained with the passive *effusae*, cf. 3.307n. Cf. Theocr. 5.91 λιπαρὰ δὲ παρ' αὐχένα σείετ' ἔθειρα, 'brightly waves the hair on his neck'.

[338] The line is not found in the best MSS, and is clearly an importation from *A.* 5.826. Damning proof against it (if needed) is the fact that these nymphs, unlike the rest (333–86n.), *are* Homeric – they appear, over two lines which the later V. incorporated into one, at *Il.* 18.39–40.

339 Cydippe: not otherwise a nymph, unless Callimachus made her one; she is the heroine of his 'Acontius and Cydippe' (*Aet.* 3, frr. 67–75 Pf.).

Lycorias: from Lycoreia, a town near Delphi, which appeared in the *Aetia* of Callimachus (*Aet.* 3, fr. 62 Pf.), and which, through association with the oracle, is first used as an epithet for Apollo at Callim. *H.* 2.19 (Λυκωρέος ... Φοίβου). If Callimachus had her as a nymph, with associations with Apollo, Gallus' choice of the name Lycoris for his elegiac mistress would be a natural one (cf. Propertius' Cynthia and the Callimachean Κύνθιος; 3.36n.).

339–40 altera uirgo, | altera: the cadence of this epanalepsis is much favoured by Catullus in his epyllion: 64.61–2 *prospicit, eheu,* | *prospicit,* 132–3 *perfide, ab aris,* | *perfide,* 186–7 *omnia muta,* | *omnia,* 259–60 *orgia cistis,* | *orgia,* 321–2 *carmine fata,* | *carmine,* 403–4 *impia nato* | *impia*. It otherwise occurs in all his dactylic verse only at 62.63–4 and 66.75–6, and would therefore seem to be a characteristic of neoteric epyllion (the context of this instance; cf. 315–558n.). V. avoids it: there is one other occurrence in the *Georgics* (297–8 and n.); at *E.* 9.27–8 it evokes the pathos evident in many of the Catullan examples (*Mantua nobis,* | *Mantua*), and the same may be said of the only instance of this precise type in the *Aeneid*: 2.405–6 (the death of Cassandra) *lumina frustra,* | *lumina*. *E.* 8.49–50 is a more complex and distinct instance (*an puer improbus ille?* | *improbus ille puer*.). Those who read *ex omnia* at *E.* 6.33 (where there is no pathos) should do so with an awareness of these patterns.

340 'the other having for the first time just experienced the pangs of childbirth'; either a purely ornamental and unnecessary detail, or (no doubt) a literary reference, with a larger context now lost to us (perhaps involving a story of an affair between Lycorias and some mortal or divine figure).

341 Clioque: not otherwise a nymph; the muse is suggested, and through her, poetry.

Beroe: a complete mystery, as is the Beroe at Ov. *M.* 3.278 (the nurse of Semele).

341–2 Oceanitides ambae, | ambae auro, pictis incinctae pellibus ambae: an adaptation of Callim. *H.* 3.42–3 (where Artemis visits Oceanus and chooses a group of his daughters as attendants – cf. *Oceanitides*) πολέας δ' ἐπελέξατο νύμφας, | πάσας εἰνέτεας, πάσας ἔτι παῖδας ἀμίτρους, 'and she chose many nymphs, all nine years old, all girls still ungirdled'. Apart from the thematic similarities, V. reproduces the anaphora of πάσας with that of *ambae*, and *incinctae* answers ἀμίτρους, though with affirmative instead of privative suffix. It is noteworthy that Callimachus and V. both combine sylvan nymphs and Oceanids (cf. 344, 383nn.).

Oceanitides: not otherwise in Latin (except in Hyginus); in Greek it survives only as an adjective in the singular ('Ωκεανῖτις), 'of, in the Ocean'. Possibly Callimachean, though at *H.* 3.13, 62 he uses the Hesiodic patronymic 'Ωκεανῖναι.

343 Ephyre: according to Pausanias (2.1.1) the archaic Corinthian poet Eumelus claimed that Ephyre was an Oceanid and the first inhabitant of Corinth, of which the old name is also Ephyra (the only name by which Callimachus and Apollonius call the city); Callimachus will have had an antiquarian interest in her.

The hiatus between *Ephyre* and *atque* is doubtless to be seen as an appropriate Graecism (as at 463).

Opis: the name (var. Upis) became an epithet of Artemis, transferred from one of her band of nymphs; cf. *A.* 11.532–3 *Opim, | unam ex uirginibus sociis sacraque caterua.* Callimachus mentions her at *H.* 3.204–5 (341–2n.), and she is a good candidate for his treatise on nymphs (333–86n.).

Deiopeia: the form does not survive in Greek, but Deiope, like Clio and Lycorias, is connected with poetry – she is married to Musaeus at [Aristot.] *Mirab.* 143b.

344   Arethusa: not attested in Greek as a nymph (or personal name) until Apollodorus, where she is one of the Hesperides (2.5.11). She has already attained great status as a poetic nymph at *E.* 10.1, and it looks as if she too is associated with Artemis (*positis ... sagittis*), while at *E.* 10.4 she is a sea-nymph – a Callimachean conflation (cf. 341–2, 383nn.)? See 351n. Ov. *M.* 5.572–641 treats her story at some length.

345-7   After the catalogue proper of nymphs (cf. 344 *tandem*), which demonstrates clear traces of the influence of Callimachus and Hellenistic poetry and is studiously non-Homeric, V. introduces a nymph who *is* Homeric, namely Clymene (cf. *Il.* 18.47); and he has her sitting in their midst singing, naturally, a Homeric song, the account of the affair between Ares and Aphrodite from *Od.* 8.266–366 (but see 347n.). That song was sung by the bard Demodocus, referred to at *Od.* 8.367 as the 'renowned singer' (περικλυτός), which may account for V.'s choice of Clymene (κλυμένη). A tradition on the island of Ios (Paus. 10.24.2) makes her the mother of Homer, and if V. was aware of this fact it too could have motivated his choice, given the Homeric tone of the passage.

345   inter quas: like *tandem* in 344, has the effect of separating Clymene from the rest of the nymphs.

curam ... inanem: this is generally taken to refer to the futility of Vulcan's precautions to prevent Venus' affair, but it is somewhat oddly put since in the *Odyssey* his concern and his plan is to catch his wife in bed with Ares, and as such it works. Some take it as a reference to his own unrequited love for Venus; if so the focus of Clymene's story is changed from the Homeric version, and has become more Alexandrian and more in line with the story of Orpheus (cf. 347n.).

346   dulcia furta: i.e. 'stolen joys'; the noun belongs to the language of elegy, and is first found in an amatory sense in Catullus: 68.136 *rara uerecundae furta feremus erae*, 140 *furta Iouis*; cf *A.* 4.171–2.

347   The Homeric status of Clymene's song recedes as she sings a divine erotology, an account of the numerous affairs of the gods. While no such poem is known (an abridged version of Ovid's *Metamorphoses* would qualify), an Alexandrian or neoteric setting is suggested (cf. e.g. the theme of Calvus' *Io*).

348   carmine quo captae: in the light of the theme of Clymene's *carmen*, cf. 3.285 (and n.) *capti ... amore*; *E.* 6.9–10 *haec ... si quis | captus amore leget.*

348-9   dum ... deuoluunt 'as they twist down [i.e. spin] the soft coils with their spindles' – as they were doing at 334–5.

349–50   iterum maternas impulit auris | luctus: cf. 333–4 *mater sonitum . . . | sensit.*

350   uitreisque: implying a greenish colour and a glassy opaqueness, as suits the locale; their wool is of the same colour (cf. 335 and n.).

351   obstipuere: the enjambment and the strong break which follows enforce the sense of the word; they are startled, and doubtless stop their weaving.

ante alias Arethusa sorores: cf. 344n. Arethusa, who stood in for the Muses in *E.* 10 (on the elegiac grief of Gallus), now takes the chief role in communicating to Cyrene the grief of Aristaeus, who has similarities with Gallus in *E.* 6; it is reasonable to suspect that Arethusa, otherwise mentioned by V. only in passing at *A.* 3.696, played a role in the poetry of Gallus (319, 354–6nn.).

352   Cf. *A.* 1.127 (of Neptune) *prospiciens summa placidum caput extulit unda.* Cf. the graphic description of the Nereids at Cat. 64.14 *emersere freti candenti e gurgite uultus,* 18 *nutricum tenus exstantes e gurgite cano.*

353   non frustra: the litotes *nec frustra* occurs at 1.257, and cf. 1.95–6 *neque . . . nequiquam.*

354–6   ipse . . . dicit: the reminiscence of *E.* 10, again difficult to define (cf. 319, 355nn.), intensifies; cf. 22 [*Galle*] *tua cura Lycoris* – this use of *cura* is frequent in elegy (e.g. Prop. 1.1.35–6 *sua quemque moretur | cura,* 28–9 *Amor non talia curat,| nec lacrimis crudelis Amor . . .* [*saturatur*]). Cf. too *A.* 1.678 (Venus of Ascanius) *mea maxima cura.* Ross (1975) 68–9 argues plausibly that the word *cura* played a prominent part in the poetry of Gallus.

355   tristis: cf. 319 and n.

Penei genitoris ad undam: oddly put; the words naturally mean 'by the wave of *his* sire Peneus' (as e.g. at 363 *domum mirans genetricis,* of Cyrene's home), but must be read as = 'by the wave of *the* sire Peneus'. Various adjectives have been suggested to replace *Penei* (*magni* Bentley, *nostri* Peerlkamp, perhaps better *sacram* Ribbeck), but emendation is probably not justified. The words would be suitable to a treatment of Daphne, the daughter of Peneus, who reaches his banks and asks for help; cf. Ov. *M.* 1.544 *uicta labore fugae spectans Peneidas undas.* For a similarly 'inappropriate' reference cf. 323n. Possibly V. is referring to a context now lost, for Aristaeus here resembles the Virgilian Gallus of *E.* 6.64 (319n.), as well as the grieving Orpheus of 508–9 *deserti ad Strymonis undam | flesse sibi,* himself a figure depicted in elegiac terms (453–527n.).

Penêi: scanned as a spondee by synizesis.

356   lacrimans: like Orpheus at 509 (*flesse*).

te crudelem nomine dicit 'is calling on you by name for your cruelty'; see 354–6n. Cf. *E.* 5.23 (at the death of Daphnis) *atque deos atque astra uocat crudelia mater*.

357   percussa ... mentem 'her mind stricken'; for the retained accusative, cf. 3.306–7n., and cf. the more normal ablative absolute at *A.* 9.292 *percussa mente*. Some see it, less satisfactorily, as an accusative of respect. Cf. *A.* 3.47 *ancipiti mentem formidine pressus*.

noua: i.e. sudden; cf. *A.* 3.259 *subita ... formidine*.

358   duc age, duc: the only instance in V. where the imperative preceding *age* is repeated; it obviously conveys great urgency.

359   ait: V.'s use of *ait* to close direct speech is oddly restricted to Cyrene (here and at 381) and to two instances in the *Aeneid* (3.543; 5.551); in each case the speech is brief.

360   qua iuuenis gressus inferret 'in order that the young man could enter there'; relative clause of purpose.

360–1   at illum | curuata in montis faciem circumstetit unda: as it did for Thetis and Iris at Hom. *Il.* 24.96, though they went in the other direction, ἀμφὶ δ' ἄρα σφι λιάζετο κῦμα θαλάσσης, 'and the wave of the sea opened about them'. For both of the Virgilian details cf. Hom. *Od.* 11.243 (where the water rises up to conceal the love-making of Poseidon and Tyro) πορφύρεον δ' ἄρα κῦμα περιστάθη, οὔρεϊ ἶσον, 'and the blue wave, like a mountain, curved up to enclose them'.

362   acceptque sinu uasto: the words suggest a nurturing of Aristaeus, appropriate since it is his mother who ultimately receives him; cf. *A.* 1.685 *cum te gremio accipiet laetissima Dido*.

363–73 In a sentence of 11 lines (the longest of the poem) V. introduces a catalogue of eight rivers, matching the 10-line catalogue of 12 nymphs at 334–44. If those lines are likely to have been based on Callimachus' treatise 'On Nymphs' (333–86n.), it seems even more probable that these are indebted to his better-known 'On the Rivers of the Known World' (367, 370, 371–3nn.). At *M.* 2.241–59 Ovid has a catalogue of 27 rivers which dried up when Phaethon lost control of the sun-chariot. He includes the Peneus and four of V.'s rivers (the Phasis, Tiber and Caicus and Po), and he treats in order the rivers of the north, the east, the south and the west – in other words the 'rivers of the known world'. He and V. perhaps share, as often, a common source.

V. here stresses the moist nature of Cyrene's setting, as he presently stresses the heat of Proteus' environment (401–2, 425–8) and the cold of Orpheus' (517–20).

363   domum mirans: cf. the admiration of Telemachus and his men as they enter the house of Menelaus at Hom. *Od.* 4.43–4 οἱ δὲ ἰδόντες | θαύμαζον κατὰ δῶμα, 'as they saw it they marvelled at the house'. Cf. 376–9n.

mirans defines the whole setting as fantastical or miraculous (Gr. θαυμάζω).

364   speluncisque lacus clausos 'and pools confined in caves'; if the words are intended to do more than indicate the watery nature of the place (363–73n.), they perhaps refer to the pools as sources of the rivers.

lucosque sonantis: so at *E.* 10.58 (spoken by Gallus).

365   ibat: in the same position at 430 (of Proteus), and not otherwise in the poem; it is common in the *Aeneid.*

stupefactus: similar to, but stronger than, *mirans* at 363; cf. 351 *obstipuere.*

366   Some see this merely as a reference to the underground sources of the rivers (cf. 368 *caput*), but *labentia* suggests that they actually flow underground, a view found elsewhere in antiquity.

A golden line (1.117n.).

367   diuersa locis 'in different places' (lit. 'distinct in positions'); Ovid (*M.* 1.40) uses the same words in describing the creation of the rivers of the world. See following n.

Phasimque Lycumque: there are various rivers Lycus, but V. doubtless means the one in Colchis, where the Phasis also flows; they are mentioned together by Apollonius (*Arg.* 4.131–4) and Strabo (11.14.7). The former states that the Lycus flows into the Phasis and that they emerge together in the Black Sea, Strabo that they do so separately. V.'s *diuersa locis* may imply support for ?Callimachus, who will certainly have treated the question, perhaps in the same way as Strabo, who preserves one of the three fragments of Callimachus' treatise on the rivers of the world (fr. 458 Pf.).

368   caput: cf. 319n.

se erumpit: the verb is normally intransitive (some MSS accordingly omit *se*, while others have *se rumpit/rupit*), but the reflexive occurs a number of times in republican Latin authors (Accius, Varro, Lucretius, Caesar); after V. it is found only once in Scribonius Largus.

Enipeus: a tributary of the Peneus (317n.) in Thessaly.

369   The Tiber and the Anio, two Italian rivers, occupy the centre of the catalogue (with three foreign rivers preceding and following – the Eridanus is of course the Po, but V.'s use of the Greek name sets it apart from the Tiber and Anio). The Anio flows into the Tiber.

pater Tiberinus: cf. *A.* 8.540; 10.421 *Thybri pater*; 8.72 *Thybri … genitor*.

Aniena fluenta 'the streams of the Anio'; cf. *A.* 12.35 *Thybrina fluenta*.

370   saxosusque sonans: sound reflects sense; cf. 50; *A.* 12.592 *saxa sonant*; *A.* 7.566–7 *fragosus | dat sonitum saxis et torto uertice torrens*. Servius' reading *saxosumque sonans* has some merit.

Hypanis: the Scythian river, which flows into the northern waters of the Black Sea, was one of the dividing lines of Europe and Asia; cf. Gallus, *uno tellures diuidit amne duas*, p. 99 Morel.

Mysusque Caicus: the river has this epithet as early as Aeschylus: ἰὼ Κάικε Μύσιαί τ' ἐπιρροαί, 'Caicus with your Mysian streams' (cf. 369 *fluenta*), *Mysoi* fr. 143 Radt. The literary reference is preserved in Strabo (13.1.70; he reports that some take it of two rivers, the Caicus and the Mysus) and Photius, and may well have been disseminated by Callimachus (who discussed the river; cf. *frag. gram.*, fr. 404 Pf.). That seems a likely source for both V. and Ovid, who uses an epithet (*Teuthranteusque* [i.e. *Mysusque*] *Caicus*, *M.* 2.243; see 363–73n.) not otherwise found in Greek or Latin; also *A.A.* 3.196 *Myse Caice*.

371–3   The Eridanus, originally a mythical northern European river and later identified by Greeks with the Po, was one of the three rivers known to have figured in the treatise of Callimachus (*frag. gram.*, fr. 458). According to Strabo (9.1.19), he claimed to laugh at the maxim that even the virgins of Athens 'could drink from the pure stream of the Eridanus', since it was in his view so muddy that even herds shunned it. V.'s description also perhaps suggests that the river was silt-filled; cf. 126 *qua niger umectat flauentia culta Galaesus*.

371–2   et … | Eridanus 'and Eridanus, with both horns of his bull's brow gilded'. Cf. *A.* 8.77 (the Tiber) *corniger Hesperidum fluuius regnator aquarum*. The association is old and comes from the sound made by rivers; cf. Hom. *Il.* 21.237 (of the Scamander) μεμυκὼς ἠΰτε ταῦρος, 'bellowing like a bull'. At Ov. *M.* 9.80–8 the river-god Achelous, while fighting Hercules, assumes the form of a bull, which results in his losing a horn.

372–3   quo … amnis: cf. 371–3n.; adapted from Hom *Il.* 16.391 ἐς δ' ἅλα πορφυρέην μεγάλα στενάχουσι ῥέουσαι, 'sweeping in flood with a great din down to the dark sea'. When used of the sea the epithet *purpureus*, like πορφύρεος, seems to denote movement ('seething', 'troubled') as much as colour.

The Po in flood behaves similarly at 1.481–2.

374   thalami: cf. 333–4n.

pendentia pumice tecta 'the hanging pumice ceiling'; it hangs without support from below, i.e. 'arches'; cf. *A.* 1.166 *scopulis pendentibus antrum*.

375   fletus … inanis: cf. 345 *curam … inanem; A.* 4.449 *lacrimae … inanes;* 10.465 *lacrimasque … inanis.*

376–9   A miniature vignette, heavily indebted to Homeric poetry, describing the reception and entertainment of Aristaeus. At *Od.* 4.47–58, a context already recalled (363n.), Telemachus and his men are received in a similar way: they are bathed, anointed with oil, dressed in fleecy garments, they wash their hands and are served with food and wine. At *A.* 1.701–6 there is a very similar scene, with much verbal repetition from the present lines.

376   ordine: implies that it is a part of a ritual, reflecting the formulaic nature of such Homeric scenes (376–9n.).

377   tonsisque … mantelia uillis 'close-shorn napkins'. As they are for the hands, V. may intend a gloss, reflecting the etymology found at Varro, *L.L.* 6.85 *mantelium, ubi manus terguntur.*

378   epulis onerant mensas: cf. 133 *dapibus mensas onerabat.*

378–9   plena reponunt | pocula 'they lay and fill the goblets'; *plena* is proleptic, and *reponunt = ponunt.* Cf. 3.527 *epulae … repostae;* also 2.528 (and n.) *cratera coronant.*

379   Panchaeis … ignibus: they burn incense from Arabia; cf. 2.139 *turiferis Panchaia pinguis harenis.*

adolescunt 'blaze up'; the verb, meaning 'to grow up', is best seen as transferred to *arae* from *ignibus*, and though it seems unusual in such a context, cf. Frontin. *Strat.* 1.5.28 *adolescente flamma* 'as the flame spread'. Some see it as a distinct verb, *adoleo* + *-sco.*

380   Maeonii carchesia Bacchi: cf. *A.* 5.77 *mero libans carchesia Baccho* (cf. 381 *Oceano libemus*). *Maeonii* could suggest Homer, given the Homeric surroundings.

381   ait: cf. 359n.

382   Oceanumque patrem rerum: developed from Hom. *Il.*
14.245–6 ποταμοῖο ῥέεθρα | Ὠκεανοῦ, ὅς περ γένεσις πάντεσσι τέτυκται,
'streams of the river Ocean, from whom all take their origin'; cf. too
14.201. With *rerum* V. also alludes to the theory of water as the original
element.

Nymphasque sorores: somewhat odd as objects of the libation,
since the nymphs, Cyrene's sisters (cf. 354 *Cyrene soror*) are *participants* in
the libation. Did V. write *Oceanum patrem rerum Nymphaeque sorores*, which
would give point to the otherwise colourless *ipsa*? Cf. *ipse* at 391–2
(where Cyrene and the Nymphs venerate together) *hunc et Nymphae
ueneramur et ipse | grandaeuus Nereus*; cf. also 2.494 (which could perhaps
have caused the corruption) *Nymphasque sorores*.

383   centum quae siluas, centum quae flumina seruant: the
combination of sylvan and water nymphs, here elegantly expressed,
looks back to the catalogue of nymphs (341–2, 344nn.); at *H.* 3.40–5
Callimachus has Artemis choose her woodland companions from the
nymphs of Ocean and the rivers.

384–5   ter ... | ter: for the same anaphora cf. *A.* 4.690–1; also,
though not in consecutive lines, 1.281–3. The flaring up of fire when
wine is poured on it is a good omen, as is a triple response; so, at *A.*
7.141–2, after Aeneas' prayer, Jupiter responds favourably: *ter ...
intonuit.*

384   Vestam 'hearth'; this may be the first instance of the word as a
pure metonymy.

385   summum tecti: for *summum tectum*; cf. 321–2 (and n.) *gurgitis
... ima.*

386   firmans animum: cf. *A.* 3.611 *animum ... firmat.*

387–414   Cyrene's instructions

In this section, and in the next (415–52), though the characters and
situation are changed to suit the new context, V. adapts a poetic model
as closely as anywhere in his corpus. Cyrene's instructions, and Aristaeus' execution of them, are based closely on the famous incident from
Hom. *Od.* 4.351–570, where Menelaus, instructed by the nymph Eidothea, secures Proteus and learns from him the fate of the other Greeks
following the fall of Troy, and is also told of his own future. In spite of
V.'s close attention to this text, he both abbreviates and (where it suits

his purpose) embellishes his model (cf. 425–8n.), and deliberately varies the details (407–10n.). At the same time he seems to have imposed secondary references upon the Homeric fabric (390–1, 392–3, 395, 404). It is presumably coincidental that Eidothea's speech begins at *Od.* 4.383, Cyrene's at *G.* 4.387, though V., like many others, may well have felt *Od.* 1–4 (the *Telemachy*) to be in part a separable section of the epic – in which case the structural parallelism is perhaps intended (see 3.1–48n. for such structural imitation).

Ovid has an amusing and neat reversal of the incident at *M.* 11.229–65, where the mortal Peleus, with advice from the god Proteus, captures the nymph Thetis.

387–8 Est in Carpathio Neptuni gurgite uates | caeruleus Proteus: the speech begins in high style, and in the form of an ecphrasis (3.146–7n.), the only one of the 15 Virgilian examples of the device to have a human or divine being as its subject (see also 418n.). The mannered style is reminiscent of the opening of Cat. 64 (*Peliaco quondam prognatae uertice pinus*), and may well have been a characteristic opening feature of epyllia.

uates: also used at 392, where the sense of 'seer' is uppermost. Though Proteus is not so called by Homer, Callimachus refers to him as Παλληνέα μά[ντιν, 'the seer of Pallene', *SH* fr. 254.5 (390–1, 395nn.). Given the nature of Proteus' song (453–527 and n.; *uates* is repeated at 450, as Proteus begins), V. perhaps intends a more contemporary reference to *uates* as the new term for the ideal Roman poet.

caeruleus Proteus: cf. *A.* 8.64 *caeruleus Thybris.*

388–9 magnum ... equorum 'who traverses the great sea with his fishes and his yoked team of two-footed horses', i.e. his team of hippocampi. *piscibus et curru* ['team'; cf. 3.91] *equorum* is a hendiadys to describe the half-fish, half-horse creature (ἱππόκαμπος) which traditionally drew the chariots of sea gods.

magnum ... aequor | ... metitur: exactly as Hom. *Od.* 3.179 πέλαγος μέγα μετρήσαντες, 'measuring the great open sea'; also Lucil. 996 M. *uir mare metitur magnum.*

390–1 hic ... | Pallenen: Aristaeus does not have to travel to Egypt, since Proteus is visiting Thessaly and Pallene, the western peninsula of Chalcidice, across from Thessaly. Before 1975 the tradition connecting Proteus with this area was known only from Lycophron (*Alex.* 126–7) and later from Nonnus (*Dion.* 43.334); but it is now clear that V. took the detail from Callimachus who, at the beginning of the *Victoria Berenices* (3.1–48n.), referred to Proteus as the seer from Pallene (387–8n.) – though Lycophron, who came to Alexandria from Chalcis in Euboea (which colonized most of Chalcidice), may have brought the detail with him. V. has Pallene as Proteus' fatherland, while Lycophron states that he visited Pallene *from* his fatherland, Egypt (*Alex.* 126 πάτραν). The reversal, and V.'s insistence, might suggest a Callimachean correction of Lycophron.

392–3 nouit ... trahantur: V. adapts Homer, not, however, *Od.* 4, where Proteus is not treated as a seer (387–8n.), but *Il.* 1.70, describing the abilities of Calchas, the prime Homeric seer, ὃς ᾔδη τά τ' ἐόντα τά τ' ἐσσόμενα πρό τ' ἐόντα, 'who knew what was, what would be and what had passed before'. The Muses are assigned the same capability at Hes. *Theog.* 38.

quae mox uentura trahantur 'what is being drawn forward, yet to happen'.

394–5   An elaboration of the designation of Proteus as 'servant of Poseidon' (Ποσειδάωνος ὑποδμώς, *Od.* 4.386).

395 armenta et ... phocas: one and the same.

turpis: a typically restrained reference to the acrid smell of the seals on which Homer dilates (*Od.* 4.404–6, 441–3); see also 415, 417nn.

pascit ... phocas: at *Od.* 4.413 Homer has a brief simile (adapted and expanded at 433–6; see n.) comparing Proteus to a shepherd. For the bolder designation here implied (*pastor phocarum*) V. is surely indebted to Callimachus, who gives Proteus (without naming him) this very title: ποιμένα [φωκάων], *SH* fr. 254.6 (cf. 387–8, 390–1nn.) – V.'s line confirms Lloyd-Jones's conjecture, if confirmation be needed.

396 uinclis capiendus: cf. 399–400, 405. In *E.* 6 Silenus must be treated similarly before singing his song: 19 *iniciunt ipsis ex uincula sertis*, 23 *'quo uincula nectitis?'*; cf. 404n.

396–7 ut omnem | expediat morbi causam euentusque secundet: Servius notes: *duo enim ista requiruntur in oraculis, causa mali et remedium.* Proteus does not in fact give any remedy, as Cyrene implies in her framing speech at 532 *haec omnis causa morbi.* The remedy, if it can be so called, is *bugonia.*

398 sine ui non ulla dabit praecepta: cf. 399, 450; from Hom. *Od.* 4.415 καὶ τότ' ἔπειθ' ὑμῖν μελέτω κάρτος τε βίη τε, 'that will be the moment for you to use strength and force'.

praecepta: cf. 448 *deum praecepta*, 548 *matris praecepta*; otherwise in the poem only at 1.176 (of ancient agricultural precepts) *ueterum praecepta*.

398–9 neque illum | orando flectes 'he is not one you will bend with prayer'; cf. *A.* 6.376 (the Sibyl to the shade of Palinurus) *desine fata deum flecti sperare precando*.

399–400 uim duram et uincula capto | tende: cf. 412 *contende tenacia uincla*. *tende* goes more easily with *uincula* than *uim*, but the two nouns can be seen as a hendiadys: 'the forceful chains'.

400 doli ... inanes 'against these alone his wiles will vainly shatter themselves'; for this use of *demum* (= 'alone', qualifying *haec*) cf. 1.47 *illa ... demum*. The image is of a wave breaking on the rocks; cf. Sen. *Med.* 392 (the nurse, of Medea's frenzy) *ubi se iste fluctus franget? exundat furor.*

401 medios cum sol accenderit aestus 'when the sun has kindled the heat of midday'; from Hom. *Od.* 4.400 ἦμος δ' ἠέλιος μέσον οὐρανὸν ἀμφιβεβήκῃ, 'when the sun in its course has reached mid-heaven' – so that Proteus, as a *pastor*, will be sleeping. Cf. 426–7 *medium sol igneus orbem | hauserat.* V.'s emphasis on pastoral heat, here and at 425–8 (see n.), far exceeds that of the Homeric model, and contrasts with the excessive cold of Orpheus' landscape (517–18); see also 363–73n.

402 The language of pastoral begins (433–6n.); cf. 3.325–7.

403 in secreta senis ducam: so Eidothea at Hom. *Od.* 4.407 ἔνθα σ' ἐγὼν ἀγαγοῦσα, 'I shall take you there myself'.

senis: cf. 438 *senem*; in *Od.* 4 he is consistently called ὁ γέρων.

404 facile ut somno adgrediare iacentem: recalling the sleep of Silenus, which likewise precedes his capture and his song: *E.* 6.14 *Silenum pueri somno uidere iacentem*. In both cases the sleep precedes and perhaps creates poetic inspiration; cf. Hor. *Epist.* 2.2.77–8 *scriptorum chorus ... | rite cliens Bacchi somno gaudentis et umbra.*

405 ubi correptum manibus uinclisque tenebis: cf. 396n.

406 'then will a variety of forms confuse you, and the shapes of wild beasts'; for the opening of the line cf. 1.181 (and n.) *tum uariae inludunt pestes.*

407–10 At Hom. *Od.* 4.417–18 Eidothea warns Menelaus that Proteus will turn into all the creatures of the earth, and into water and fire, but at 456–8 he in fact turns into a lion, a serpent, a leopard, a boar, water and a tree. V. reverses the two passages: Cyrene warns of a boar, a tigress, a serpent, a lioness, fire and water (exactly reversing Homer's order), but at 441–2 Proteus in fact turns into fire, beast and water. He omits the Homeric tree altogether, doubtless feeling it to be out of place, and each animal receives an epithet, while in Homer that is true only of the lion ('bearded') and the boar ('large'). V. may have sensed that the specific list of animals (407–10) should precede rather than follow the general reference, 442 *feram* (i.e. *Od.* 4.418 ἑρπετά). For a very similar alteration of the details of a Homeric list at *A.* 7.15–18, see Thomas (1985) 66–7.

407   horridus 'bristly'; cf. *A.* 7.17 *saetigerique sues.*

atraque tigris 'a deadly tiger', representing the Homeric leopard (πάρδαλις); for this use of *ater*, cf. 1.129 (and n.) *serpentibus . . . atris.*

408   squamosusque: only here in V.; he elsewhere uses *squameus* (2.154; 3.426), or a periphrasis with *squama*.

fulua ceruice leaena: though Page tries to exonerate V. by taking *leaena = leo*, this looks like a lapse, resulting from V.'s alteration of the gender, but not the appearance, of the Homeric lion: *Od.* 4.456 λέων . . . ἠϋγένειος, 'a bearded lion'. Valerius Flaccus likewise has a lioness (*lea*) with a mane (*iuba*) at *Arg.* 3.740.

409–10 V. speaks of fire and water, where Homer mentioned water and a tree (*Od.* 4.458); not only is fire more appropriate (407–10n.), but it better suits the emphasis on extremes of the various elements in the second half of the book (363–73n.).

409   flammae sonitum dabit: normally the phrase *sonitum dare* is absolute; e.g. *A.* 12.524 *dant sonitum . . . amnes.*

410   in aquas tenuis dilapsus abibit: adapted by Ovid at *A.A.* 1.761 *utque leues Proteus modo se tenuabit in undas.*

excidet . . . abibit: conatives: 'he will seek to . . .'

411–12 Developed from Hom. *Od.* 4.419 ὑμεῖς δ' ἀστεμφέως ἐχέμεν μᾶλλόν τε πιέζειν, 'you must hold him fast and press him all the more'.

contende tenacia uincla: cf. 396, 399–400.

413–14 'until through physical transformation he is such as he was when he closed his eyes as he first fell asleep'; from Hom. *Od.* 4.420–1 ἀλλ' ὅτε . . . | τοῖος ἐὼν οἷόν κε κατευνηθέντα ἴδησθε, 'but when . . . being just as he was when you saw him sleeping'.

tegeret cum lumina somno: for the more normal construction *tegeret cum lumina somnus*; cf. Cat. 51.11–12 *gemina teguntur | lumina nocte.*

415–52   Aristaeus and Proteus

As in the preceding section (387–414n.) the Homeric model is closely adapted, though modified in various ways (415, 425–8, 433–6nn.).

415   liquidum ambrosiae defundit odorem: Homer has Eidothea bring ambrosial unguent to Menelaus and his men (*Od.* 4.445–6), but its function there is to combat the foul odour of the seals. V., who has virtually suppressed this detail (cf. 395 (and n.) *turpis* – it may, however, be implied at 417 *dulcis … aura*; also 431n.), has Cyrene use it mainly to invigorate Aristaeus (418); in this the passage most resembles Homeric contexts where a deity infuses strength into a mortal (e.g. *Od.* 8.18–23); cf. *A.* 12.418–19.

416   perduxit 'coated'.

417   Somewhat rare in the poem, a golden line which does not serve as a clausula (1.117n.).

dulcis … aura 'a sweet scent'; see 395 (and n.) *turpis*, 415n.

compositis … crinibus: the effects of the oil; an elegiac attribute, going with the use of perfume (Prop. 1.15.5 *et potes hesterno manibus componere crinis*; also 1.2.1–6).

418   habilis membris uenit uigor: cf. 415n.

est specus ingens: another ecphrasis (cf. 387–8; 3.145–6nn.), the only one in V. beginning within a line. It is perhaps suggested by Hom. *Od.* 4.354 (of Pharos, the home of Proteus) νῆσος ἔπειτά τις ἔστι ..., 'now, there is an island ...', but it is closer in diction to *Il.* 13.32 (of the cave used by Poseidon; and cf. 430–1n.) ἔστι δέ τι σπέος εὐρύ ..., 'there is a broad cave ...'

419   exesi latere in montis: cf. 44 *exesaeque arboris antro*; *A.* 8.418–19 *specus et Cyclopum exesa caminis | antra Aetnaea tonant.*

419–20   quo … reductos 'to which numerous breakers are driven by the wind and dissipate into the withdrawn bays'; cf. *A.* 1.160–1 (which also expands on an ecphrasis, 159 *est in secessu longo locus*; see 421n.) *laterum, quibus omnis ab alto | frangitur inque sinus scindit sese unda reductos.* In both passages the alliteration represents the hissing of the shallow waves over the sand.

421   deprensis olim statio tutissima nautis: suggested by Hom. *Od.* 4.358–9 (where the geographical ecphrasis is also connected with seafaring; cf. 418n.) 'and there is a harbour there with good mooring, from which men put their well-balanced ships out to sea after drawing dark water'. Cf. *A.* 2.23 (which, like *A.* 1.160–1, expands on another ecphrasis; cf. 419–20n.) *nunc tantum sinus et statio male fida carinis*, 5.128 (which also follows an ecphrasis) *apricis statio gratissima mergis*.

deprensis 'caught [in a storm]'; cf. *A.* 5.52 *Argolicoue mari deprensus*.
olim 'sometimes', as at 433.

422   obice: the first syllable is scanned long (*objice*).

424   ipsa procul nebulis obscura resistit: Cyrene is present throughout, like Athena in the *Odyssey*; her part is resumed after the story of Orpheus and Eurydice: 530 *at non Cyrene* . . . . Aeneas and his men are similarly made invisible by Venus at *A.* 1.411–12.

425–8 See 401n. on V.'s (non-Homeric) emphasis on the heat of Proteus' setting. Almost every word conveys the intensity of heat: *rapidus, torrens, sitientis, ardebat, igneus, hauserat, arebant, siccis, tepefacta, coquebant.* For a similar concentration cf. 1.84–93 and n.

425–6   iam ... caelo: i.e. after the summer solstice, in July or August, the hottest times of the year. V. may intend a reference to Ap. Rhod. *Arg.* 2.516–17 (of the plague which Aristaeus cured) 'when from heaven Sirius scorched the Minoan islands'; cf. the plague at *A.* 3.141–2 *tum sterilis exurere Sirius agros,* | *arebant herbae* . . . (cf. 427n.).

rapidus 'consuming'; cf. 1.92 *rapidiue potentia solis*; *E.* 2.10 *rapido aestu*.
sitientis ... Indos: cf. 402 *cum sitiunt herbae.*

426–7   medium sol igneus orbem | hauserat: i.e. at midday; cf. 401 *medios cum sol accenderit aestus*; the sun is depicted as having 'consumed' half its course, a striking extension of the more usual notion of the consuming power of fire; e.g. Livy 5.7.3 *aggerem ac uineas . . . incendium hausit.*

427   arebant herbae: repeated at *A.* 3.142 (425–6n.).

427–8   caua ... coquebant 'and the hollow rivers with their dry channels were heated and baked down to the mud by the rays'; this is no normal summer heat.

429–30   cum ... | ibat: cf. Hom. *Od.* 4.403 ἐκ δ' ἐλθὼν κοιμᾶται ὑπὸ σπέσσι γλαφυροῖσιν, 'when he comes out [from the sea] he will sleep beneath his hollow caverns'.

ibat: cf. 365n.

430–1   eum uasti circum gens umida ponti | exsultans ...: at first sight an adaptation of *Od.* 4.404–5 (429–30n.) ἀμφὶ δέ μιν φῶκαι . . . εὕδουσιν, 'and about him the seals sleep'; but that detail comes at 432, and the reminiscence seems rather to be of *Il.* 13.27–8 (a context to which V. has already referred; 418n.) ἄταλλε δὲ κήτε' ὑπ' αὐτοῦ | πάντοθεν ἐκ κευθμῶν, 'and the sea-creatures came up from the depths and sported about him on all sides'.

uasti: in the same position at 422.

431   rorem late dispergit amarum: V. returns to the primary model, again suppressing the Homeric reference to odour (395, 415nn.): *Od.* 4.406 πικρὸν ἀποπνείουσαι ἁλὸς πολυβενθέος ὀδμήν, 'giving off the bitter smell of the deep sea'; *rorem ... amarum* may imply a smell, but essentially means 'briny spray' (cf. *E.* 10.5 *Doris amara*).

432   Cf. *Od.* 4.405 ἀθρόαι εὕδουσιν, 'they sleep in a huddle'; V. alters the detail (*diuersae in litore*, 'scattered about the shore').

somno: dative: '[lie down] for sleep'.

433–6   At *Od.* 4.411–13 Eidothea says that Proteus will go among his seals and count them, and will then lie among them (436n.) 'like a herdsman among his flocks of sheep' (νομεὺς ὣς πώεσι μήλων). V. expands this to give a vivid three-line simile (*preceding* the outer action of 436) comparing Proteus to a shepherd in the mountains on the lookout for wolves (395n.).

Proteus, then, is strongly associated with a *pastor*, both through the elaboration of this simile and through the intensely hot landscape in which he is set (401, 402, 425–8nn.). This is all intended to prepare the reader for his song (453–527), itself a poem with strong affinities to Virgilian bucolic, and doubtless to the poetry of Gallus which had been merged with Virgilian bucolic in *E.* 6 and 10 (see n.).

433   stabuli custos: cf. 1.17 *Pan, ouium custos*; *E.* 5.44 *pecoris custos*; 10.36 *custos gregis*.

olim: cf. 421n.

434   Cf. 186–7 (and n.) *Vesper ubi e pastu tandem decedere campis* | *admonuit*; the notion forms a pastoral closing: cf. *E.* 6.85–6; 10.77.

435   'and with the sound of their bleating the lambs sharpen the wolves' hunger'; an elegant reversal of the more normal order of subject and object ('the wolves hunger for the lambs').

436   consedit scopulo medius: Homer has him lying down in their midst to sleep: λέξεται ἐν μέσσῃσι, *Od.* 4.413. Cf. *A.* 7.169 *solio medius consedit auito*.

numerumque recenset: a pastoral act; cf. *E.* 6.85 (434n.) *numerumque referre*, 3.34 (excess) *bisque die numerant ambo pecus, alter et haedos*. V.

takes it from *Od.* 4.411 φώκας ... ἀριθμήσει, 'he will count his seals', and 451 λέκτο δ' ἀριθμόν, 'he tallied their number'.

437 The expression is rather odd: 'as soon as the opportunity of [catching] him offered itself to Aristaeus'; Conington has 'as soon as P. gave him the opportunity'.

438 senem: cf. 403n.

439-40 cum clamore ruit magno, manicisque iacentem | occupat: a close adaptation of *Od.* 4.454-5 ἡμεῖς δὲ ἰάχοντες ἐπεσσύμεθ', ἀμφὶ δὲ χεῖρας | βάλλομεν, 'with a cry we rushed upon him, and locked our arms around him'. V.'s enjambed verb *occupat* responds precisely in position and scansion to the Homeric βάλλομεν (cf. 447n.).

440 ille suae contra non immemor artis: a translation of *Od.* 4.455 οὐδ' ὁ γέρων δολίης ἐπελήθετο τέχνης, 'nor did the old man forget his devious skill'.

441-2 Cf. 407-10n. V. returns from the immediate Homeric context to *Od.* 4.417-18 'he will test you by turning into all the creatures which are born and crawl upon the earth, and into water and prodigious fire'. *omnia* matches Homer's πάντα in sense and initial position, and *miracula rerum* is probably intended to mean 'the wondrous things of the earth' (cf. *rerum* at 2.534, and see n.), rather than merely *miras res*, thus representing Homer's ἐπὶ γαῖαν. The second line therefore represents in detail the generality of the first with Homer's ἑρπετά (now *feram*) enclosed by the important Virgilian pair (inverted from the Homeric model), *ignem* and *fluuium* (363-73n.); a similar rearrangement occurred at 261-3 (see n.).

441 transformat sese in ...: cf. *A.* 7.416 (of Allecto) *in uultus sese transformat anilis.*

443 uerum ubi nulla fugam reperit fallacia: V. returns to the later section of *Od.* 4: ἀλλ' ὅτε δή ῥ' ἀνίαζ' ὁ γέρων ὀλοφώια εἰδώς, 'but when the old man, though skilled in wiles, grew weary', 460.

444 in sese redit: cf. 441 *transformat sese in ...*

445 nam quis te: for Homeric τίς νύ τοι (*Od.* 4.462); *nam quis* is similar to *quisnam*, but stronger 'why, who ...?'

confidentissime 'most impudent'; the word belongs to comedy, and to prose, and the superlative is not otherwise found before Apuleius. This is the only instance in the poem of a word extending from the third-foot main caesura to the end of the fifth foot; the effect is one of great weight.

446 quidue hinc petis?: cf. *Od.* 4.463 τέο σε χρή, 'what do you want?'

447 scis, Proteu: imitates *Od.* 4.465 in sense and shape and position, οἶσθα, γέρον, 'you know, old man' (cf. 439–40n.).
ipse: i.e. you (a *uates*) do not need to be told.

447–8 neque ... uelle 'nor is it possible to deceive you in anything: but [likewise] *you* should stop wanting [to deceive me]'; some have taken 447 'nor can you deceive me in anything', but that would require *quare* rather than *sed* in 448.
est = *potest* (impersonal); a Graecism.

448 deum praecepta: cf. 398n.

449 lassis quaesitum oracula rebus 'to seek oracular solutions for our weary fortunes'; cf. *A.* 3.145 *fessis ... rebus*; 11.335 *rebus ... fessis.* The supine (*quaesitum*) expresses purpose after a verb of motion.

450 uates: cf. 387–8n.
ui denique multa 'finally under the compulsion of great force'; cf. 398n.

451 ardentis oculos intorsit: Aristaeus is understood as the object of his gaze; cf. *A.* 12.670 *ardentis oculorum orbis ad moenia torsit.* Proteus has the appearance of a divine figure with oracular power; cf. *A.* 5.647–8 *diuini signa decoris | ardentisque notate oculos.*

452 frendens: the verb appears only here in V., and contributes to the depiction of Proteus' oracular ecstasy.
fatis ora resoluit 'opened his lips with [words of] destiny'.

453–527 The song of Proteus: Orpheus and Eurydice

The *causa morbi* in fact turns out to be Orpheus' and the nymphs' anger at Aristaeus for his pursuit of Eurydice, the ultimate cause of her death. Proteus, who offers no solutions to Aristaeus, merely sings the song which, after the opening lines, is concerned solely with Orpheus' recovery and second loss of Eurydice. It is a version which is not found before V. (Orpheus traditionally succeeds), in theme, style and emphasis absolutely typical of epyllion, and is to be seen as V.'s venture into that genre. The themes are success and failure, themes which reflect on a higher and more lyrical level the very essence of the poem (491–2, 511–15nn.).

Though in nature original the song shows a debt to Cat. 64 (Crabbe

(1977)), and doubtless is indebted to other neoteric epyllia. Coincidences with *E.* 6 and 10, and with the elegists (cf. 461–3, 464, 465–6, 466, 488, 498, 508–9, 514, 525–7nn.), strongly suggest that V. was also looking to the poetry of Gallus. It is particularly noteworthy that in the poetic genealogy of the Sixth Eclogue Orpheus and Gallus were connected (cf. Ross (1975) 23–38), while here in the story of Orpheus V. seems to recall the type of verse represented by Gallus. See Introduction, pp. 15–16.

453 'you are hounded by the anger of a considerable spirit'; for the emphatic double negative (never *nonnullus* or juxtaposed in V.) cf. 1.83 *nec nulla*; *A.* 11.725 *non ... nullis.* The final syllable of *nullius* is scanned long at the point of ictus.

The anger is chiefly that of the nymphs, who must be appeased at 535.

Non ... nullius ... numinis: Conington notes the Greek manner of asserting divine interest: οὐκ ἄνευ θεῶν, 'not without the gods', Eur. *I.A.* 809.

454   magna luis commissa: cf. *A.* 1.136 (Jupiter to the unruly winds) *post mihi non simili poena commissa luetis*; also 11.841–2, 849.

miserabilis: cf. 514 and n.

Orpheus: mentioned by name only here and at 494, where Eurydice addresses him.

455   haudquaquam ob meritum poenas: taken in three ways: (*a*) 'penalties which you have by no means deserved [because you did not intend Eurydice's death]'; (*b*) (with the Palatinus reading *ad* for *ob*) 'penalties which are by no means as severe as you deserve'; (*c*) (taking the phrase with *miserabilis*) 'Orpheus, wretched by no means according to his deserts'; (*b*) seems excessive and (*c*) somewhat harsh grammatically.

ni fata resistant: the thought of the apodosis is compressed: 'he stirs up punishments [which would be exacted] were not the fates to resist'.

456   rapta ... pro coniuge: cf. 3.67–8n. on the frequent association of *raptus*, etc. with death; see also 504 *rapta bis coniuge.*

grauiter: cf. 452; a casual reminiscence.

457–8   illa ... puella: for the demonstrative beginning the sentence and its noun coming at the end of the next line cf. *A.* 5.609–10 *illa ... uirgo*; 10.522–3 *ille ... supplex*; 12.901–2 *ille ... heros*; it is perhaps a feature of epic, and occurs in Homer (with the definite article doing the job of the demonstrative, to which it is often equivalent): *Il.* 1.488–9 αὐτὰρ ὁ ... Ἀχιλλεύς. Cf. also Callim. *Epigr.* 55.1–2 τῶι ... θεῶι.

457   illa quidem: changes the subject and provides emphasis; cf. 3.217n.; and see 506 (and n.), where the focus moves from Orpheus to Eurydice.

dum te fugeret: the subjunctive implies an end to the action of the main clause: 'if only she might escape you'.

458–9   hydrum ... non uidit in herba: once again a *pestis* (3.414–39n.). Cf. *E.* 3.93 *frigidus ... latet anguis in herba.*

seruantem ripas 'hugging the banks'.

460   chorus aequalis Dryadum: *aequalis* is transferred: 'the band of her companion Dryads'.

461   impleuit: preferable to the better-supported *implerunt,* which produces with *flerunt* (by which it may have been generated) a rhyme that is not typical of V.

461–3   flerunt ... Orithyia: the empathy and grief of nature look to *E.* 10.13–15 (where the cause is Gallus' dying of love) *illum etiam lauri, etiam fleuere myricae ...*

The places mentioned are Scythian and Thracian locales, balanced by those at 517–19 (towards the end of the story), where Orpheus wanders in the northern wastes.

461   Rhodopeiae arces: cf. 1.240 *Riphaeasque ... arces.* Rhodope is associated with Orpheus at *E.* 6.30 *nec tantum Rhodope miratur et Ismarus Orphea.* The adjective (scanned *Rhōdŏpēĭaĕ,* with the last syllable treated as short in hiatus – 'epic correption'), though a Greek formation, is not found in Greek; cf. 317n.

463   The line looks Greek (an effect produced elsewhere, without there being a specific model; 1.279n.); there is hiatus after *Getae,* and *Orithyia* creates a *spondeiazon.* The Getae are a people, Hebrus the river down which Orpheus' head will roll (523–7), and Attic Orithyia was the daughter of Erechtheus who married the North wind (mentioned with these details at Ap. Rhod. *Arg.* 1.212, also a *spondeiazon*).

464   He attempts to use song, or poetry, as a solace for his love; somewhat similar is *E.* 6.46 *Pasiphaen niuei solatur amore iuuenci*; cf. too *A.* 10.191 (of Cycnus, on the loss of Phaethon) *dum canit et maestum Musa solatur amorem.* Cf. Horace of the poet Anacreon at *Epd.* 14.11 *qui persaepe caua testudine fleuit amorem.*

aegrum: used of Dido at *A.* 4.35, 389.

465–6   A sonorous and studied couplet, shaped by the repetition of *te* (elegantly placed at line-beginning and following the main caesura in each line), with *t, s* and *l* sounds predominating in the first line, *t, d* and *c* in the second. In its mannered effect it is somewhat reminiscent of a couplet from Cinna's epyllion, the *Zmyrna*: *te matutinus flentem conspexit Eous | et flentem paulo uidit post Hesperus idem*, p. 88 Morel. Such mannerism may well have appealed to Gallus, if Ov. *Am.* 1.15.29–30 in some way reflects his style: *Gallus et Hesperiis et Gallus notus Eois, | et sua cum Gallo nota Lycoris erit* (525–7n.).

466   te solo in litore secum: cf. 1.389 *et sola in sicca secum spatiatur harena*; Cat. 64.133 *deserto . . . in litore*; see 319n. on the lone lament beside water, a feature it seems of Gallus' poetry – certainly the words are reminiscent of the lament of the elegist in general; cf. Prop. 1.18.1 *haec certe deserta loca et taciturna querenti*, 2 *uacuum . . . nemus*, 4 *sola . . . saxa*.

467   Taenarias . . . fauces: Taenarus, the southern tip of Laconia, had a cave reputed to be an entrance to the Underworld.

468   caligantem nigra formidine lucum 'the grove which was shrouded with dark terror'; a fine blending of the physical and spiritual appearance of the place.

469   adiit 'dared to approach', 'actually approached'.

470   nesciaque humanis precibus mansuescere corda: cf. 489 *ignoscenda quidem, scirent si ignoscere Manes*. The thought is traditional; cf. Hom. *Il.* 9.158 Ἀίδης τοι ἀμείλιχος ἠδ᾽ ἀδάμαστος, 'Hades is implacable and inflexible'.

471–80   Developed from Hom. *Od.* 11.34–43, where the host of the Underworld crowd in on the blood of the sheep sacrificed by Odysseus. V. softens the ghoulish nature of the original by having the souls respond to the music of Orpheus. The image is repeated at *A.* 6.305–12, with 306–8 identical to 475–7 here, and with the simile (6.309–12) slightly changed from that of 473–4 and following instead of preceding the repeated lines.

471   Erebi de sedibus imis: from *Od.* 11.37 ὑπὲξ Ἐρέβευς, 'up out of Erebus'.

472   tenues: cf. 499–500 (of Eurydice's shade) *ceu fumus in auras | commixtus tenuis*; also *A.* 6.292 *tenuis sine corpore uitas*.

simulacraque luce carentum: from Lucr. 4.39; and cf. 255 (of the dead bees) *corpora luce carentum*.

473–4   The shades are compared to the number of birds which settle in the foliage when evening or rain approaches; at *A.* 6.309–12 (471–80n.) this is expanded as they are compared to the number of falling leaves, *or* to the birds which leave in winter for warmer climates.

473 quam multa: cf. 2.103–6 *quam multae … quam multae*; V. uses the phrase as often as he uses *quot*.

474 Vesper ubi …: cf. 434, with the same personification.

475 uita: ablative of separation with *defuncta:* 'bereft of life'.

476 magnanimum: the only 2nd decl. adjective in V. with a gen. pl. in *-um* (a feature common enough with some 2nd decl. nouns and especially proper names); the form is archaic, but by this time is felt as an epicism.

pueri innuptaeque puellae: a more or less formulaic phrase for the innocent young; cf. *A.* 2.238; 6.307.

477 A notion of extreme pathos and tragedy throughout V.; the detail is not found in the Homeric model.

478 deformis 'unsightly'; only here in V.

479 tardaque palus inamabilis unda 'the hateful marsh with its sluggish water'; cf. *A.* 6.438 *tristisque palus inamabilis undae* (480n.). Hades is called *inamabile regnum* at Ov. *M.* 4.477. The *palus* is presumably the Styx of the next line.

480 Repeated at *A.* 6.439.

nouies … interfusa 'which flows nine times around them'.

481–4 Orpheus' music affects not only the shades (471 *cantu commotae*) but the very halls of the Underworld, the Furies, Cerberus and the wind which drives the wheel of Ixion. The lines suggest the triumph of poetry over Hades, a theme which V. had already developed in a programmatic context at 3.37–9 (see n.). Orpheus' success is, however, temporary, doomed to be reversed by his emotional lapse (485–91), a lapse which results in the extinction of his *labor* (491–2n.).

481 quin ipsae stupuere domus 'what is more the halls themselves were amazed'.

481–2 intima Leti | Tartara 'innermost Tartarus, seat of Death'; or possibly, since Tartarus is the pit of Hades, 'the innermost pit of Death'. The expression is somewhat obscure.

482–3 caeruleosque implexae crinibus anguis | Eumenides: a standard feature of the Furies; cf. Cat. 64.193 *Eumenides, quibus anguino redimita capillo | frons exspirantis praeportat pectoris iras*; *A.* 7.346–7. *anguis* is a retained accusative with *implexae* (which has reflexive force) 'with snakes entwined in their hair' (lit. 'having had snakes entwined').

483–4 Eumenides … Ixionii: the same two are found (with Cocytus; cf. 479) at 3.37–8 *Furias … Cocyti … Ixionis* (481–4n.).

483   tenuitque inhians tria Cerberus ora: cf. *A.* 6.417–18 *Cerberus haec ingens latratu regna trifauci | personat*; there the beast is tamed by the drugged food of the Sibyl. For *tenuit ... ora* cf. *A.* 2.1 *ora tenebant.*

484   uento ... constitit 'was stopped in the wind' (since the wind had stopped); cf. *E.* 2.26 *cum placidum uentis staret mare.*

rota ... orbis 'the wheel of his [Ixion's] turning'; *orbis rotae* might seem the more natural expression; Ovid (*M.* 10.42) has *Ixionis orbis.* Ixion was attached to a revolving wheel in punishment for his attempt to seduce Juno.

485   iamque pedem referens ...: V. proceeds immediately to the departure of Orpheus and Eurydice, referring only obliquely to the success of the petition (486 *reddita*). Ovid, perhaps providing a commentary on the compression, has Orpheus deliver a persuasive speech of 23 lines to Pluto and Persephone (*M.* 10.17–39).

486   superas ueniebat ad auras: cf. *A.* 6.128–9 *reuocare gradum superasque euadere* (cf. 485 *euaserat*) *ad auras, | hoc opus, hic labor est.*

487   hanc ... legem: as at 485, the reference to actual negotiation is oblique; cf. Ov. *M.* 10.50–1 *hanc simul et legem Rhodopeius accipit Orpheus, | ne flectat retro sua lumina.*

488   cum subita incautum dementia cepit amantem: the *cum*-clause, which carries the main action of the sentence, effectively reverses the success which Orpheus had been enjoying. V. uses the amatory language of the *Eclogues*; cf. *E.* 2.69 *a, Corydon, Corydon, quae te dementia cepit*; 6.47 (of Pasiphae) *a, uirgo infelix, quae te dementia cepit.* Orpheus' failure is emotional, a loss of control caused by *amor* (cf. 494–5n.).

incautum: cf. 2.303 and n., where heedlessness leads to the destruction of the farmer's *labor.*

489   See 470 and n.

490–1   restitit ... respexit: a climactic sentence with the two crucial actions beginning and ending the sentence, and with what lies between creating a suspension of action which drives home the enormity of Orpheus' error. The effect is stressed by the rare pause after *respexit* at the fifth-foot trochee.

Eurydicenque suam 'his own [dear] Eurydice'.

immemor heu!: cf. Cat. 64.135 (Ariadne of Theseus' desertion) *immemor a!.* Cf. 3.215–16n. on the connection between *amor* and forgetfulness.

uictusque animi 'defeated in his purpose'; for the genitive of respect cf. 3.289 *animi dubius.*

491–2 **ibi omnis | effusus labor:** words crucial to the poem, and indicating one of the main connections between Orpheus and the participants of the agricultural *Georgics*; Orpheus, paradigm for the man who controls not only nature, but even the powers of the Underworld, finds his own *labor* destroyed by a momentary lapse – a lapse caused by *amor*, one of the very forces of nature which destroyed man's work in Book 3. Cf. 1.325–6 (of the storm) *sata laeta boumque labores | diluit*; 3.525 *quid labor aut benefacta iuuant?*

492–3 **rupta ... | foedera:** a political phrase; cf. *A.* 8.540; 12.202, 582.

493 **stagnis ... Auernis** 'the pools of Avernus'; adjectival *Auernus* is more common than *Auernalis* (cf. 2.164 *fretis ... Auernis*).

494–5 **quis et me ... miseram et te perdidit, Orpheu, | quis tantus furor?:** cf. the questions posed to the afflicted Gallus at *E.* 10.21–2 *omnes 'unde amor iste' rogant 'tibi?' uenit Apollo: | 'Galle quid insanis?'* The language is similar to that of elegy; cf. Prop. 2.28A.7 *hoc perdit miseras, hoc perdidit ante puellas.* And the answer to the second question, *amor*, looks back to the treatment of love in the third book, and foreshadows the love-madness of Dido in the *Aeneid*. Cf. also *A.* 5.670 *'quis furor iste nouus?'*

495 **en iterum** 'look, once again ...'; she recedes as she speaks.

496 **conditque natantia lumina somnus:** cf. *A.* 5.856 (where the deity Somnus descends on Palinurus) *cunctantique natantia lumina soluit.* In both lines the unusual coincidence of accent and ictus perhaps reflects the harmony of the power of sleep.

lumina condere is commonly used of closing the eyes of a corpse; e.g. Prop. 4.11.64 *condita sunt uestro lumina nostra sinu.*

497 **iamque uale:** V. reserves the words for the dead and dying: *A.* 2.789 (Creusa to Aeneas); 5.738 (Anchises to Aeneas); 11.827 (Camilla to Acca).

feror 'I am carried off'.

498 **tendens ... palmas:** like the shades of *A.* 6.314 *tendebantque manus ripae ulterioris amore*; see 471–8on.

heu non tua: the appositional phrase disrupts the natural word-order and has high emotional effect.

499–502 Closely adapted from Hom. *Il.* 23.99–101, where Achilles tries vainly to embrace the ghost of Patroclus: 'so he spoke and reached out with his own hands, but could not grasp him; for his spirit departed like smoke beneath the ground, squeaking as it went'. The motif is later developed at *A.* 2.790–4 and 6.699–702, as Aeneas tries to embrace the apparition of Creusa, and the shade of Anchises; these two, however, are strongly influenced by another Homeric scene, that at *Od.* 11.204–8, where Odysseus makes a similar attempt to embrace his mother in the Underworld.

499–500   ceu fumus in auras | commixtus tenuis: cf. 472 (and n.) *umbrae ... tenues*; also *A.* 2.791 *tenuisque recessit in auras* – in both passages *tenuis* modifies *auras*.

500   fugit diuersa: cf. *A.* 12.742 *ergo amens diuersa fuga petit aequora Turnus.*

500–2   neque ... dicere: cf. *A.* 2.790–1 *lacrimantem et multa uolentem | dicere deseruit* (499–502, 499–500nn.); also *A.* 4. 390–1 (as Dido leaves Aeneas) *linquens multa metu cunctantem et multa parantem | dicere.* Ovid conflated these lines with 502–3: *M.* 10.72–3 *orantem frustraque iterum transire uolentem | portitor arcuerat.*

umbras: probably 'the shadows' (Conington) rather than 'her shade' (Forbiger), which would normally be in the singular; cf. *A.* 2.772 *umbra Creusae*, etc.

502   portitor Orci: cf. *A.* 6.326 *portitor ille Charon.*

503   obiectam ... paludem 'the barrier of the marsh'.

504–5   The despairing deliberative question seems to have been a requirement of epyllion; cf. Cat. 64.177–83 *nam quo me referam? quali spe perdita nitor? ... an patris auxilium sperem?*, etc. See 322–5n.

rapta bis coniuge: cf. 456 (and n.) *rapta ... pro coniuge.*

qua: *quae* has better MS support and is preferred by most editors, but *qua* is perhaps more elegant and gives greater force to the question – and has good parallels; cf. 2.95 *quo te carmine dicam?*; *A.* 4.283–4 *quo nunc reginam ambire furentem | audeat adfatu?*; 6.506 *magna* (syntactically parallel to *qua*) *manis ter uoce uocaui.*

506   A golden line depicts the last glimpse of Eurydice and ends the subsection (1.117n.). The imperfect *nabat* presents the action from Orpheus' point of view.

illa quidem: cf. 457 and n.; the words form a frame, introducing the first and last lines on Eurydice. Cf. Cat. 64.167, where Ariadne sees Theseus for the last time, *ille autem prope iam mediis uersatur in undis.*

507   totos ... ex ordine: stressing the duration: 'seven whole months, one after the other'.

perhibent: the oblique manner of narration is characteristic of epyllion; cf. Cat. 64.76 *nam perhibent ...*, 124 *saepe illam perhibent.*

508–9 rupe sub aëria deserti ad Strymonis undam | flesse sibi: cf. 319n. Cf. Theocr. 7.72–7, where Tityrus sings of the lovelorn Daphnis wasting away beside the river Himeras, also in the presence of an empathetic nature (cf. 510). And the parallels with *E.* 10 and the role of Gallus are close and significant (461–3n.).

509 haec euoluisse: Orpheus is more than just a character in the action; Proteus suggests that he is responsible for the actual poem – *haec* refers to the entire song.

astris: slightly preferable to *antris* (somewhat flat after *rupe* in 508); cf. Prop. 1.16.23–4 (also a lamenting lover) *me mediae noctes, me sidera plena iacentem, | frigidaque Eoo me dolet aura gelu.*

510 The traditional role of Orpheus; cf. Hor. *Odes* 3.11.23–24 (addressed to the lyre, but referring to Orpheus) *tu potes tigris comitesque siluas | ducere et riuos celeris morari*; at *E.* 6.69–71 (*calamos ... quibus ille solebat | cantando rigidas deducere montibus ornos*) the reference is either to Orpheus or Orphic qualities; see Ross (1975) 26–7.

511–15 V. has conflated two Homeric passages: the primary model is *Od.* 19.518–23, where Penelope compares herself to Philomela, whose lament for her son Itys became the song of the nightingale; the secondary reference is to *Od.* 16.216–18, where the lamentations of Odysseus and Telemachus are compared to the cry of birds whose young have been taken away by farmers. More important than this, however, is the Virgilian self-reference of the lines; they immediately recall 2.207–11, where the successful farmer, who has control over his environment, uproots and destroys the birds' home as he converts the woods to ploughlands (see n.). Orpheus, who traditionally controls nature, has through a failure of emotion become identified with the victim of the ethics which earlier in the poem represent that same control (512n., Introduction, pp. 23–4).

511 populea: the noun *populus* ('poplar') can only be used in the nominative in dactylic poetry; hence the frequency of this adjective in V. (*A.* 5.134; 8.32, 286; 10.190).

512 queritur: cf. 515 (and n.) *questibus.*

durus arator: looks to 2.207 (see n.) *iratus ... arator*; cf. 511–15n.

513 implumis: from Hom. *Od.* 16.218 πάρος πετεηνὰ γενέσθαι, 'before their wings were fully-grown' (511–15n.).

514   miserabile carmen: V. has altered the Homeric model (*Od.* 19.521 πολυήχεα φωνήν, 'many-toned song') so as to suggest the elegiac associations of Orpheus' song; cf. Hor. *Odes* 1.33.2–3 (of Tibullus' poetry) *miserabilis | ... elegos.*

515   maestis late loca questibus implet: cf. 460–1 *clamore ... | impleuit montis*; also *A.* 9.480 (the lament of Euryalus' mother for her dead son) *caelum dehinc questibus implet.* V. surely has in mind Cat. 64.130 (just before the lament of Ariadne) *haec extremis maestam dixisse querellis.*

516   nulla Venus, non ulli animum flexere hymenaei: the effect is parallel to that of the plague at 3.520–1 *non umbrae altorum nemorum, non mollia possunt | prata mouere animum*; and cf. *A.* 4.35 (of Dido) *aegram nulli quondam flexere mariti* (the form *flexere* appears nowhere else in the corpus); also Cat. 64.330 [*coniunx*] *quae tibi flexanimo mentem perfundat amore.*

517–19   solus ... | lustrabat: Orpheus wanders alone (466 and n.) in a frozen landscape, matching, but more intense than, that of 461–3 (see n.) – the reverse of the intensely hot setting of Proteus (401–2, 425–8 and nn.). Ross (1975) 94 notes: 'the unending cold of the landscape suggests vividly the impotence of the pure magic of [Orpheus'] song when faced with the reality of personal loss'. There is a reminiscence of the end of the song of Gallus at *E.* 10.65–6, where the poet states that Amor will be implacable, regardless of the hardship he (Gallus) undergoes: *nec si frigoribus mediis Hebrumque bibamus | Sithoniasque niues hiemis subeamus aquosae.*

The lines, especially *Hyperboreas* and *Riphaeis*, also evoke the frigid Scythia of Book 3 (cf. 3.381–2).

518   aruaque ... numquam uiduata pruinis: cf. 3.356 *semper hiems, semper spirantes frigora Cauri*; see 517–19n.

519–20   raptam Eurydicen ... querens: cf. 512 *amissos queritur fetus*; also 456 *rapta ... pro coniuge*, 504 *rapta bis coniuge*, and see 3.67–8n.

**520–2   **Orpheus is conflated with Pentheus, who was torn apart by maenads (traditionally Thracian as here) for his refusal to believe in Dionysus. The present cause is Orpheus' preoccupation with his own grief, which is taken as a slight by the women. In Aeschylus' *Bassarides* Dionysus sent these Bassarid women against Orpheus, whom they apparently tore apart; cf. [Eratosth.] *Catast.* 24.

520   Ciconum ... matres: the Cicones were a people of southern Thrace. *matres* is somewhat odd if *spretae* refers to their sense of a personal

slight (rather than his slighting their cult activities), and Ovid makes a
pointed change: *M.* 11.3 *nurus Ciconum.*

quo munere 'for which tribute [to the dead Eurydice]'.

521   inter sacra deum: cf. 3.486 *saepe in honore deum.*

nocturnique orgia Bacchi: the words carry a hint of the Roman
disapproval of these activities, evident in the *Senatus Consultum de Bac-
chanalibus*, and in the embellishment of Livy 39.8–18; cf. 39.8.4 (of the
Greek who imported the rite) *occultorum et nocturnorum antistes sacrorum.*

522   discerptum ... sparsere 'tore him apart and scattered him'.
V. perhaps intends a gloss on σπαραγμός (related to *spargo*), the technical
term for the Bacchants' tearing to pieces of their victims; cf. Eur. *Bacch.*
1127 (the fate of Pentheus) ἀπεσπάραξεν ὦμον, 'she [Agave] tore his
shoulder off', 1134–5 γυμνοῦντο δὲ | πλευραὶ σπαραγμοῖς, 'his ribs were
stripped by their tearing'.

523–7   The climax and conclusion of the song: Orpheus' head goes
rolling down the icy Hebrus, his dying voice still singing of Eurydice.

523   caput a ceruice reuulsum: taken from Ennius, *Ann.* 483
Skutsch, where the context is similar: the eyes of a severed head still
flicker (484 *semianimesque micant oculi*); Servius, who preserves the Ennian
lines (ad *A.* 10.396), states that this second line (484) was taken over
intact by Varro of Atax (p. 96 Morel), and it is possible that V. is
referring to more than one model. Cf. *A.* 2.558 (of the death of Priam)
auulsumque umeris caput.

524   Oeagrius Hebrus: cf. Ov. *M.* 2.219 *Oeagrius Haemus*; the
adjective (= 'Thracian') is appropriate in that it derives from Oeagrus,
king of Thrace and father of Orpheus. The poet of the *Culex* brings out
this connection by altering the Virgilian combination: 117–18 *tantum
non Oeagrius Hebrum | restantem tenuit ripis siluasque canendo.*
At 463 the Hebrus wept for Eurydice, and it is evoked by Gallus as a
paradigm for the frozen north at *E.* 10.65; see Ross (1975) 93.

525–7   Eurydicen ... ripae: the words of Orpheus' final song are
reported. The double repetition of *Eurydicen*, and the pathetic exclamation *a* (which occurs elsewhere in the *Georgics* only at 2.252, not at all in
the *Aeneid*, and in the *Eclogues* usually in situations which recall neoteric
poetry) are features of the high neoteric style, and, it seems, of the style of
Gallus; cf. *E.* 10.47–9, where *a!* occurs three times in as many lines –
lines which Servius says were taken over from Gallus. Perhaps the final
words of Orpheus are also the final element of the *laudes Galli* (*poetae*).

526 a miseram Eurydicen: cf. the exclamation from Calvus' *Io* (p. 85 Morel), developed by V. at *E.* 6.47, 52 *a uirgo infelix.*

527 Elegant word-order (not quite a golden line) closes the song. The echoing of Orpheus' words perhaps suggests the same empathy as at 460–3. This too is a feature of elegy; cf. Prop. 1.18.21 *a quotiens teneras resonant mea uerba sub umbras!*; also *E.* 1.4–5 *tu, Tityre, lentus in umbra | formosam resonare doces Amaryllida siluas.*

528–58   Proteus, Cyrene, Aristaeus and bugonia

The narrative retreats from the centrally placed song of Orpheus, retracing in reverse order the subjects of 281–452 – the *bugonia* and the roles of Aristaeus, Cyrene and Proteus.

528–9 From Hom. *Od.* 4.570 (immediately following Proteus' prophecy) ὣς εἰπὼν ὑπὸ πόντον ἐδύσετο κυμαίνοντα, 'so he spoke, and dived back under the surging sea'.

spumantem undam sub uertice torsit: cf. Cat. 64.13 *tortaque remigio spumis incanuit unda.*

530 at non Cyrene: at *Od.* 4.571 the contrast is rather between Proteus and Menelaus (Eidothea, unlike Cyrene, was not present for the prophecy) αὐτὰρ ἐγών, 'but as for me, I . . .'

timentem: like Menelaus after hearing the words of Proteus: *Od.* 4.572 πολλὰ δέ μοι κραδίη πόρφυρε κιόντι, 'as I went my heart was greatly troubled'.

531 nate: her exclusive way of addressing him (cf. 396, 412).

tristis: cf. 319n.

532 haec omnis morbi causa: cause and remedy had been promised at 396–7, but only the former is given; the remedy is again to be the *bugonia*, described in even more excessive terms than previously (538–58 and n.).

miserabile: modifies *exitium.*

Nymphae: the Dryad companions of Eurydice who mourned her loss at 460–1; cf. 535n.

533 Cf. 460 *chorus aequalis Dryadum*; also *A.* 1.498–9 *per iuga Cynthi | exercet Diana choros.*

534 exitium misere apibus: cf. 318 *amissis . . . apibus morboque fameque.*

535   facilis uenerare Napaeas: V. returns to the solution of 1.338 *in primis uenerare deos* – a solution which has had little to do with the real problems of the *Georgics* (1.335–50n.).

The *Napaeae* are nymphs of the vales (νάπαι), who make their first appearance here. They are not found at all in Greek, though Aelian (*N.A.* 6.42) refers to a 'god of the woods and vales' (θεὸν ὑλαῖόν τε καὶ ναπαῖον). Columella (10.264) has them separate from the Dryads, but it looks as if V. made no distinction; see 460, 533.

facilis 'easily appeased'; cf. *E.* 3.9 *faciles Nymphae risere.*

536   irasque remittent: cf. 453 *te ... exercent ... irae.*

537   modus orandi: the *bugonia*, ostensibly a scientific procedure at 281–314 (see n.), has now become a religious function – whose details, moreover, differ fundamentally from the previous description (538–58n.); this removes it even further from the realities of the poem (1.335–50n.).

ordine: as at 376; Cyrene and her nymphs are careful with their rituals.

538–58   As at 387–452, Cyrene's instructions to her son are followed by his execution of them. The *bugonia* looks little like that of 281–314: there is no attempt to prevent puncturing the carcass (542), and there is no special structure into which it is put. Moreover, this is even less economically rational as a means of restoring a hive of bees: Aristaeus must slaughter a total of ten animals – four choice bulls, the same number of heifers, a ewe and a calf. This is a religious ceremony, somewhat resembling the *suouetaurilia* of Cato, *Agr.* 141; cf. 537n.

538–42   quattuor ... | quattuor: matches the anaphora *quattuor ... | quattuor* at 297–8 (see n.).

538   The line is repeated exactly at 550, giving a sense of correct religious procedure (cf. 540, 544, 549–53nn.). It is also used (with *a stabulis* for *eximios*) of the bulls stolen from Hercules by Cacus at *A.* 8.207 – with *totidem ... iuuencas* in the following line (as in 540 and 551).

praestanti corpore: also of Nymphs at *A.* 1.71, of Turnus at 7.783.

539   depascunt summa Lycaei: on *depascunt* cf. 1.112n.; Mt Lycaeus is appropriate to the designation *Arcadii ... magistri* (283), but not to the fact that Aristaeus is now in Thessaly. At 1.14 his herds are grazing on the island of Cea.

540   delige: cf. 296 (of the setting of the *bugonia*) *eligitur locus.*

et ... iuuencas: cf. the sacral repetition at 551, and cf. 538n.

intacta ... ceruice: i.e. not yet used in ploughing; cf. the sacrifice at *A.* 6.38–9 *nunc grege de intacto septem mactare iuuencos | praestiterit.*

541–2   quattuor ... aras ... | constitue: cf. 549 *monstratas excitat aras* (cf. 538n.); these have taken the place of the four-windowed enclosure described at 296–8.

dearum: i.e. the nymphs.

542   sacrum iugulis demitte cruorem: at odds with the precepts given at 302; see 538–58n.

543   frondoso ... luco: as befits a sacrifice to the nymphs, but not mentioned at 281–314.

544   Repeated, with *induxerat* for *ostenderit*, at 552; cf. 538n.

post, ubi ...: see 3.235n.

**545–6   The shade of Orpheus is to be appeased with poppies and a black ewe; the former are connected with Ceres and Proserpina (1.212n.), while black victims are traditional offerings to the shades: at *Od.* 11.32–3 Odysseus offers a black ram before proceeding to the Underworld, at *A.* 5.97 Aeneas offers black-backed steers to Anchises, and he is told by the Sibyl to prepare for his descent to the Underworld in the same way: *duc nigras pecudes*, 6.153; also 6.243.

inferias Orphei ... papauera mittes 'send poppies as funeral offerings to Orpheus'; cf. Lucr. 3.52–3 *pecudes ... manibu' diuis | inferias mittunt. Orphēī* is a Greek dative, scanned by synizesis as a spondee, like the accusative *Orphĕā* at *E.* 6.30. Cf. 553 and 538n. for the repetition of these words and of *lucumque reuises/reuisit.*

Lethaea papauera: cf. 1.78 (and 1.77–8n.) *Lethaeo perfusa papauera somno.*

mittes | ... mactabis ... reuises: like *uenabere* in 547, didactic futures for the imperative.

**547   Placed by Bentley before 546, since it seems at first sight awkward following *lucumque reuises*; but the tense of *placatam* implies that the preceding sacrifices and offerings have appeased Eurydice, and the calf is merely a thank-offering after the success of the *bugonia*. It might seem rather curious that this sacrifice is the only item not repeated in 549–58 (cf. 538n.), but it would belong logically after 558, and V. clearly wished to end the section with the appearance of the bees.

uitula: the animal used for the *bugonia* at 299–300 (there a male: *uitulus ... | quaeritur*), but that is not its function here.

548 haud mora: cf. 185n., and *A.* 3.548 *haud mora, continuo* ...
matris praecepta: cf. 398n.

549–53 Virtually every word is repeated from 538–47, as Aristaeus
carries out Cyrene's instructions (cf. 537 *ordine*, and see 538n.); such a
style is epic (Homeric).

549 monstratas: cf. Dido's preparations at *A.* 4.498 *monstratque
sacerdos*, 636 *monstrata piacula ducat* [sc. *Anna*].

554–5 subitum ac dictu mirabile monstrum | aspiciunt: so
described at 309 *uisenda modis animalia miris*; see n. See too *A.* 7.64–6 *huius
apes summum densae (mirabile dictu) | ... | obsedere apicem.*

555 liquefacta ... per uiscera: cf. 302 *soluuntur uiscera*, 308 *tepefactus in ossibus umor.*

556 stridere: cf. 310 *stridentia pennis*; for *strideo/strido* in V. see 262n.;
on *(ef)ferueo/feruo* see 1.455–6n.

557 immensasque trahi nubes: so of the bees at 60 *obscuramque
trahi uento mirabere nubem*; also 312 (the simile for their emergence from
the carcass) *ut aestiuis effusus nubibus imber.*

558 et lentis uuam demittere ramis 'and hang in a cluster from
the pliant boughs'; cf. Hom. *Il.* 2.89 (also of bees) βοτρυδόν, 'like a
bunch of grapes'.

559–66 The poet's sphragis

The *Georgics* is the only Virgilian poem or collection which concludes
with a *sphragis* ('seal', 'signature'), though these lines refer also to the
Eclogues (565–6n.). The device, which is a vehicle for discussion of the
poet's literary achievement, immortality, etc., gained prominence in
Hellenistic literature, and V. may have been chiefly motivated by the
fact that the four-book collection of Callimachus' *Aetia* concluded in this
way (*Aet.* 4, fr. 112 Pf.). Mention of Caesar (560) may be intended to
parallel the prominence of Berenice at the end of that poem (fr. 110 Pf.);
cf. 3.16n. In Augustan poetry the *sphragis* is fairly common; e.g. Prop.
1.22; Hor. *Odes* 3.30 (*Sat.* 1.10 and *Epist.* 1.20 are variations on the
theme, adapted to the genres in which they appear); Ovid, *M.*
15.871–9. The *Eclogues* end with a coda, if not a *sphragis*, which like this
passage extends over eight lines (*E.* 10.70–7) and begins with *haec* –
referring to the entire collection.

559–60   Haec... arboribus: cf. 2.143–4n. on the couplet referring
to the topics of Books 1–3. Since (as always in such instances) the topic of
Book 4 is omitted (Servius noticed, and thought *pecora* could include
apes!), *haec super* ... is somewhat ambiguous: either 'this [the whole
poem] is what I sang concerning [agriculture]', or 'this [Book 4] is what
I sang over and above [agriculture]' – V. could easily have intended
both meanings.

Haec... canebam: the 'epistolary' imperfect; cf. Hor. *Epist.* 1.10.49
(at the end of the letter) *haec tibi dictabam.*

**560–1   Caesar dum magnus ad altum | fulminat Euphraten
bello:** cf. 1.509n. for the importance of placement of the Euphrates in
V., and for the connections he thereby establishes with Callimachus.
The wording *Caesar ... fulminat* is of interest; though Lucretius (3.1034)
referred to Scipio Africanus as *belli fulmen* (adapted by V. at *A.* 6.842–3),
the verb *fulmino* occurs here for the first time with a personal subject
other than Jupiter. At the beginning of the *Georgics* there was a suggestion that Jupiter (towards whom V. is ambivalent throughout the
poem) had in some way been supplanted by Octavian (1.1–42n.; also
562n.). If the same implication emerges from the present use of *fulminare*,
it may be that V. was also thinking of another prominent Callimachean
context, *Aet.* 1, fr. 1.20 βροντᾶν οὐκ ἐμόν, ἀλλὰ Διός, 'thundering is for
Zeus, not for me'. Octavian's military operations (*bello*) are at 564
contrasted (with excessive self-deprecation) with Virgilian leisure: *ignobilis oti.* For the ambiguity with which V. treats Octavian's activities
in the East, cf. 2.170–2n.

561–2   uictorque... iura: a foreshadowing of the famous words of
Anchises at *A.* 6.851–3 '*tu regere imperio populos, Romane, memento* | ...'

562   uiamque adfectat Olympo: forms a frame with the beginning of the poem (1.24–42 and n.). The words strengthen the sense that
Octavian in some way supplants, rather than merely joins, Jupiter
(560–1n.).

563–6   Four lines on Octavian are balanced by four on V.

563   Vergilium: V. does not elsewhere mention himself by name
(but cf. 1.427–37n.).

564   Parthenope: i.e. Naples (so named for a Siren supposed to be
buried there), where V. was buried; cf. the epitaph reported at *Vita
Donati* 36 *Mantua me genuit, Calabri rapuere, tenet nunc* | *Parthenope; cecini
pascua rura duces.*

ignobilis oti: cf. 2.486 (and n.) *inglorius*; the self-deprecatory reference is in marked contrast to the 'glorious' achievements of Octavian (560–1n.).

565–6   The end of the *Georgics* refers to the beginning of the *Eclogues*, with 566 only slightly and necessarily altered from *E.* 1.1 *Tityre, tu patulae recubans sub tegmine fagi.*

lusi: appropriate to the *Eclogues*; cf. *E.* 1.10 *ludere quae uellem calamo . . . agresti.*

audaxque iuuenta 'and in the boldness of my youth'; the adjective is very general, but presumably refers to the generic, dictional and metrical audacity and innovation of the *Eclogues* – and, ultimately, to that of Virgilian poetry in general: 1.40 *da facilem cursum atque audacibus adnue coeptis.*

BIBLIOGRAPHY

The list includes only those works cited in the Introduction or Commentary. These are generally cited in order to resolve textual or interpretative issues, and the list is therefore selective in the extreme. For a full bibliography of scholarship on the *Georgics* from 1875 to 1975 see W. Suerbaum in H. Temporini and W. Haase, edd., *Aufstieg und Niedergang der römischen Welt* II 31.1 (Berlin and New York 1980) 395–499; for works since 1975 see the bibliographies published in each issue of *Vergilius*.

1 Abbreviations

K–S	R. Kühner and C. Stegman, *Ausführliche Grammatik der lateinischen Sprache*, Zweiter Teil (Hanover 1971)
LS	C. T. Lewis and C. Short, *A Latin dictionary* (Oxford 1879)
OLD	P. G. W. Glare, ed., *Oxford Latin dictionary* (Oxford 1982)
PGL	*Papiri greci e latini* (Florence 1912–)
SH	H. Lloyd-Jones and P. Parsons, edd., *Supplementum Hellenisticum* (Berlin 1983)
ThLL	*Thesaurus linguae latinae* (Leipzig 1900–)

2 Editions, commentaries, etc.

Büchner	K. Büchner, rev. edn of Morel (Leipzig 1982)
Conington	J. Conington and H. Nettleship, rev. F. Haverfield, *The works of Virgil, with a commentary* I, 5th edn (London 1898)
Forbiger	A. Forbiger, ed. with comm., *P. Vergili Maronis Opera* I, 4th edn (Leipzig 1872)
Geymonat	M. Geymonat, *P. Vergili Maronis opera* (Paravia 1973)
Gow	A. S. F. Gow, ed. with trans. and comm., *Theocritus*, 2 vols. (Cambridge 1952)
Gow and Scholfield	A. S. F. Gow and A. F. Scholfield, ed. with trans. and notes, *Nicander. The poems and poetical fragments* (Cambridge 1953)
Malcovati	H. Malcovati, *Oratorum Romanorum fragmenta liberae rei publicae* I (Paravia 1953)

242

Martyn	J. Martyn, *Publii Virgilii Maronis Georgicorum libri quatuor*, 5th edn (Oxford 1827)
Morel	W. Morel, *Fragmenta poetarum Latinorum epicorum et lyricorum praeter Ennium et Lucilium* (Stuttgart 1963)
Mynors	R. A. B. Mynors, *P. Vergili Maronis opera* (Oxford 1980)
Nisbet–Hubbard	R. G. M. Nisbet and M. Hubbard, *A commentary on Horace: Odes Book 1, Book 2* (Oxford 1975, 1978)
Norden	E. Norden, *P. Vergilius Maro, Aeneis Buch VI*, 5th edn (Stuttgart 1970)
Page	T. E. Page, ed. with intro. and notes, *P. Vergili Maronis Bucolica et Georgica* (London 1898)
Pfeiffer	R. Pfeiffer, ed., *Callimachus*, 2 vols. (Oxford 1965)
Powell	J. U. Powell, ed., *Collectanea Alexandrina* (Oxford 1925)
Richter	W. Richter, ed. with intro. and comm., *P. Vergilii Maronis Georgica*, Das Wort der Antike 5 (1957)
Skutsch	O. Skutsch, ed. with intro. and comm. *The Annals of Quintus Ennius* (Oxford 1985)
Williams	R. D. Williams, ed. with intro. and notes, *Virgil, The Eclogues and Georgics* (New York 1979)

3 Other works

Abbe, E. (1965). *The plants of Virgil's Georgics*. Ithaca.

Adams, J. N. (1982). *The Latin sexual vocabulary*. London.

Aitken, R. (1956). 'Virgil's plough', *J.R.S.* 46:97–106.

Allen, W. S. (1973). *Accent and rhythm. Prosodic features of Latin and Greek: a study in theory and reconstruction*. Cambridge.

Altevogt, H. (1952). *Labor improbus. Eine Vergilstudie*. Orbis Antiquus 8. Münster.

Anderson, W. B. (1933). 'Gallus and the Fourth *Georgic*', *C.Q.* 27:36–45.

Axelson, B. (1945). *Unpoetische Wörter. Ein Beitrag zur Kenntnis der lateinischen Dichtersprache*. Skrifter utgivna av Vetenskaps-societeten i Lund 29. Lund.

Bennett, C. E. (1898). 'What was ictus in Latin prosody?', *A.J.P.* 19:361–83.

Brown, E. (1963). *Numeri Vergilianae. Studies in Eclogues and Georgics*. Coll. Latomus 63. Brussels.

Clausen, W. V. (1955). '*Silua coniecturarum*', *A.J.P.* 77:47–62.
  (1976). 'Cynthia', *A.J.P.* 97:245–7.
  (1982). 'Theocritus and Virgil', in E. J. Kenney and W. V. Clausen, edd., *The age of Augustus* (Cambridge History of Classical Literature II 3). Cambridge.

Coleman, R. (1962). 'Gallus, the *Bucolics*, and the end of the Fourth *Georgic*', *A.J.P.* 83:55–71.

Crabbe, A. M. (1977). '*Ignoscenda quidem* . . . Catullus 64 and the Fourth *Georgic*', *C.Q.* N.S. 27:342–51.

Dahlmann, H. (1954). *Der Bienenstaat in Vergils Georgica*. Akad. der Wissen. und der Lit. Mainz 10. Mainz.

Flintoff, E. (1983). 'The Noric cattle plague', *Q.U.U.C.* 42:85–111.

Frentz, W. (1967). *Mythologisches in Vergils Georgica*. Beitr. zur klass. Philol. 21. Meisenheim.

Garner, R. J. (1958). *The grafter's handbook*. Oxford.

Getty, R. J. (1948). 'Some astronomical cruces in the *Georgics*', *T.A.P.A.* 79:24–45.

Griffin, J. (1976). 'Augustan poetry and the life of luxury', *J.R.S.* 66:87–105.
  (1979). 'The Fourth *Georgic*, Virgil and Rome', *G. & R.* 26:61–80.

Hardie, C. (1971). *The Georgics. A transitional poem*. Abingdon-on-Thames, Berkshire.

Harrison, E. L. (1979). 'The Noric plague and Vergil's Third *Georgic*', *P.L.L.S.* 2:1–65.

Hopkinson, N. (1984), ed. *Callimachus, Hymn to Demeter*. Cambridge.

Jacobson, H. (1982). 'Vergil, *Georgics* 3.280–281', *M.H.* 39:217.
  (1984). 'Aristaeus, Orpheus, and the *laudes Galli*', *A.J.P.* 105:271–300.

Jahn, P. (1903). 'Eine Prosaquelle Vergils und ihre Umsetzung in Poesie durch den Dichter', *Hermes* 38:244–64.

Jermyn, L. A. S. (1951). 'Weather-signs in Virgil', *G. & R.* 20:46–69.
  (1954). *The ostrakon*. Sanderstead, Surrey.

Kenney, E. J. (1971), ed. *Lucretius, De Rerum Natura Book III*. Cambridge.
  (1984), ed. *The ploughman's lunch. Moretum. A poem ascribed to Virgil*. Bristol.
  (1986). 'Prodelided *est*: a note on orthography,' *C.Q.* N.S. 36:542.

Kent, R. G. (1920). 'The alleged conflict of accents in Latin verse', *T.A.P.A.* 51:19–29.

Knight, W. F. J. (1939). *Accentual symmetry in Vergil.* Oxford.

Koenen, L. (1976). 'Egyptian influence in Tibullus', *I.C.S.* 1:127–59.

Klingner, F. (1931). 'Über das Lob des Landlebens in Virgils Georgica', *Hermes* 66:159–89.

    (1963). *Virgils Georgica.* Zurich.

Leach, E. W. (1977). '*Sedes apibus*: from the *Georgics* to the *Aeneid*', *Vergilius* 23:2–16.

Lyne, R. O. A. M. (1978), ed. *Ciris. A poem attributed to Vergil.* Cambridge.

McDermott, E. (1977). '*Horatius callidus*', *A.J.P.* 98:363–80.

Mackail, J. W. (1912). 'Virgil's use of the word *ingens*', *C.R.* 26:251–4.

McKay, A. J. (1972). 'Vergil's glorification of Italy (*Georgics* II 136–174)', in J. R. C. Martyn, ed., *Cicero and Virgil.* Amsterdam.

Merrill, W. A. (1916). 'Parallels and coincidences in Lucretius and Virgil', *U. Calif. Public. in Class. Philol.* 3:135–247.

Miles, G. B. (1980). *Virgil's Georgics. A new interpretation.* Berkeley and Los Angeles.

Mittsdörffer, W. (1938). 'Vergils Georgica und Theophrast', *Philol.* 93:449–75.

Norden, E. (1934). 'Orpheus und Eurydice. Ein nachträgliches Gedenkblatt für Vergil', *Sitzb. preuss. Akad. Wiss.* 22:626–83. Berlin.

Nougaret, L. (1946). 'Les fins d'hexamètre et l'accent', *R.E.L.* 24:261–71.

Ogilvie, R. M. and Richmond, I. (1967), edd. *Cornelii Taciti de uita Agricolae.* Oxford.

Otis, B. (1964). *Virgil. A study in civilized poetry.* Oxford.

Perkell, C. G. (1981). 'On the Corycian farmer of Virgil's Fourth *Georgic*', *T.A.P.A.* 111:167–77.

Pickard-Cambridge, A. (1962). *Dithyramb, tragedy and comedy*, 2nd edn, rev. T. B. L. Webster. Oxford.

Putnam, M. C. J. (1975). 'Italian Virgil and the idea of Rome', in *Janus. Essays in ancient and modern studies*, 171–99. Ann Arbor.

    (1979). *Virgil's poem of the earth. Studies in the Georgics.* Princeton.

Race, W. H. (1982). *The classical priamel from Homer to Boethius. Mnemos.* Supp. 74. Leiden.

Renehan, R. (1981). 'Anthologia Latina 14 Riese', *C.Q.* N.S. 31:471–2.

Ross, D. O. (1969). *Style and tradition in Catullus*. Cambridge, Mass.

(1975). *Backgrounds to Augustan poetry. Gallus, elegy and Rome*. Cambridge.

(1979). 'Ancient logs and old saws (Horace, *Epode* 2.43)', *A.J.P.* 100:241–4.

(1980). '*Non sua poma*. Varro, Virgil and grafting', *I.C.S.* 5:63–71.

(1987). *Virgil's elements. Physics and poetry in the Georgics*. Princeton.

Sargeaunt, J. (1920). *The trees, shrubs and plants of Virgil*. Oxford.

Schechter, S. (1975). 'The "aition" and Virgil's "Georgics" ', *T.A.P.A.* 105:347–91.

Schroeder, A. (1921). *De ethnographiae antiquae locis quibusdam communibus obseruationes*. Diss. Halle.

Scodel, R. S. and Thomas, R. F. (1984). 'Virgil and the Euphrates', *A.J.P.* 105:339.

Shackleton Bailey, D. R. (1976). Rev. of L. Håkanson, *Textkritische Studien zu den grösseren pseudoquintilianischen Deklamationen*, in *A.J.P.* 97:73–9.

(1982). *Profile of Horace*. London.

(1983). '*Anth. Lat.* 24.3 (Riese)', *C.Q.* N.S. 33:301.

Speranza, F. (1974). *Scriptorum Romanorum de re rustica reliquiae* I. Messina.

Stinton, T. C. W. (1976). ' "Si credere dignum est": some expressions of disbelief in Euripides and others', *P.C.P.S.* 22:60–89.

Syme, R. (1939). *The Roman revolution*. Oxford.

Tarrant, R. J. (1976), ed. *Seneca, Agamemnon*. Cambridge.

Thomas, G. S. (1961). *The old shrub roses*. London.

Thomas, R. F. (1978). 'Ovid's attempt at tragedy (*Amores* 3.1.63–64)', *A.J.P.* 99:175–8.

(1979). 'Theocritus, Calvus and *Eclogue* 6', *C.P.* 74:337–9.

(1982a). *Lands and peoples in Roman poetry. The ethnographical tradition*. Camb. Philol. Soc. Supp. 7. Cambridge.

(1982b). 'Gadflies (Virg. *Geo.* 3.146–148)', *H.S.C.P.* 86:81–5.

(1982c). 'Catullus and the polemics of poetic reference (64.1–18)', *A.J.P.* 103:144–64.

(1983a). 'Virgil's ecphrastic centrepieces', *H.S.C.P.* 87:175–84.

(1983b). 'Callimachus, the *Victoria Berenices* and Roman poetry', *C.Q.* N.S. 33:92–113.

(1985). 'From *recusatio* to commitment. The evolution of the Virgilian programme', *P.L.L.S.* 5 (1986) 61–73.

(1986a). 'Unwanted mice (Arat. *Phaen.* 1140–1)', *H.S.C.P.* 90:91–2.

(1986b). 'Virgil's *Georgics* and the art of reference', *H.S.C.P.* 90:171–98.

Wellesley, K. (1985). 'Virgil, *Georgics* 3.44, emended', *L.C.M.* 10.3:35.

West, D. (1979). 'Two plagues: Virgil, *Georgics* 3.478–566 and Lucretius 6.1090–1286', in D. West and T. Woodman, edd., *Creative imitation and Latin literature*. Cambridge.

Whatmough, J. (1931). 'The *Osi* of Tacitus – Germanic or Illyrian?', *H.S.C.P.* 42:139–55.

White, K. D. (1967). *Agricultural implements of the Roman world.* Cambridge.

(1970). *Roman farming.* London.

Wild, J. P. (1970). *Textile manufacture in the northern Roman provinces.* Cambridge.

Wilkinson, L. P. (1946). *Horace and his lyric poetry.* Cambridge.

(1963). *Golden Latin artistry.* Cambridge.

(1969). *The Georgics of Virgil. A critical survey.* Cambridge.

(1970). 'Pindar and the proem to the Third Georgic', *Festschr. K. Büchner.* Wiesbaden: 286–90.

(1982). 'The *Georgics*', in E. J. Kenney and W. V. Clausen, edd., *The age of Augustus* (Cambridge History of Classical Literature II 3). Cambridge.

Williams, F. (1978), ed. *Callimachus, Hymn to Apollo.* Oxford.

Williams, R. D. (1956). Rev. of Dahlmann (1954) in *C.R.* N.S. 6:170.

Wimmel, W. (1960) *Kallimachos in Rom. Die Nachfolge seines apologetischen Dichtens in der Augusteerzeit.* Hermes Einzelschriften 16. Wiesbaden.

INDEXES

References are to lemmata in the commentary, or page numbers in the Introduction (Vol. 1).

INDEXES

253

2 Latin words

Lightning Source UK Ltd.
Milton Keynes UK
UKOW050601100812

197334UK00001B/6/A